D0475967

The
# OBSERVER
## ON CRICKET

**AN ANTHOLOGY OF THE BEST CRICKET WRITING**

# The OBSERVER ON CRICKET

## AN ANTHOLOGY OF THE BEST CRICKET WRITING

*Edited and Compiled*

by

**SCYLD BERRY**

UNWIN HYMAN
London          Sydney

First published in Great Britain by Unwin Hyman,
an imprint of Unwin Hyman Limited, 1987.

**UNWIN HYMAN LIMITED**
**Denmark House, 37–39 Queen Elizabeth Street, London SE1 2QB**
**and**
**40 Museum Street, London WC1A 1LU**

Allen & Unwin Australia Pty Ltd
8 Napier Street, North Sydney, NSW 2060, Australia

Allen & Unwin New Zealand Ltd with the Port Nicholson Press
60 Cambridge Terrace, Wellington, New Zealand

**British Library Cataloguing in Publication Data**

The Observer on cricket: an anthology of
    the best cricket writing.
1. Cricket
I. Berry, Scyld
796.35'8        GV917
ISBN 0–04–440034–9

Typeset in 11 on 13 point Garamond by
Nene Phototypesetters Ltd, Northampton
and printed in Great Britain by
Biddles Ltd, Guildford & King's Lynn

*To*
*all the sub-editors*
*unknown and unthanked*

## On being dropped

Standing
on a still summer's day,
eye watching swallows
earth-hugging
insect-chasing way,
wondering what to do,
knowing that it always happens
and now it's happened to you.
What not again? Yes.
Feeling like laughing at the fable
yet not being able
because you have no middle
and life waits watching behind
having given you the casual twiddle.
Yet as your world revolved
it spun you through a wider sky,
opened further open eye,
it's a game.
So come on, who's king of the castle
now I'm the dirty rascal,
standing,
on a still summer's day
eye watching swallows
insect-chasing way.

*John Snow* (first published in *The Observer*)

# Contents

## PART 3    *Matches*

## PART 4    *Occasional Pieces*

# Contents

## PART 5    *Obituaries*

# Illustrations

# Acknowledgement

To Paddy in the library for all the assistance
that was rendered.

# *Foreword*

## by Donald Trelford
### Editor, *The Observer*

One summer evening over thirty years ago, two *Observer* journalists were enjoying a pint of Guinness in an Irish pub in Fleet Street when their attention was caught by a paragraph in the evening paper. It reported that Groucho Marx, the famous Hollywood comedian, was visiting London and seemed to be rather bored. So, doubtless fortified by the Guinness, they decided to invite him to join them for a day's cricket at Lord's. They wrote out a note in the bar, extracted an envelope from the landlord, and took a taxi to the Savoy Hotel to deliver it. And that, they thought, would be the end of it.

So much so that when the telephone rang next day on the desk of one of the journalists, John Gale, he had no idea whom he was talking to when an American voice said, 'This is Mr Marx.'

'I don't know any Mr Marks,' said Gale.

'Yes, you do,' rapped the voice, 'you wrote to me.'

The stunning realisation then dawned that the great man himself was on the line. 'Meet me at the Berkeley Hotel,' he said.

Gale grabbed his colleague of the night before, Michael Davie, and off they dashed. They could hardly miss their guest when they arrived – 'He actually walked like Groucho in the movies,' Davie recalls, 'and smoked a big cigar.' He was wearing a white cap of the kind made famous by Gene Sarazen, the golfer.

Groucho's opening remark to them was disconcerting: 'Have you brought the Benzedrine?' He introduced his beautiful 'secretary', Miss Hartford, later to be consecrated – very briefly – as Mrs Marx. The four of them piled into a taxi, Gale and Davie on the jump seats, the film star and friend in the back. Davie thought he'd better start describing the game and leaned forward to explain that one side batted while the other was fielding.

'Fielding?' said Groucho, staring out of the window: 'Didn't he write *Tom Brown's Schooldays*?'

As they arrived at Lord's, Groucho pointed to a sign reading 'Members and Friends' and said, 'That's the most ambiguous notice I've ever seen.' There was only a handful of spectators in the ground, watching a dullish mid-week county match in a reverent silence. A young man recognised the star and asked for his autograph. As he signed it, Groucho glowered at him and growled, 'Were you the guy making all the noise back there?' – at which the young man jumped away in alarm protesting, 'No, no, sir.'

They signed Groucho in at the pavilion, where his name was recognised by the doorman, who passed the word along the corridors of power. Down came the formidable MCC Secretary, Ronald Aird, MC, TD, and found them in the Long Room, Groucho still in his white cap. 'Are you over here on holiday, Mr Marx?' said Aird in his plummiest tones.

Groucho, suspecting that he was being patronised by the British, snapped back, 'I was until I saw *this* game' – at which point the Secretary turned on his heel and left. As Gale apologised, Groucho replied, 'Never mind, I've met stuffed shirts before.'

Then he pointed with his cigar at a picture of a young, willowy long-haired cricketer in a picture on the wall. 'Cricket, eh? Circa 1780, eh? I guess this homo business started earlier than we thought.'

According to the account I heard, the journalists turned to Groucho after about half an hour of watching the cricket and asked him uncertainly, 'How do you like the game?' To which he replied, taking his cigar out of his mouth, 'Great, just great.' Pause. 'When does it start?' Alas, Michael Davie does not recall this last bit, though he confirms the rest.

I am very glad to see that he and the late John Gale are both represented in this first anthology of *Observer* cricket. In fact, Michael Davie deserves a special mention in this context, for it was chiefly through his infectious enthusiasm for the game – as Sports Editor in the 1950s and as Deputy Editor in the 1960s – that so many of the distinguished writers represented here were first introduced to the paper. And what a remarkable team they make!

A Regular Contributors XI could read: Len Hutton, Jack Fingleton, C. G. Macartney, Douglas Jardine, Donald Knight, Ted Dexter, Harry Altham, Percy Fender, Tony Pawson, Frank Tyson and R. C. Robertson-Glasgow. The captaincy might be a subject of fierce debate between Hutton and Jardine. There is no wicket-keeper, but Tony Pawson, who illustrated fielding in the first MCC coaching manual after the war (a copy of which I still possess), would doubtless oblige.

An Occasional Contributors XI could read: Colin McDonald, Mike Brearley, Colin Cowdrey, Frank Worrell, Bobby Simpson, Trevor Bailey, Frank Lee, Henry Blofeld ('keeper), John Snow, Mike Selvey and Ian Peebles. Four Test captains to choose from there!

An All-Time XI of those who have contributed to *The Observer* would be a formidable team of all the talents: Hutton, Simpson, Macartney, Cowdrey, Worrell, Jardine, Dexter, Fender, Snow, Tyson and Peebles. Again there is no 'keeper, but with such a batting order they might not be dismissed in time to field at all!

It is surely no coincidence that so many of the best writers on cricket were themselves great practitioners of the game. The Press in general has paid lip-service to that idea through countless 'ghosted' columns, in which a celebrity loans out his name while a hack puts clichés in his mouth. *The Observer* can reasonably claim to have been one of the first newspapers to recognise that cricketers were bright enough to write for themselves and that their own words often had a ready-made freshness and originality that were missing in their 'ghosts'. The novelist Leslie Thomas, who used to pen 'Len Hutton' columns many years ago for a London evening paper, told me recently, 'I realised, listening to Len talk, that he could do the job better himself, but in those days papers thought only journalists could write.' There was a shaming period in Fleet Street when trade union restrictions prevented ex-sportsmen from writing their own copy unless they held a union card; otherwise their words had to be 'told to' an accredited journalist. Thankfully, as these pages show, *The Observer* chose to ignore such restrictions.

Had it not done so, it is doubtful whether Scyld Berry – our present cricket correspondent, who edited this collection and whose idea it was – could ever have been appointed in the first place, since he had no qualifications and certainly no union card. He came to us in 1976 with little more to recommend him than a degree in Arabic Studies, a name that is in the first line of *Beowulf* (his father was a Professor of Anglo-Saxon) and a consuming passion for cricket. The credit for this remarkably shrewd piece of selection should go to a former Sports Editor, Geoffrey Nicholson. The line of *Observer* cricket correspondents from R. C. Robertson-Glasgow through Alan Ross to Scyld Berry is a distinguished one. I regret that Scyld, with characteristic shyness, has included relatively little of himself in this book.

Personally, I also regret the ungenerous profile of my friend Len Hutton that appeared in the paper in 1951, though its inclusion here can be justified as a matter of historical record. To say that Len, like the poet Milton, was 'not very lovable' is surely one of the great misjudgements of cricket history. Fortunately, Len didn't hold that against the paper, and his insights and dry wit have been a feature of our sports pages for a quarter of a century since.

I recently discovered a surprising link between Len Hutton and the chairman of *The Observer*, 'Tiny' Rowland. It turns out that Mr Rowland travelled out on the same ship to South Africa as the MCC team of 1948/49 and struck up a friendship with some of the players. When they reached Cape Town he gave Len a gold watch in exchange for one of his bats, which he wanted to keep as a memento.

'Do you know this Rowland?' Len said to me 35 years later when Lonrho bought the paper.

'Yes, of course,' I replied.

The Yorkshireman grinned, 'Then tell him the watch has just run out and I need a new one!'

Finally, no *Observer* book on cricket would be complete without an extract from the interview that playwright Harold Pinter once gave to Miriam Gross:

MG: Why does cricket appeal to you so much?
HP: I tend to believe that cricket is the greatest thing that God ever created on earth.
MG: Greater than sex, for example?

HP: Certainly greater than sex, although sex isn't too bad either. But everyone knows which comes first when it's a question of cricket or sex – all discerning people recognise that. Anyway, don't forget one doesn't have to do two things at the same time. You can either have sex before cricket or after cricket – the fundamental fact is that cricket must be there at the centre of things.

This, of course, must account for *The Observer*'s otherwise mysterious decision to publish an anthology on cricket rather than an anthology on sex.

# *Preface*

Cricket *writing* has not existed for most of the time that cricket has been played or *The Observer* published. When the oldest of Sunday newspapers first appeared in 1791, the capital of the game was the windswept hill called Broadhalfpenny Down outside the Hampshire village of Hambledon, and those parochial proceedings were never going to merit space in the few pages that stamp duty and the cost of newsprint allowed. Even the matches played for high stakes by a new club of London beaux, at Thomas Lord's Ground, did not command the paper's attention – not, at any rate, until the early nineteenth century when Marylebone Cricket Club was recognised as the sport's pre-eminent authority.

Any matches that rated space were described cursorily, and it may be safely generalised that until the First World War the method was all reporting as opposed to writing. The first Test match in England was staged in 1880, and great public enthusiasm was aroused, but *The Observer* did not pander to its readers by publishing a Profile of the England captain Lord Harris, or a match preview, or an interview with the three brothers Grace ('Tell us, William, are you, Ted and Fred going to give it 110 per cent?'). The notice that did appear was a fairly formal announcement, brief and to the point: 'a truly representative team, to which little exception can be taken, will meet the colonists at The Oval on the first three days of the week. An immense amount of interest is manifest in the affair, which bids fair to far outrival all previous contests in attractiveness, for there can be little doubt that it will be the match of the age.'

In nineteenth-century coverage of the game (*The Young Cricketer's Tutor*, by John Nyren, always excepted), the style was formulaic, the vocabulary stock: 'Fry turned his attention to Richardson and cracked him to the confines, before being palpably lbw. Surrey were thus left the victors by one run.' Were this quotation genuine, it would typify the manner of the staid Victorian chronicler. Everything might be recorded, save the atmosphere, the excitement, the drama.

Should any reader remain to be convinced, he may read in the following pages the agency account of the Old Trafford Test in 1902 between England and Australia. It was the closest finish known to Test cricket up to that point, yet the report hardly encourages us to feel as though we were present at the climax. The 1902 series was indeed one of the finest encounters for the Ashes: Hirst and Rhodes dismissed Australia for their lowest ever total of 36 in one Test, England fell short by three runs in another, and edged home by one wicket in another. Victor Trumper was enjoying his greatest hour; Ranji, Fry and a host of Golden Age cricketers bedecked the England team. Then on the Saturday of the Lord's Test, not for the last time, it rained all day. *The Observer*'s report, in full, was as follows: 'Weather of the worst description was experienced at Lord's yesterday, and it was soon officially announced that this match was abandoned as a draw.'

Happy, leisurely days! If the same were to happen now, the Sports Editor would be on the phone to say he needed a piece of the same length as if there had been play: bring in some 'colour', talk about the cricket so far, single out an outstanding player and give us a few fine phrases about him. In 1902, on the other hand, with the England captain Archibald MacLaren available in the pavilion to offer his thoughts and numerous Immortals present to provide 'quotes', our agency man packed up his sandwiches, filed his 24 words, and went home to watch the highlights of the Boer War.

The Great Leap Forward began after the First World War with, as I interpret, two developments. One was the appearance in 1921 of a bespectacled young man from the *Manchester Guardian* with more literary and musical than sporting interests. His match reports may now seem to us to have been self-indulgently vague, the author more concerned with getting off whatever might have been on his chest than with telling the reader what happened. But again, the pace of cricket and of newspapers was more leisurely, unhurried; and there can be no question that the powers of empathy and imagination which Neville Cardus brought to cricket writing created a new half-acre plot in the field of English Literature. (By comparison, boxing, the only other English sport to have inspired a corpus of literary writing, would only claim a few square yards.)

It is thanks to Cardus that the Old Trafford Test of 1902 became a legend – no thanks at all to the newspapers of the time. Perhaps Fred Tate's teeth did not actually chatter when he went in with eight runs to win, and he may not have uttered the words Cardus ascribed to him: being poetic truth, that matters little. What is important was that Cardus stood back to see the wood, and painted it with a rich palette of colours. In the early 1930s the Editor of *The Observer*, J. L. Garvin, tried to tempt Cardus to London. But he felt himself to be immutably Mancunian, though he did write numerous cricket commentaries for *The Observer*, including the two on the Bodyline tour anthologised here.

If Cardus had never existed, however, I'm inclined to think that cricket reporting would still have developed into writing, albeit far more gradually (Nyren, after all, had shown it could be done). Just as the English play was taking root before the advent of Shakespeare, cricket correspondence was developing – simultaneously yet independently of Cardus – in order to deal with the 1921 tour of England by Warwick Armstrong's Australians. The previous winter England had lost all five Test matches in Australia, unprecedentedly, and their war-weary batsmen were rapidly routed three more times at home by Gregory and McDonald. The nation's bosom was beaten; and Australian strengths were compared to English frailties at enormous length. In *The Observer* alone, essays poured forth from 'A Former County Player', 'An Australian Correspondent' and that hardy annual 'A Special Correspondent', all analysing the visitors' superiority ever more discursively and expansively. At least it helped to take the minds of the survivors off the war.

One such survivor was a former Oxford student, Donald Knight. As a batsman, he had been a prodigy and had played for Surrey for two seasons while still at school. His father, however, would not allow him to join in the general sacrifice – and this parental refusal of permission, it is said, profoundly disturbed Knight for the rest of his life. In any event, Knight was one of the lucky young men to survive the war, and he became *The*

*Observer*'s first cricket correspondent when he covered the Ashes series of 1926, having played twice himself in the previous home series against Australia.

Another Surrey and England amateur, Percy Fender, provided reports and comments of the 1930 Ashes series – whenever his duties as county captain allowed, one would have liked to add, but Fender in fact missed several important Surrey matches and was criticised for taking on the assignment. The astuteness of Fender's cricketing brain can be gauged here from his analysis of Don Bradman's batting. A third Surrey and England player, one Douglas Jardine, covered the 1938 series, without having to abscond from playing as he had already been drummed out of the Establishment regiment. By now Test cricket demanded a large amount of space, and to help satisfy the readers' appetite that highly individual Australian Charlie Macartney was hired to provide his comments alongside Jardine's match reports. Together they covered the record-breaking innings of 364 by a future *Observer* contributor.

These all seem to have been temporary arrangements. In 1939, the first regular cricket correspondent was appointed, Raymond Robertson-Glasgow. He had been a fine fast-medium bowler for Oxford University and Somerset; he had already done some journalism; he was a great wit; and in this editorial view he became the finest of cricket writers (whereas Cardus was the best writer of English on cricket, among other subjects). Robertson-Glasgow was felicitously funny, knowledgeable, and perceptive both about the game and the characters of the men who played it. His output was not large, which may have helped in keeping the quality high, and the best of it appeared originally in *The Observer* during his eight seasons as cricket correspondent: 1939, and from 1946 to 1952.

After some neglect since his death – like many a great wit, Robertson-Glasgow was manic depressive and ultimately suicidal – his writings are being appreciated by the wider readership they deserve and his few books have been reprinted. After the Second World War his 'Sporting Prints' were a special feature of the sports page (there could only be one in that era of rationing), often accompanied by a cartoon from Hiro. It is recalled that 'Crusoe' would come into the office with a crumpled piece of handwritten paper – unless his wife had typed it for him – in his old raincoat, and another pearl would be added to his string of sketches of the cricketers of his day. Simply because these 'Sporting Prints' have appeared in book form, and have recently been reprinted, none has been selected here, except for one on the Australian 'mystery' bowler Jack Iverson, to give any new-comer an idea of their flavour. (Neither was there justification for selecting such delightful pieces as the essay on Arthur Wellard by Harold Pinter, which appeared as an extract in the colour magazine and can also be found in book form.)

The good news is that plenty of Robertson-Glasgow writing has been unearthed in the Profiles that he wrote for the editorial pages of the newspaper. The first of such Profiles was of Hitler, in January 1943, and was written by one of the European refugees from Fascism and Nazism that had found intellectual breathing-space in the Astor fold, Arthur Koestler. These Profiles, usually of a topical personality of international standing (particularly in those years when *The Observer* abounded with everyone but Englishmen), are unsigned by custom: but from the style it is quite apparent that those of Lord's, Don Bradman and Denis Compton were written by Robertson-Glasgow. So lovely is the Profile of Lord's, celebrating as it did the return of the summer game after six years of war, that it alone may be considered to make this anthology worthwhile.

After the Profiles come the Portraits of the renowned and famous, some of them by the famous. Beginning with those wartime refugees from Europe, *The Observer* has welcomed a wide spread of contributors, in its sports department as else-where. Hence the presence of some surprising names like Barry Norman and Clement Freud.

In the third section, Matches, selection was made easier by the fact that only one-sixth of the cricket played before the 1960s took place on a Saturday, and nowadays one-seventh. But even when a famous innings or incident did fall right for a Sabbath newspaper, it has not automatically been included, for the quality of writing has throughout been the chief criterion. Macartney once hit 345 against Nottinghamshire, the largest innings ever scored in a day, let alone on a Saturday: but the report does not generate quite as much excitement as his hitting no doubt did. In

1934, Don Bradman and Bill Ponsford shared a record- and heart-breaking partnership against England at The Oval: but it must be said that the editor of *Wisden*, S. J. Southerton, in his faithful chronicle of the day's play for *The Observer*, was about as daunting to the reader as Bradman was to the bowlers.

Some might dismiss match reports as too ephemeral to be worth immortalising in book form (scores, too – thus the original scoreboards have only been appended in full where desirable). Against that, they do help clarify the way in which the game has altered over the decades. Bouncers, for instance: in 1921, we read, one England batsman was bowled by an 'almost vulgar resemblance of a long hop' from McDonald; while in 1946–47 in Brisbane a single 'bumper' was bowled by England during their two days in the field. By 1960, however, it is reported by the cricket correspondent of the time, Alan Ross, that the West Indian pace attack was delivering short, rib-cage stuff as a general rule.

In the Occasional Pieces I have tried to focus on some of the major issues cricket has faced since the First World War, and would like to think that somewhere or other most of the main personalities, problems and aspects of the game have been treated. A village cricketer and a female cricketer are portrayed; umpiring and throwing and Kerry Packer and the burgeoning influence of the subcontinent are discussed. For the sake of this catholicity, I have included two pieces of mine about cricket on radio and television: this has to be my defence against the common accusation that an editor only composes an anthology in order to see his own work made permanent in book-form.

Sir Leonard Hutton is the principal contributor to the Obituaries section, having known or seen or played with all the great names of the last half-century and more. He was covering England's 1958–59 tour of Australia for another newspaper, with a 'ghost' in attendance, when he nodded to *The Observer* correspondent on the tour, Michael Davie, and said in his cryptic way, 'You've got a typewriter.' A pause followed, after which the master batsman added, 'When I was batting, I had my bat.' Another pause, and eventually the realisation dawned that Sir Leonard was effectively saying he wouldn't mind being in control of his own destiny instead of relying on a 'ghost'. *The Observer* was only too happy to take the hint, sign him up, and let him write his own comments thereafter.

The articles within each section appear in the order they were printed, although an eyebrow might be raised at the sight of Sydney Barnes or Jack Gregory coming after Basil d'Oliveira. But I should not say 'articles': my first Sports Editor, Geoffrey Nicholson, told me that an article was something you kept under a bed. He then suggested to the keen and callow 21-year-old that he might like to write a 'piece' about cricket, and so I have been doing since. It has been good to be in the employ of a newspaper that has been a microcosm of post-war England: not exactly streamlined and efficient, even exasperating in its ethereal failure to make the most business-like use of its resources; but respected nevertheless and regarded with good will, even affection, by those who know it, and especially by those abroad to whom it seems an encapsulation of certain liberal and fair-minded values.

A great deal has changed merely in my decade, let alone the period which this anthology spans. Yet I have reason to hope that both this game and this newspaper will continue to be sturdy institutions, whether the reports are filed by telephone, as at home, or by telegram, as in the distant past from overseas, or by telex, as in the recent past, or by Tandy as in the hi-tech present. But enough trumpet-blowing: let this collection of cricket writing, plus a selection from the best of *Observer* photography, do the rest of the talking.

SCYLD BERRY

# PART 1

# *Profiles*

*After the loss of six seasons, and more, to the Second World War,* The Observer *celebrated the return of a traditional English summer with this Profile, not of a person, but of something inanimate for once. The style is that of the cricket correspondent of the time, Raymond Robertson-Glasgow, whose career-best bowling figures were achieved at the ground celebrated here: 9 wickets for 38 runs, for Somerset against Middlesex, in 1924.*

# Lord's Cricket Ground

The procession of cricket worshippers is on the move again. At the game's House of Commons, The Oval, there are to be centenary honours this season. This should mean bunting all over the local landmark, the famous gasometer; as well as the usual Cockney mirth on the back benches.

The union of cricket and ceremony suggests the Upper House of the fancy, the turf so aptly and so augustly known as Lord's. There was, indeed, nothing baronial about its origin. Its name might just as well have been Mudd's, had a pioneer called Mr Mudd, a familiar London patronymic, instead of a pioneer called Mr Lord, developed some real estate for the sportsmen of Marylebone.

Mr Lord, a Yorkshireman from Thirsk – there was early a White Rose in the pleasance of St John's Wood – laid out a ground in what is now Dorset Square. With a proper Yorkshire distaste for rent-raising landlords he moved nor'-west in 1811, only to find 'Progress' intersecting his new meadow with the still newer Regent Canal. So he picked up his turves and walked yet again, this time to rest on the site of the present temple, later taken over from Mr Lord by Mr Dark. Here the Marylebone gentlemen continued to bat and bowl, oblivious of Napoleon. Nowadays wars make more interruption. But the rites have remained and are restored.

Of course, the splendour of these rites is diminished. The heavy roller of austerity naturally flattens out the old rich goodness of a day at Lord's. The Forsyte assemblage, the mid-season panoply of top-hats, barouches, hampers, blazers in hue, ladies in the mode, chicken in aspic, strawberries in cream, and banners in the air – these are not easily recoverable glories. None the less that castle of dalliance, the Pavilion, erected in 1890, will be seigneurial as long as it stands. With its picture gallery of happy English fields and whiskered cricket veterans, its boxes for the rival teams, its tier on tier of spacious spectatorium, it is the grandee of all our sporting premises. Cricket may be, in essence, a humble matter, a growth of the village green, elm-tree shaded, river-flanked, tavern-mellow, something earthy and in-digenous. To that sort of cricket Lord's stands as Norman Castle to the cottage home. Here, on the great days, 'with its flutter of flags and dames', cricket has made blazon of its blood and state. Old and private things like royal or real tennis rightly belong there in the dark timeless seclusion of the court behind the pavilion. There, if anywhere or nowhere else, is the haunt, the air, the life, and perhaps the death of the old and tawny Conservatism. Each stroke of the dim player is like a vain whack at Mr Dalton's Death Duties, a farewell gesture to a fleeting world.

It would be unfair to suggest that Lord's is (or always was) simply a paradise of privilege. It has been justly ridiculed for its class-distinction between Gentlemen and Players, but that snob-bery dwindles and a 'Pro' is now permitted to have his initials on the scorecard. It has always given felicity and fair comfort to the ordinary man, especially to the ordinary schoolboy: it is not so vastly long ago that a lad who came bowling up on a seat beside the coachman of a green Atlas bus with a shilling and a few sandwiches in his pocket could make it a day indeed. Entrance sixpence, scorecard a penny, fivepence for the gastronomic extras; now it takes three shillings or more for boys to have the same fun – and they have it. Not that Lord's is just an abode of bliss. It can be the rack of young ambition. When one thinks of all the torture undergone by players on probation in the sacred arena, schoolboys, Blues, and new County or 'Test' choices, when one thinks of the ignominious 'duck' and the dropped catch on the great occasion, one can hear wailing and lamentation as well as cheers and laughter in the ghosted air.

Now in Maytime to the wicket
Out I march with bat and pad
See the son of grief at cricket
Trying to be glad.

Lord's has known that mood too. A missed catch, like a missed putt, can leave a lifetime legacy of sudden shivers in the night.

During the 1860s Lord's grew in size and value. Since the Marylebone gentry had neglected to buy their freehold a smart investor did quite nicely out of what is now called 'betterment', buying for £7000 in 1860 that which he sold six years later for £18,000.

Cricket, like prices, was 'on the up and up'. The first Australian team came there in 1878 and MCC were skittled by Boyle and Spofforth; the former took nine wickets for 17, the latter ten for 20. (That would be front-page news twice over nowadays. But then the Press gave sport only the bare figures and hardly any colour, comment, or build-up.) However, MCC were avenged 18 years later when they put out the Australians for 18 runs. But now we are moving into the age of the still living giants, on from the vast Victorian face-fungus to mere moustaches and into the epoch of clean-shaven masters.

Do you want the true Lord's – Lord's as you would like to have it if you knew that you could never see it again? Some would not have it during a Test match, not even if Frank Woolley were walking back to the echoing pavilion from his solitary mag-nificence against Gregory and McDonald, or Hammond were driving the dominant O'Reilly smack against the railings, or Hedley Verity were luring Don Bradman to a rare, incredible doom. For Test matches at Lord's are too like Test matches that you can see on grounds more spacious but less grand; and, truth to tell, on the spectators' side of the argument, Lord's emerges from the battles a little ruffled and breathless, like some old lady who has felt it her seasonal duty to take part in a game of blind man's buff.

Many a cricketer's love is for Lord's on the more private and intimate occasion when the ground is, so to speak, superior or at least equal to the cricket. For some, the Eton and Harrow; for others, perhaps some military, clerical, or theatrical occasion ('band if possible' as the old announcement said) or just the local needle-match, parochial grapple, Middlesex against the chocolate caps from Kennington, Cockney North v. Cockney South. Many will think of a long June day with cool Hearne and bustling Hendren (the feast of reason and the flow of soul) scourging the invader's attack and suggesting that St John's churchyard nearby was designed as a proper recipient for the broken hearts and limbs of such as came to bowl there. Not that Lord's has ever been a penitentiary for bowlers like The Oval. Mr Lord did seem to plant some devilry in his turves that no treatment has ever wholly exorcised.

So there it is, a home of all sorts, with its vintage cricket and its beery purlieus, its solemn devotees, its notable bores, its hero-worship, its autograph-hunters, its overwhelming difference from any other cricket ground in the world. It has (and it must retain even in these thieving times) an inherent honesty. A cricket-starved senior recently said, 'It will be nice to go to Lord's again and prove that there's somewhere in England where you can fall asleep and wake up without finding that your hat and stick have gone.' Its management has never practised the subtler arts of salesmanship. Marylebone has not loved change; it eludes the ringer-up. A mere member of the public cannot phone MCC. Yet therein has lain and grown its strength. It has been guided and guarded by men of dignity and of a certain not inappropriate divorcement from affairs. These are the right doctors to be in charge of cricket's heart; even if they have often been a little absent-minded in feeling its pulse.

But we shall not end on any dismal diagnosis. Once more there shall be the flash of style (and the mighty window-smashing swipe as well), once more great surging of speech-demanding crowds outside the Pavilion after the day has been won, and once more the noble unreason of a Harlequin cap, that most un-English bedizenment, so oddly beloved of very English people (and even of staid Scots like Douglas Jardine), and so long the sign and shelter of him who is, in skill and dedication, the embodiment of Lord's, Sir Pelham Warner.

5 May 1946

*When England toured Australia in 1946–47, it was widely suspected that Don Bradman had 'gone'. He was, after all, 38 and in the warm-up games he did little. Then came the First Test, and one late November morning listeners to the wireless heard that 'The Don' had done it again. Two days later this Profile appeared, unsigned as usual but unquestionably by R. C. Robertson-Glasgow.*

# Don Bradman

Just over eight years ago Don Bradman was carried from the field at The Oval, in a vast silence, with a vast score by England on the board.

He had injured his leg when bowling; a function which, as matters then stood, might more successfully, if less legally, have been delegated to any willing spectator of either sex; underarm, overarm, or roundarm; roll, bowl, or pitch.

Then, at the sepulchral hour of seven last Friday morning, a Voice, striving heroically for tact, stated that Bradman had made a century at Brisbane; his sixteenth, single, double, or treble, against England. Later and ample, such very ample, reports sought to ease disappointment's bread with the margarine of comfort. Bradman had started shakily; he had offered what would have been chances if they had happened to go to hand; he had even been caught at slip, but it had proved not to be a catch. And it all boiled down to this, that Bradman had done it again. The most devastating return since Sherlock Holmes surprised the iniquitous Colonel Sebastian Moran.

In a purely cricketing, and Pickwickian, sense the obituary of Bradman has several times been written of recent years. At the start of this Australian cricket season, rays of rumour flickered through clouds of mystery. Bradman was an old man, with no interest except for commerce. He had batted in the nets at Adelaide, where some found him as wonderful as ever, while to others he was just a memory of splendour, a husk of genius, or even a different man altogether, batting under the same name.

He proved his identity by playing against MCC. But his performance was, for him, only moderate. He was grey and tired and
wizened. He might conceivably appear in the First Test, but not as
captain. So much for rumour.

Donald George Bradman, lord in the nonpareilage of New South
Wales and South Australia, was born on 27 August 1908, at
Cootamundra, a small up-country town in New South Wales.
When he was still not much higher than a short-handled bat he
moved, with his parents, to Bowral, 50 miles or so from Sydney.
Here, in the backyard, against a wall, with himself as batsman,
bowler, and ten fielders, and the sky as sole spectator, he taught
himself cricket. From this one-man show he graduated to pick-up
matches with the Bowral High School. In 1926, at the request of
the New South Wales State selectors, he appeared in the practice-
nets on the Sydney Cricket Ground. His style of batting was
described as uncouth, even eccentric. But the less hilarious
judges noticed that hardly a single ball reached the back-netting.
Arthur Mailey, one of the subtlest dealers in the leg-break that
cricket has known, was called in to tax this turbulent novice and
was treated as just another practice-bowler.
    When the Australian team came here in 1930, there was a quiet
confidence that the 'Ashes' would not sail away with the challengers. Bradman was the exploder-in-chief of that comfortable
view. He began, reasonably enough, with only 131 in the first
Test, at Nottingham. He followed with 254 at Lord's, 334 (a new
record) at Leeds, and 232 in the deciding match at The Oval. The
pundits might argue about his right place in the galaxy of the
great, or even deny him greatness. But they had to admit that he
had set a new standard of arithmetic. Once, batsmen, even in Test
matches, had tended to depart, decently or with a flourish,
somewhere between the first and second century. But Bradman
batted on.
    Few, if any, had so disciplined themselves to physical excel-
lence, or fielded and thrown with such agility and accuracy. The
critics were not educated to such perfection, and it was fashion-
able to decry the supreme artist as an automaton. But Bradman,
the breaker of records, was but reflecting the spirit, even the
demands, of a record-hunting age. He was only 21, but he knew

the market. He was something new and strange, an Australian Test cricketer who could capitalise his skill and even dare, successfully, to defy authority and contractual clauses.

Bradman was now the greatest figure in world sport. Envious fate sent to Australia Larwood and Jardine, a very fast and accurate bowler directed by a very able and realistic captain. Under the leg-theory attack Bradman's art wilted but never wholly collapsed. It may be allowed that he was reduced, numerically, to the ordinary; but ordinary is no epithet for square cuts played past point from mobile headquarters on and outside the leg stump.

In 1934 Australia again arrived as challengers. At the start of the season a different Bradman was seen on English grounds. He was in a perpetual hurry. Was it nerves? or weariness of being Bradman? or just an agreeable expression of *joie de vivre*? There was a wonderful 160 against Middlesex; then a failure in the First Test; then, on a sticky pitch in the second Test at Lord's – Verity's match – a catastrophe, which profoundly shocked the wise and paternal Woodfull. Bradman's answer was to play innings of 304 and 244 in the last two Tests, he and the scarcely less magnificent Ponsford aggregating over 800 in two partnerships. As soon as the tour ended, Bradman was operated on for appendicitis.

In the last two series of Tests before the Hitler war Bradman was captain of Australia. Against Allen's visiting team he led Australia to victory after losing the first two Tests. Then, eight or 80 years ago, according to taste, he had to content himself with three single Test centuries and a drawn rubber, saw Leonard Hutton beat the Bradman record of 334 and sustained the heaviest defeat in any single Test match. As to his place among captains, the argument still awaits full evidence. But, whatever verdict the immediate future begets, none who saw that Oval Test of 1938 will forget the difference between Australia fielding under Bradman and Australia on the field without him.

To the connoisseur, the most exquisite duel in cricket was between Bradman and the left-handed Verity; the back-chatting urchin versus the Professor of Logic, Don against don. The last time that it was fought, or, alas, can be fought, was in the 1938 match between the Australians and Yorkshire at smoky Bramall Lane. The pitch varied from the sportive to the cantankerous.

Verity used every trick of spin and flight; stuff that might have won two matches in a day, and Bradman played him, for over after over, in the middle of the bat. 'Don't ever tell me,' Verity used to say, 'that Don is just ordinary on the sticky ones.'

So, the story is 'to be concluded', perhaps in England in 1948, of the slight, high-shouldered batsman, walking out from the pavilion, slowly, pensively, to slice the enemy into ribbons.

1 December 1946

---

*This Profile, of the 'golden boy' of English post-war cricket, was published on the Sunday before the First Test of 1948 against Australia. In the second innings of that game Denis Compton was out, famously, 'hit wkt b Miller 184'. The style of the author is the style of Robertson-Glasgow.*

# Denis Compton

Everybody knows who is the *Boy's Own* Hero of Australia: and the Men's, Women's and Wallabies' Hero, too. Bradman, about whom everything possible has been said, has a powerful English rival for the championship of the young heart.

He is Denis Compton, ten years younger, still on the record-makers' up-and-up, but outreaching even 'The Don' in width of favour because of his excellence at football, too.

The possession of 'all eyes' will be shared by these two at Nottingham on Thursday when the First Test is held, on a wicket long known as' sweet, serene and fruitful for the batsman and a source of affliction to the bowler. Facing Denis as well as Donald, if the sun shines, is a task for the pertinacious, the imperturbable, the optimist.

Compton, the most entertaining of great batsmen today, cannot help his abundance. The song of his bat is as natural as summer's warmth. But he is like those natural wits whose sayings are waited for by professional joke-gatherers. The statisticians prowl and prowl around.

Arithmetical digits are provocative things. They beget comparisons; and the last thing to do with Denis Compton is to compare him, as if he were an adjective or a length of linoleum. He is, in the strictest sense, incomparable, though Captain C. B. Fry has been heard to compare him, without final judgement, to Victor Trumper.

No athlete of modern times has been so popular with the young. The shout that greets Denis Compton when he walks out to bat at Lord's is mainly of treble and alto pitch. He is, of course, what each shouter would himself like to be; and these hero-worshippers, while their eyes watch him moving in white flannels, call up also the image of Compton (D.) dribbling down the left touchline at Highbury and cracking it across into the top corner of the net. These are the more obvious attractions. But the deeper alliance is in the kinship of temperament. Compton is just 30 years old, as years are officially measured. But his youth does not mean to listen to that old nagger, Time, and keeps easy company with the skill and strength of the man.

In the grimmest Test Compton cannot quite shake off the half-holiday idea. A match lost is still in the nature of 'a swizz', and an immortal century is 'a bit of a fluke'. Thus, at a time when others would be awaiting their innings, padded and silent, Compton is engaged far from the dressing-room, in a delirious finish at shove-ha'penny.

What of the style, the technique? Above all, easy; natural, concealing – but strengthened by – hours of study and practice. In all great batsmen there is the distinguishing trait; in Ranjitsinhji, the glide to leg; in Frank Woolley, the length ball driven over the despairing bowler's head; in Macartney, the half-volley chopped late, crack to the rails behind third man; in Bradman, the prolific diversion of worthy balls to the space wide of mid-on. Compton, above all batsmen, is a teaser of cover point. No one has quite his gift of so delaying or advancing the impact of the off-drive that the fielder needs to run both ways at once.

Denis Charles Scott Compton is a Londoner. His home and

school and first cricket were at Hendon. His father, a competent club cricketer, took the boy to matches, as scorer and occasional filler-up of a gap. 'We can't play against such a small lad,' said an opposing captain. 'Don't worry,' said the father, 'just bowl normally.'

On 13 September 1932, at the age of 14, Compton played his first match at Lord's, captaining the Elementary Schools against Mr C. F. Tufnell's Public School XI. He scored 114. His partner, A. McIntyre, now the Surrey wicket-keeper, scored 44. The Elementary Schools won by 148. Compton, slow left-hand, took two wickets.

Luck went paired with skill. Sir Pelham Warner was watching, and soon Compton joined the ground staff at Lord's. He sold scorecards; with Young, Robertson and Brown, today his companions in the Middlesex team, he helped to pull the heavy roller over the pitch on which Hedley Verity overthrew Australia, and, at the end of that match, found that, by foregoing lunch, he had netted a profit of £14 6s 1½d from the sale of cards. The money was banked. He also bowled in the nets; and once, at request, batted in them to the bowling of Mr P. G. H. Fender. Good practice for a boy.

Compton began, like the great Hendren before him, as no. 11 for Middlesex, and helped G. O. Allen to head the Sussex total in the Whitsun match at Lord's. Ten years afterwards, with Godfrey Evans, in the breathless heat of Adelaide, he was to control the last-wicket stand of latter years. In his third county match, he made 82 against Northamptonshire. By the end of this season, 1936, he had arrived. A year later he had settled in as an England batsman, scoring 65 against New Zealand at The Oval Test.

In 1938 came 'the Tiger', W. J. O'Reilly, and that erratic genius, L. O'B. Fleetwood-Smith, whose experiments with the left-handed googly Compton is still following up, as yet some way behind. At Nottingham, in his first Test against Australia, Compton scored 102. Arithmetically, this innings was swamped by the concurrent triumphs of Paynter, Barnett, and Hutton. Temperamentally, it was significant. For here was a batsman with care but no cares. And, at Lord's, in the Second Test, came the sealing answer: a 76 not out in the second innings, against bowlers who scented victory near.

Then the war; with Army service, cricket in India; football in 'war' internationals; the 1946 summer; and the one 'bad patch' with which fortune chastises her favourites. And so to the Test matches in Australia, heavy, argumentative matches, in which even Compton for some time lost his bearings and, almost, his spirit, till the Test at Adelaide, where, after struggling each painful inch to 50, he reached that famous hundred, then added another.

Last summer, light returned. With W. J. Edrich, he perplexed and caned the bowlers of South Africa and the English counties. Crash went the records of those old masters, Hayward and Hobbs. The Championship came South. A perfect physique surmounted the strain; a perfect balance met the fame. Above all, whether for Middlesex or England, he remains a team man. There's nothing of the showman about him, and, in his highest triumphs, he has kept that happiness without which no game is worth playing or watching.

6 June 1948

---

*By mid-February 1951, Australia were 4–0 up against England, and had beaten them eleven times in all since the war, without a defeat. The one English beacon was Len Hutton's batting, which is here eulogised in a piece commissioned from J. M. Kilburn of the* Yorkshire Post. *The human side of his character is less warmly eulogised, and the piece has never met with Sir Leonard's ardent approval.*

# Len Hutton

Len Hutton's unique fame throughout the cricketing world rests on his cricket alone. He is the very opposite of a man like Patsy Hendren, who purveyed a personality through cricket – almost used cricket as a means to this end. Hutton's name is austerely untouched by anecdote. He is the greatest living batsman, and – behind this – he is the greatest living batsman.

To any cricketing enthusiast, a formal acknowledgement of Hutton's achievements would seem an entirely inadequate form of tribute. But the figures are impressive. During the first four Test matches of the present tour Hutton's batting average has been 79 runs, which is fifty runs more than the next highest average in the England team. His 364 made at The Oval in August 1938 still stands as the highest score by any player in the 70-year-old history of Anglo-Australian Test cricket. It is (or was) the record most coveted by that incomparable run-gatherer, Sir Donald Bradman.

But to admire Len Hutton merely for the quantity of his runs is like praising Milton for the length of *Paradise Lost*, or Schubert for the quantity of his songs. In Hutton's batting there are poetry and rhythm which no critic can translate into words. It has been said that some go to see Hutton make runs, while others go to glory in the perfection of his style. The former are seldom disappointed; the latter almost never.

Leonard Hutton was born at Fulneck, a small Moravian Church community near Pudsey, on Midsummer Day of 1916. His father, a builder by trade, encouraged cricket in the family, and the young Hutton was dedicated to it from the beginning. His career as a Yorkshire professional was strictly conventional. His talent was quickly noted, and he was nursed into the right path from a very early age. From 14 to 18 he was playing for Pudsey St Lawrence in the Bradford League, and in 1934 he was chosen to play for Yorkshire against Cambridge University. Two years later he played for England in his first Test, at Lord's against New Zealand, and was caught out for nought. But, and this is an early mark of his imperturbability, he scored a faultless century in the Second Test. And so to 1938 and the innings which would have made Hutton immortal, even if he had never scored another run. In that Fifth Test match the experiment had been made of playing a game without any time limit, and when Hutton went in he was ordered by his captain, Walter Hammond, to 'Stay there forever'. He stayed there for 13 hours and 20 minutes, slight and pale of face, to score his 364 and beat Bradman's great record.

14

So, at the age of 22 Hutton had given an exhibition of skill, restraint and endurance which, all in all, had never been seen in the game before. But he has never quite lived down the kind of reputation he acquired by it. The public and the critics refused to remember that Hutton batted under orders in that innings, and even Bradman could write some years later that Hutton's genius was purely defensive. Yet since then he has again and again proved that he can get runs as quickly in an emergency as he must, at all times, get them gracefully.

Yet it remains oddly true that Hutton is not so popular a public figure as his sheer achievement would seem to warrant. Though a greater batsman than his colleague Denis Compton, he has never become a popular figure of such high standing – nor, no doubt, does this bother him. The difference in the public's attitude to the two men is illustrated by the way each has been treated during a period of misfortune. In the present Test series, Compton has lamentably failed, and his successive failures have been rightly treated with a sort of indulgent awe. 'How are the mighty fallen!' Yet when, in the Test series of 1946–7 and of 1948, Hutton was daunted into relative failure by the fast bowling of Lindwall and Miller, the end of his career was confidently foretold.

This is the penalty of being a machine. Machines are taken for granted when they work as they should, and impatiently criticised when they go wrong. Hutton has never given the public any cosy human view of himself which will allow them to recognise him as *mon semblable, mon frère*, capable, however rarely, of the same errors of nerve and judgement as themselves. He once said at a dinner that he had never in his life played cricket for fun, an attitude which would be far less unendearing in Australia than it is in England. The implication is not, of course, that he played only for money – though certainly he has a lively enough sense of its value as a guarantee of his own independence – but that he played always with the utmost gravity, not to enjoy himself but to win. His is the stern and antique figure of the gladiator, a grim contestant, hired by the public to give them a spectacle, yet determined that the spectacle shall be good by *his* standards, even if it be also above the public's head. In his cricket Hutton is an extreme highbrow and a Puritan, a faithful follower of the high and unsensational Yorkshire tradition.

15

Like a strict professional, Hutton is never prepared to throw away future prospects just to relieve his own feelings. When he was left out of an English side in 1948, his only comment was that such an event was 'all in the game'. And from this comment, which might have been self-consciously 'sporting' in the mouth of a stiff-upper-lipped amateur, one gets an impression of sheer common sense. Hutton could afford to wait. He seemed to feel no more shame at his moment of humiliation than he had felt triumphs in the many moments of his glory.

Off the field, deprived of his single glorious element, he is a man whom it would be difficult greatly to like or dislike. He becomes a typical enough Yorkshire businessman, patient, imperturbable, determined to get good value for his money and always ready to give fair value in return. He has set up his own sports outfitters business in Bradford and made it into a limited liability company with only himself and his wife as directors. The business is as successful as one would expect. The gloomier side of such a character is that he finds it difficult to exert himself in interests which are not his own. It has been suggested that Hutton has seldom been very helpful to young players. One can tell at once that, if this has been true, it was never due to the weak and envious man's fear of being supplanted or outshone. No young batsman in Hutton's career ever threatened him with that. Hutton is simply one of those who pay primary attention to their own interests, at the expense of anything which they might consider impractical or idealistic. Yet there is no suggestion that Hutton has exhibited any such narrowness of interest in the actual playing of his cricket. There he achieves a kind of universality which excludes none of the basic human qualities. He can even, though he disclaims any sense of fun, be sprightly, gay, almost impish. Broadly he is a classical player rather than a romantic, but it is the great quality of classical masters that they can embrace the romantic within their gigantic range.

On the field, like Milton at his desk, Hutton far surpasses in imagination and ingenuity anything which he could conceivably achieve in ordinary life. Both men are universal inside the limits of their particular activities (the comparison only becomes absurd if one forgets the unthinkable difference in the range of these particular activities). Deprived of those activities, neither is

16

very lovable, if only because neither greatly cares whether he is loved or not.

18 February 1951

---

*Frank Worrell was profiled during the Second Test between England and West Indies at Lord's in 1963 – the Test that entered its final over with the television cameras interrupting the news, all four results possible, and ended in an honours-even draw. Most thought it the most thrilling finish to that point in post-war England but even before then, as evidenced by this Profile, Worrell had entered the national consciousness as one of cricket's most important captains.*

# Frank Worrell

We have been brought up to believe that international cricket captains work under pressures almost as severe as those that harass statesmen during a political crisis. We imagine them to be equally concerned about presenting an acceptable image to the world. But both these assumptions fade away in the presence of the great Frank Worrell, now leading West Indies against England in the Second Test at Lord's.

For Worrell gives an impression of absolute calmness, of utter detachment. In his London hotel bedroom, he likes to relax with his legs up and wearing a blue jersey. Nearing 39, he is now one of the oldest men still active in first-class cricket and no doubt feels the need to store up energy in his tall, strong frame.

But his relaxation is evidently total. It shows in the dead-pan look on his round, coffee-coloured face with the narrow moustache. He exposes it in the careless candour with which he answers questions.

Pressed about the source of his calm, he says, 'Oh, it's often boredom and disinterestedness.' He concedes that he finds relaxing easy. He admits that the first time he ever played in a Test match and was waiting with his pads on for his turn to bat, he went to sleep in the dressing-room. But he says it was a psychological sleepiness. The more vital the match, the sleepier he got.

Even in the exciting early days of his career as a cricketer, he let it be known that for him cricket was not enough. He would wander round the university in Jamaica, asking his friends there to tell him what he should read to widen his scope. Later he went to Manchester University, first with the idea of becoming an optician and then studying, of all things, social anthropology.

Today, he no longer claims any personal cricketing ambitions. He doesn't mind if he takes ten wickets or none, makes a hundred or a duck. He scarcely minds who wins, provided the crowd gets its money's worth. He is almost a fatalist, accepting the outcome of a game as what was in the cards from the beginning.

Yet these characteristics have helped to make Frank Worrell one of the great cricketers of our time. The roots of his nature are to be found in his West Indian boyhood, in events which might very well have destroyed him but which seem instead to have been splendidly refining fires.

He was born in Barbados in 1924. He himself says that close family affection is an important part of West Indian life. But Worrell was not yet 3 when his parents went off to the United States, leaving him to be brought up by his grandmother. In spite of this childhood, which might have left him diffident and un-certain, there is now nothing more remarkable about Worrell than his self-reliance, his independent spirit.

Climate makes the West Indies a natural home of cricket and Worrell was involved in it from the start. He soon began to show exceptional talent as a player and it was this, together with his easy-going ways, that led him at the age of 13 into the most upsetting experience of his life.

He was at Combermere School and by far the youngest player in the school XI. At that time he was thought to be primarily a bowler and so was put to bat last man in. Where any other small boy might have waited his turn with mounting tension as the

18

wickets fell, Worrell asked the captain if he could fill in the time by going down-town to the cinema. The sports master met him on the way and reported him to the Head, who then paid off a longish score of similar small offences by formally dressing Worrell down in front of the assembled school, calling him 'unbearably conceited'.

For years thereafter, Worrell believed that everywhere people were unjustly deriding him as 'big-headed' behind his back. No doubt this helped to spur him on, making him determined obviously to deserve a high reputation. His stature as a batsman grew steadily. He reached the heights in 1945 when he scored 308 not out for Barbados against Trinidad, in a fourth-wicket stand with Goddard that put on 502.

Yet the legend of his conceit still haunted him. Because of it, he tried several times to leave Barbados and did, in fact, move permanently to Jamaica in 1947. When Test cricket started again after the war, Worrell was an obvious choice for the West Indian side and was, indeed, selected. But he was so afraid people would say 'There goes Big-Head Worrell' that he thought of bolting to America. One thing alone deterred him. 'There's no cricket there,' he says, 'so I couldn't be bothered.'

It may be the legend is not entirely groundless. At all events, a curious mutual antipathy seems still to exist between Worrell and Barbados and whenever he returns there, reluctantly, he is apt to be barracked and abused. But once again, the lasting effect of an experience full of stress has turned out to be good where it might have been extremely bad. It helps to explain Worrell's present disengagement from group emotions, his strange placidity.

Worrell's rise to fame as a cricketer may be traced through Wisden's. He became one in that company of marvellous professionals – a kind of mercenary-champion heading each team – who have brought a special vitality to league cricket in the North of England. The place where most small boys have clamoured for Worrell's autograph is indubitably Radcliffe in Lancashire. At the same time, he played Test cricket for his country and has emerged as one of the very greatest – a formidable, silky bat and an effective left-arm bowler.

But it was in Australia in 1960–61 that all Worrell's peculiar virtues combined to win him lasting fame. For countless Australians he is the first non-white hero they ever worshipped.

Cricket was then in a bad way. The preceding English tour of Australia had been a flop, unendurably dull. People were saying that if *this* tour, by the West Indians, was no good, then Test cricket might grind to a halt, might even disappear from the sporting calendar.

As captain of the West Indians, Worrell set the tour alight. His side didn't win, but they made every game flash and sparkle with excitement. Cricket writers the world over gleefully wrote the word 'renaissance' into their copy. When Worrell and his players left for home there were wildly emotional scenes. Australians were demanding that Worrell should be appointed Australia's special agent in the West Indies, that he should be knighted.

Worrell may feel a bored detachment between games, and even when the game is on may never suffer the anguish that troubles other captains. But he brings to every interesting match an alert and subtle mind. His standing is so high with his side that he can tell the gifted Hall how to bowl and the magnificent Sobers how to remedy a faulty shot. His confidence has released the talents of his volatile and sometimes excitable players. Yet by balanced and composed example, with an air of authority that would become a Governor-General, he has always held them together.

Frank Worrell will no doubt retire from cricket when this Test series in England is over. He has, in the end, found other and agreeable things to do. Independent Jamaica has sensibly made him a Senator. He is popular and successful as warden of a hall of residence at the University of the West Indies, where his study has a chair full of footballs and the air smells faintly of bat-oil. He lives contentedly with his wife and tomboy daughter and busies himself quietly with good works.

And when he leaves our cricket grounds for good, thousands who have watched him through long days with knotted handkerchief on their heads will be glad to know he has found his cricketing life 'very, very satisfying' and that it has given him 'peace of mind'.

23 June 1963

*This profile was published under the headline of 'The Young Lochinvar'. At the time, the subject of it was England's vice-captain, about to be raised to the full captaincy in succession to Bob Willis. He did not, however, enjoy a happy first season, suffering from blood poisoning and a 5–0 home defeat by West Indies.*

# David Gower

Seven weeks ago today the bus carrying the England cricket team from Lahore to Faisalabad broke down. So, too, did the captain Bob Willis, thanks to some viral fever, and shortly afterwards he left Pakistan for home, leaving in charge a blond and curly-haired young man, not then 27 years of age, with intensely pale eyes.

English cricket then was perhaps at its lowest ebb since the aftermath of the Second World War. The national side had just lost a series to New Zealand for the very first time, and a Test match in Pakistan for the first time, not to mention the services of Willis and Ian Botham. There were thirteen players left, whose morale might have disintegrated. But they were rallied and led home, with some honour restored, by David Ivon Gower.

It is mainly because of Gower that English cricket faces the start of a new season with any optimism at all. West Indies, the world champions in everything but name, will arrive in the middle of May with more fast bowlers than ever brought to this country before – most of them faster than anyone England can offer – and they have not lost a Test match to England for over ten years.

To spike these West Indian guns, the best that England can place in the firing line is Gower's promising captaincy and nonchalantly majestic batting. Misled by the cherubic appearance, female admirers may fear for him, but it is a task for which Gower – subconsciously or not – has long prepared himself. At the age of 15 he was called to his housemaster's study at The King's School, Canterbury (though he himself says he does not remember the incident), and was there asked what he thought he would be in ten years time. 'Captain of England' came the pat, even offhand, reply.

Gower has so far led England in three Test matches, but his experience of leadership otherwise extends to a mere handful of first-class games (including MCC's match against Essex last week) and he only took over the Leicestershire captaincy at the start of this season. Yet he was born to rule – or at least he was born in what used to be the ruling class, his family history being full of naval officers and consuls, lawyers and colonial officials, the most eminent of them being Admiral Sir Erasmus Gower, former Governor and Commander-in-Chief of Newfoundland (d. 1814). In this democratic age, however, when it is not the done thing to tell your fast bowler that you are related to the Gowers of Castell Malgwyn in Pembrokeshire and your family motto is 'frangas non flectes' (you can break but not bend us), Gower himself, not surprisingly, is reticent about his background.

He was born in Tunbridge Wells on April Fools' Day 1957, when his parents were home on leave from Tanganyika, where his father had been a District Officer since 1942. From those early years Gower recalls a house on stilts outside Dar-es-Salaam, servants and the occasion in the garden there when he first picked up a bat – left-handed, although he is otherwise right-handed. Following independence, his father was appointed Registrar of Loughborough University – dying soon afterwards – and David was brought back to England a day before his sixth birthday. He first went to school in Quorn, then to Marlborough House, the preparatory school in Kent; from there, as a scholar, to King's, Canterbury.

The period abroad, although occurring in his infancy, can be seen as formative: for he has something of the expansive, colonial attitude to life. Gower might have been more at home in the 1920s or 1930s, cracking a dashing hundred for MCC, the darling of the crowds, before speeding away in a Bugatti and cravat for a night on the town. The spirit is essentially amateur but, to his credit, he has buckled down to modern times. He used to have his own Range Rover; he still has a taste for champagne, a keen interest in other wines, a delight in foreign parts (especially the Caribbean), and the attitude that cricket – while a serious matter on the field – is not the be-all and end-all.

This attitude of Gower's – 'laid back' in current idiom, 'relaxed' or even 'flippant' in the past – has not always endeared him to England's selectors who, old soldiers themselves, would prefer a more forelock-tugging, 'yes sir' kind of cricketer. Indeed, Gower's casual approach to discipline has done more than anything to retard his progress towards the highest office in the game: in his two years as England's vice-captain he was not adept at the sergeant-major's role of cracking the whip and getting his players early to bed.

Here the contrast in character with his father is striking. Richard Gower was a model of studious application (four years in the King's 1st XIs for cricket and hockey, three in the 1st XV, a scholarship to Cambridge, a hockey Blue and two books on East African languages). The father was captain of King's; David was not even a school monitor. He glided into the 1st XI at 14 – impressing his coach, the Oxford Blue A. W. Dyer, with his skill of timing – but never made runs in a quantity commensurate with his ability.

He had his father's talent but has only recently developed his application. It was perhaps characteristic that when he did the Oxford entry exam (after gaining eight 'O' levels and three 'A' levels), he answered one question in the History paper – out of sheer whimsy – that was completely outside his syllabus ('about King Arthur or King Alfred, I can't remember which' in his own disarming words).

He went instead to University College, London, dabbling in law (his grandfather had been a judge in Tanganyika) and – with rather more enthusiasm – hockey, before joining Leicestershire to see if he fancied a career in cricket; during school holidays, while playing for Loughborough Town, he had been recommended to the county by a Leicestershire committeeman. It has frequently been wondered why Kent let such a prodigy slip through their fingers, but, as the cricket historian E. E. Snow (brother of C.P.) points out, Gower's family ties have always been with Leicestershire.

At Leicester two old Yorkshire professionals, Jack Birkenshaw and Ray Illingworth, liked what they saw of his batting but were occasionally taken aback by his 'amateur attitude'. (It was about this time that Illingworth told Gower to dress more smartly, and

23

saw him appear for breakfast next morning in a dinner jacket.) Gower's maiden first-class century, a good one at Lord's, came during his first half-season of 1976 but he usually found batting easier in one-day games when he could indulge his talent for improvising a scoring stroke from every ball. It was his potential, not achievement, that was recognised in 1978 with the award of an England cap – his 58 on début against Pakistan being only his eighth score of 50 in first-class cricket.

Anybody who was at Edgbaston that June day can recall Gower's beginning, for perhaps no one has announced himself to Test cricket with such élan. He pivoted, hooked a short first ball to the boundary and looked around, pink-faced and startled that Test cricket was just a game after all.

Off the field, Gower's interests include photography, travel with his live-in girlfriend, and music. He takes *The Daily Telegraph* and, like most county cricketers, loves a crossword. His taste in reading may be classified as general middle-brow; he himself writes a regular column in a cricket magazine that is droll but may sometimes – a habit he must kill when captain – be openly facetious.

His future as captain, assuming the selectors do appoint him this summer? While some may judge by the cherubic appearance that he is too soft or mild-mannered, he has developed a veneer of hardness, if only to deal with those hangers-on who want to tell him at length that he reminds them of Woolley. The accusation of mental laziness – quite aside from the fact that he did not make the most of his brain academically, and has been known, like many a cricketer, to doze off while fielding in front of three men and a dog – is a more serious one.

Enormously gifted cricketers, like Ian Botham or Colin Cowdrey, tend not to make the best captains: for they cannot conceive what it is like for lesser mortals to struggle. But Gower, already second as a batsman only to Viv Richards, may be young enough, and innately intelligent enough, to make that leap and to lead English cricket away from the depths it touched last winter.

29 April 1984

*Immediately after the 5–0 victory by West Indies over England in 1984, the first time England had been comprehensively swept aside at home, the victorious captain Clive Lloyd was profiled. Shortly afterwards Lloyd retired, having scored 7159 Test runs at 46. Of his 74 Tests in charge, he lost 12 and won 36 – the most wins achieved by any Test captain.*

# Clive Lloyd

It says much for the captaincy of Clive Lloyd that his West Indian cricketers last week put the finishing touches to the most crushing defeat that England, or any other country, has ever suffered at home in a hundred years of Test cricket. It says equally much for Lloyd's personality that his players can humiliate England's national team at the national game without our feeling the slightest animosity towards him.

After five consecutive West Indian victories, Lloyd has peered through his thick lenses and moustache at our television screens and told us not to worry, like a benevolent uncle (albeit with a touch of majesty). Arguably he has now as familiar a face as any coloured person in this country – yet it is not because of his own feats on the field that he claims our attention, although these are prodigious enough.

As a youth with sloping shoulders and loping stride, Lloyd generated electricity like no other fieldsman. He also had the habit of scoring centuries in cup finals at Lord's, whether for West Indies or his county, Lancashire. Since then, among other superlatives, he has become the longest-serving current Test player (he made his début in 1966) and by far the longest-serving captain in Test history (The Oval game last week was his sixty-ninth in charge).

But more than that, Lloyd has taken the least successful Test team in the world – it is all too easy now to forget that West Indies went from 1965 to 1974 without winning a Test match at home – and made it half as strong again as any other. In the process he has not only changed the face of Test cricket, through his use of fast bowling; he has also changed the image of the black cricketer. West Indians were renowned as flamboyant, happy-go-lucky, 'calypso' cricketers, lacking in that great Victorian virtue of temperament. Lloyd, by bridling that unbridled enthusiasm, has made them flamboyant yet utterly professional.

No wonder his players speak of him with reverence. 'Both in terms of his size (Lloyd is 6 feet 4 inches when he extends those shoulders) and his personality, Clive is a giant of a man,' says the team's wicket-keeper, Jeffrey Dujon. 'He's basically quiet – though he'll read the riot act if complacency slips in – and yet he has managed to keep us in high spirits the entire summer.'

Lloyd's impact, however, does not stop there upon the field. He has also shared in the transformation of the black cricketer from a social inferior to the peak of his profession. Their two finest before the Second World War, George Headley and Learie Constantine, had to share not only the same room but the same bed when England toured the Caribbean in 1929–30. Under Sir Frank Worrell, then Sir Garfield Sobers, and now Lloyd, that status has been exalted.

Born in British Guiana (as it was until 1966) on 31 August 1944, Lloyd's background was lower middle class, 'by no means well-to-do' as he remembers. His father worked as chauffeur for a local doctor; his mother was the aunt of Lance Gibbs, the off-spinner who for a time held the world record for most Test wickets. Together the boys grew up playing cricket in the front yard of Lloyd's two-storeyed wooden home in a humid suburb of Georgetown.

Lloyd also had a younger brother and four sisters, whom he was suddenly called upon to support when his father died in 1958. He had to leave school prematurely and took a clerical job in Georgetown Hospital at £16 a month. Responsibility, as the family breadwinner, was therefore thrust upon him at an early age.

Another childhood incident suggests a maturity beyond his years. When walking home from school at the age of 12 he saw two boys fighting: 'Always the mediator' as he describes himself, he intervened and for his pains was rewarded with a ruler jabbed into his right eye. His vision deteriorated and ever since he has worn glasses (one of only three current Test players to wear them).

Through these spectacles Lloyd has seen a profound change in the way the game is played. Indeed, he has probably had a greater hand than anyone else in this development. Whereas cricket was devised as an activity that took place below the height of the bails, the focus – at least when the West Indies are bowling – has shifted to the batsman's chest and head.

This change from a safe 'gentlemanly' sport (Sir Jack Hobbs would protest to the bowler if he were given a bouncer) into a duel between fast bowler and visored, helmeted batsman was perhaps inevitable but Clive Lloyd and his West Indians have accelerated the process over the last decade. In 1975–76 Lloyd saw his batsmen succumb to the speed of Dennis Lillee and Jeff Thomson on his first tour to Australia as captain (he lost the series 5–1, so he knows what David Gower feels like). Soon afterwards he saw his team, with three spin-bowlers in it, lose again on a turning pitch in Port-of-Spain, even though India had to score more than 400 to win. Whatever faith Lloyd had in slow bowling disappeared; speed was the thing by which he would make West Indies the world champions.

Nor was one pair of fast bowlers sufficient for his plans – like Lillee and Thomson, or Hall and Griffith, or Trueman and Statham, or Larwood and Voce. What Lloyd designed was an entirely new formation of four fast bowlers, who could keep going all day and thereby give the batsmen no respite. And by a nice irony he found the fuel for this machine in English cricket, for during the 1970s the majority of first-class counties had signed a fast bowler from the West Indies.

World Series Cricket was set up in Australia just as the plan was taking shape (Lloyd resigned as West Indies captain and, like his then poorly paid team mates, was quick to accept Kerry Packer's offer). On substandard pitches, hastily prepared for the 'circus', fast bowlers were all the more lethal. They caused the introduction of the helmet, which five years later is uniform equipment. When World Series Cricket closed down, Lloyd continued with his four-man pace attacks, to such effect that West Indies have lost only one of their past 39 Test matches.

But Lloyd has had to do more than score his share of runs and rotate his fast bowlers. In the words of Wesley Hall, who built on his reputation as a fast bowler to become a Barbados MP: 'What are not often appreciated are the psychological problems which face West Indian cricket captains because of our varied religious, political and socio-economic backgrounds compounded by the insular tendencies of island peoples.'

So strong have these 'tendencies' been that fielders were said to have missed catches if the bowler came from a different island; selection was not so much a matter of deciding relative merit as horse-trading. Yet if Guyanese and Barbadians, Jamaicans and Trinidadians have had trouble in working together, allowances should be made, according to one sociologist who explains: 'Outside the world of cricket the West Indies is not a nation and does not act as one.'

Anyone watching the present West Indians practising of a morning in their diverse tracksuits and rainbow tee-shirts might be tempted to conclude that the differences now are only outward. But much though Lloyd has done to smooth the Caribbean waters, they are still susceptible to the occasional typhoon. Lloyd himself is still regularly booed in Port-of-Spain for his role in ending the Test career of the local wicket-keeper, Deryck Murray. Antiguans, as the newest element in the equation, can be even pricklier: when their rising star Richie Richardson was dropped earlier this summer, letters accused Lloyd of being 'callous', among other less polite expressions.

Will these centrifugal forces fully reassert themselves once Lloyd has retired? The West Indian cricket journalist, Tony Cozier, for one, fears so: 'Lloyd and the success of his team have kept everyone reasonably happy, but once the next generation starts to lose, the old rivalries are likely to surface.'

And when will Lloyd retire? He has committed himself to nothing more than the next tour to Australia, but his physio-therapist, Dennis Waight, an Australian rejoicing in the nickname 'Sluggo', is well qualified to say that Lloyd could go on for 'several more years' should he feel the inclination.

The prime attraction of retirement is that it will allow Lloyd to spend more time in his adopted home of Manchester (whose university has awarded him an honorary MA) with his wife Waveney, a former nurse from Guyana, and their two daughters.

He has found an affinity with Lancashire, like many West Indian cricketers before him who played in that county's leagues, most notably Baron Constantine of Maravel and Nelson. One day it might even be Baron Lloyd of Georgetown and Manchester.

19 August 1984

PART 2

*Portraits*

**1** Sir Frank Worrell's achievements in raising the standard and status of West Indian cricketers make him the most important of post-war captains. The serenity, strength and inner conviction are here captured by 'the Gentle Eye', Jane Bown.

**2** Sir Leonard Hutton, photographed by Jane Bown on his seventieth birthday at his home in Surrey: it could be the face of a round-the-world yachtsman, single-handed of course, for he has always been his own man.

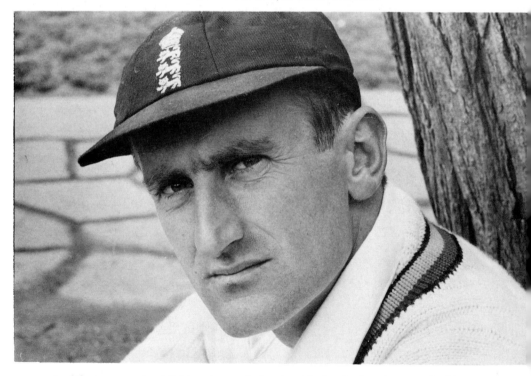

**3** 'Always use natural light and natural situations' is the single rule prescribed by Jane Bown, who took this portrait of Ted Dexter in his England and *Observer* days. 'There is no point in arriving with preconceptions, because however much you think about the subject beforehand it's nothing like that when you get there. I just arrive on a wing and a prayer, with a 35mm camera, and use the given conditions.'

*By 1938 it was acceptable for an amateur cricketer like Harry Surtees Altham (Oxford University, Surrey and Hampshire) to wax lyrical about a professional – but then appreciation of Frank Woolley's cricket always did transcend the social classes. Altham, who was an* Observer *contributor for many years, is probably the only one to be buried in Winchester Cathedral. A master at the college there, he was also a Test selector, historian of the game, coach, President of MCC and a holder of the MC, for services in the First World War. He died, aged 76, in 1965.*

# Frank Woolley

The season that is now entering its closing phase will have had much to contribute to cricket history: McCabe's defiant brilliance at Nottingham, Hammond's majestic and Augustan batsmanship at Lord's, the macabre struggle in the gloom of Leeds, Don Bradman's technical and personal dominance under the most varying conditions of wicket and situation – all these will be remembered as long as the game is played. But it may well be that, as memories turn back from ten or 20 years hence, the first words that will be spoken of the season of 1938 will be – 'Ah, that was Frank Woolley's last summer.' And summer is the word that they will use, for about Woolley's batsmanship there is a fragrance and bloom that takes the bite from the chilliest May wind and deepens the contrast between sun and shadow on the hottest field of August.

To the connoisseur his technique has always been absolutely satisfying, untrammelled by the shuffling complexities of much modern decadence, elemental in its economy and smoothness of movement, classic in its power and poise. But to the cricket world in its infinite variety, from the artisan snatching a dinner hour at Blackheath to the country parson who has come out of some sleepy parish in the Weald to the social vortex of Canterbury week, he has always been and still is the man who, more perhaps than any other, has opened their eyes to the beauty of cricket.

They cannot, even if they would, analyse the secret of his off-drive, of that devastating cut behind cover point, of the leisurely back stroke that steers the ball wide of mid-on, of the almost contemptuous flicker of the bat that glides it away to the fine-leg boundary. But so long as he is at the wicket they can sit and enjoy and absorb the beauty of an art that can be at once as serene and English as a landscape by Constable, and as instinct with style and dignity as a Gainsborough or a Reynolds.

But the appeal of his batsmanship lies in something more than its beauty: it reflects, in its unruffled ease, a singularly gracious, and, in its challenging power, a gallant personality. To Frank Woolley the bat has always been a weapon of offence, and he is the pre-eminent advertisement for his own creed that there is nothing wrong with cricket, nor ever will be, so long as it is played in the right spirit. His attitude and his art have constituted an unvarying protest against the mechanisation of the game, and the sternest struggle in a county or Test match has never found him anything but true to himself. No one who saw them will ever forget his two innings against Australia in the match at Lord's in 1921. The whirlwind of Gregory and McDonald was tearing England's batting into tatters, but only the malignity of fate denied him, by the barest margin, a century in each innings.

It is queer to reflect how many amongst the thousands who still delight to watch him at the wicket know little or nothing of his triumphs with the ball. Overshadowed for a time in the Kent XI by a supreme artist in Colin Blythe, he was nevertheless a very great bowler, with a lovely action, a fine length, and great command of spin. In the three seasons 1920–1–2 he captured 515 wickets for just over 16 apiece, and in the first of those years, with 1924 runs and 185 wickets, he came nearer than any other cricketer, before or since, to George Hirst's incomparable achievement of 2000 runs and 200 wickets in a single season. A thousand catches, the great majority at slip, are further evidence of his pre-eminence as an all-rounder.

But it has been well said that there has never been a cricketer whose contribution to the game could be less adequately assessed by statistics: transcending all his runs and wickets and catches is the fact that under his spell countless thousands of men and women have forgotten the drab preoccupations and anxieties of the day, and for an hour or more found life once again full of beauty and zest. And so, when for the last time he goes out to bat, amid the tents and flags and trees of Canterbury, the affectionate good wishes, not only of all Kent but of all the cricket world, will attend him to the wicket and beyond.

31 July 1938                                                    *H. S. Altham*

---

*Robertson-Glasgow began England's 1950–51 tour of Australia as* The Observer *correspondent and soon became correspondent for* The Times *as well, when 'Beau' Vincent fell ill. Here, in a Sporting Print, he sketches the Australian mystery bowler of that series, who took 21 wickets at 15 runs each. Jack Iverson did not play another Test match, before or afterwards, and died in 1973.*

# Jack Iverson

Other bowlers will take 6 for 27 or better in one innings of a Test match, but none, surely, will do it by spinning the ball off the thumb and bent-double middle finger with the other three fingers kept out of the way.

Till the Australian summer of 1949–50, when this quiet-minded prodigy first appeared on the field of major cricket, the Iverson way was not, so to speak, bowling within the meaning of the Act. But now, I fancy, hundreds of Australian juniors are trying to be Iverson and running in late to supper with aching fingers and diminishing hope.

Jack Iverson, son and partner of an estate agent in the Melbourne district, was born in July 1915. Before the Second World War he bowled cheerfully, but without distinction, at medium to fast-medium pace in extremely minor cricket. As a boy at Geelong College he counted himself lucky to get a game at all.

He is about 6 feet 3 inches tall, broad shouldered, well proportioned, but not athletic as to the movement of the legs, which carry him safely, rather than swiftly, in pursuit from mid-on towards the boundary. For those interested in physiognomy he has a broad brow, steady, wide-set eyes, and a strong jaw under a longish nose.

These details I send because England will not see Iverson on their cricket fields. Soon after the Third Test at Sydney he told the Australian selectors that he would gladly play in any first-class match for which he might be chosen till the end of this season. Then he would retire and no second thoughts.

When on war service with AA transport in the tropics he played in hut cricket, a game where the batsman used a ruler and the bowler a ping-pong ball. With his now famous grip Iverson made that ping-pong ball spin anyhow. Then, as now, when his middle finger tired, he folded his fourth finger as a reserve spinning agent. From celluloid he graduated to a lawn tennis ball so returning, perhaps unknowingly, to B. J. T. Bosanquet's experiments at Oxford University some 50 and more years ago.

After discovery came hours, days, weeks of practice. The penalty and the delight of genius. Then, as in such scientific stories, followed the struggle for recognition. At 30 he played for the 3rd XI of Brighton, a Melbourne suburb. After three games he was promoted to the 1st XI.

Next year his spins won the subdistrict premiership for Brighton. He stepped up to the Melbourne team. Here for a time he stuck, and he thought of returning to Brighton. But one day, as he walked with his wife through Jolimont Park, near the Melbourne Cricket Ground, he saw a sight, unforgettable and inspiring. Blinded ex-Servicemen were playing cricket with a ball that was a small round basket with a bell inside it. If they could do that, what might not he do?

Self-doubt melted. He went back to more practice. The top-spinner he had mastered; the googly came next, and last the roller from leg. So he went to his place in the Victoria State XI. Against Western Australia at Perth last season he began with one wicket only and eight catches missed off him in one innings. But soon he was taking the wickets in fingerfuls, and at the end of the season he went to New Zealand for a continuous triumph. In the present series of Tests Iverson settled the innings and the rubber with a spinning crash. Now to Adelaide and to Iverson's own Melbourne, where the wonderful story must end.

21 January 1951 *R. C. Robertson-Glasgow*

---

*Shortly after George Hirst had died, Michael Davie went to see Yorkshire's other great all-rounder in his house in Huddersfield. After the interview, Wilfred Rhodes, blind, walked down the street and was greeted with reverence by all passers-by. Such was Rhodes's dignity that the author remembers 'blubbing all the way back to London'.*

# George Hirst and Wilfred Rhodes

Hirst and Rhodes. Rhodes and Hirst. Hirst: 36,323 runs and 2739 wickets in first-class cricket. Rhodes: 39,802 runs and 4187 wickets. Apart from Grace, no one else has approached figures like these.

Both men came from the same village, played for the same county, and appeared in their first (which was also Grace's last) Test match in England at the same time, in 1899. Last Monday, Hirst, aged 82, died in his house, which is about 200 yards from where Rhodes lives in a stone suburb of Huddersfield.

Rhodes's house, like his neighbour's, looks as if it were built to last by the same men who were responsible for the imperishable mills and Methodist chapels nearby. The grass in front of it last week was a vivid green, without a weed. Inside, it is as clean as a new bat.

Rhodes is 77; clean-shaven, ruddy, upright, enduring. Mrs

Rhodes told me she was nearly 80, admitting that no one believed it. In the last two years Rhodes has lost his sight, but his blindness has provoked no self-pity.

I dared to begin by asking him about Hirst's swerve, since it is said to have been one of the deadliest weapons any bowler has possessed. 'I can tell you what it was like,' he said. He asked his wife if she would fetch a ball. She came back with a ball the reddish-mauve colour of a well-matured grape. It was mounted on a silver wicket. It was the ball with which Hirst and Rhodes, members of what people call the best side England has ever put into the field, bowled out Australia at Birmingham in 1902 for 36 runs.

Because of its fixed mount, Rhodes could not hold it properly, so his wife brought another ball. Rhodes stood. He stumbled and regained his balance. 'I'm sorry,' he said. He kept his head erect and, being handed the ball, fitted the seam between the first two fingers of his left hand. He was like a blind hero. That was the grip for the regular Hirst inswinger.

> If you were standing behind the wicket, the ball looked to be going fastish between first slip and the wicket, say a good half-yard beyond the wicket and sometimes further away. The seam stayed upright and the ball never changed direction in the air until it began its fall. Then it swung. Ideally the wind was coming in from third man. It gets the ball here, as the seam turns over, and flattens it, makes it drop quickly. I've heard fellows say it looked as if it were coming in from mid-off.
>
> Then he bowled the one which spun, the one which held itself straight.

Rhodes shifted the ball further into the palm of his hand, his fingers across the seam this time. He nipped deeply into the seams with his left index finger.

> That was the difficult part about him; that one appeared to go the other way.
>
> He always had three short legs and a fine leg. I used to field in there. I caught them out. You could go as close as you liked for the swinger because the batsman couldn't hit the ball really

hard with the face of the bat. He could hit the spun one, though. I always went back a bit for that one. I could tell which was coming by the way he gripped it, but there was lots that couldn't. I don't think Jack Hobbs knew which was which.

Aye, I'll tell you. When Hirst was waiting to go in he very rarely watched the match. I've noticed it many a time. He used to play very seriously, you know, but he hardly ever watched. Whether he was saving his eyesight or not I never knew. Myself, I always wanted to see every ball.

Would he tell me about The Oval Test match in 1902, the most famous finish in Test history, when England needed 263, five wickets fell for 48, Jessop made 104 in 75 minutes and Rhodes joined Hirst with one wicket to fall and 15 runs to get? Was he nervous?

'Well, you see, I'd been in before with Fred Tate in a situation like that in the First Test, when we needed eight to win. I'd kind of got used to it.'

Did Hirst meet him and make the most famous remark in cricket history, 'We'll get them in singles, Wilfred'?

They always tell that tale. As far as I can remember he only asked me if I was all right. It's a tale. I don't think any cricketer would believe it. There'd have been just as much sense if he'd said, 'We'll get them in sixes,' wouldn't there? I'll tell you what he might have said, though he didn't. He'd got 50, so he might have said, 'Let me have as much of the bowling as you can.' It's a pity to spoil the tale, but you can't say it's true if it isn't.

Rhodes talked on, full of cricket wisdom, demonstrating footwork, describing Yardley as the best on-side player in England, wondering why Simpson had never tumbled to the fact that Lindwall always bowled him with a fast half-volley, thinking that our fellows nowadays didn't try to swing the ball by spinning it. There were respectful references to 'this here Bedser'.

'Do you know my ideal of footwork?' I expected a name from the past. 'Hassett. Footwork doesn't mean moving your feet all over the place. It's positioning.'

'Hirst and I both learned our cricket the hard way. There were no coaches about then, but in any case you've got to reckon it up yourself, haven't you? You've got to reckon it up yourself.' He said of Hirst, 'He was stiff-built and could stand a lot of work.'

Rhodes put on his hat and took out his blind man's stick to show me to the trolleybus stop. 'I know my way back from there from the time before my sight went,' he said. He gripped my arm and I could feel the strength in the fingers of his left hand. He said he would be at some of the Tests, and at Bradford over the weekend for the Yorkshire match, although the friend who used to take him round cricket grounds had died. 'There's a puddle here,' he said. He questioned me closely about my trip back to London, and wished me a good journey.

He turned back to his house, 200 yards from Hirst's house, feeling in front of him with his stick.

Passers-by said, 'Good afternoon, sir,' and touched their hats.

16 May 1954                                                      *Michael Davie*

---

*Quotations, apart from the odd sentence, traditionally had no part in cricket writing. Then in the 'fifties reports of a New Journalism filtered over from America. A member of* The Observer *sports desk, John Gale, took up the idea and practised it in stories like the following interview with the mother of England's hero in 1954–55. Gale went on to become a general reporter and subsequently covered the Algerian War. Not long afterwards he committed suicide, partly as a result of that experience.*

# Frank Tyson

'I had a gentleman the other day who said that if every driver drove like me we would be all right,' said the taxi-driver. He was like a slightly older Al Read. We were looking for Mrs Tyson, whose son has startled Australia, and the taxi-driver wasn't wasting time. The smoke-black houses of Middleton, just outside Manchester, clung in lines to the round hills; industrial chimneys breathed into a cold sky.

'Eighteen horse-power, 17 years old,' said the taxi-driver. He came to a sudden stop and shouted to the street in general: 'Eh, Charlie.' Several people ran up to give directions. At last, we were near. A pink boy in a red cap considered heavily, and said it was No. 67. A lady said 19. It was 19, a newish house with a green door.

The taxi-driver beckoned me in impatiently. Mrs Tyson, who had grey hair and a friendly glint, said she hadn't had time to clean up in the last few days; the house looked spotless. She made us cups of tea. She was surrounded by congratulatory telegrams and letters (one from the Mayor of Bolton, where Frank was born). A music shop had sent a record of 'My Son, My Son'.

What did she think about his having increased his speed? Well, he had, so they said. 'But he was a fast bowler before. He takes a terrific long run.' Mrs Tyson said she kept telling Frank his run was too long. It took all his energy.

'Our Frank's always had a lot of treatment to keep him loose,' she said. 'He has his electric equipment with him now. They said the other day he'd pulled a pelvis. It was the first I'd heard of that.'

How did Frank get to Northamptonshire? Well, they were scouting. It was true Lancashire turned him down. 'Frank was very disappointed. They just wrote to say they would let him know when there was a vacancy. That never came off. Northants got him. You can't blame Frank. He was a keen cricketer. It was up to him.'

Frank did his Army service in the Signals. He has an elder brother who doesn't play cricket. But the brother is 'quite interested in Frank'. Mr Tyson, who died five years ago, was a foreman bleacher in a dye works. 'He would have been very proud.'

Was it true Frank quoted when he took his run-up? 'Well, I've never heard him,' said Mrs Tyson. 'But I know he was fond of poetry.' Frank was determined. 'If he sets himself to do something, he must master it.' She thought he would have got his B.A. but for cricket – and he would get it still. He took English Literature, French and History. 'He's very good at French. It's one of his pet subjects. Yet he failed in English. Isn't it funny? He failed his English by only two marks. I think it was a shame, because he was cricketing for his college.'

Just then a large clock struck 11, although it said ten to. 'Take no notice of that clock,' she said. 'It gets moved and upset every time a reporter comes. It gets moved because they take me at the wireless, and they want Frank's photo on top, where the clock usually is.'

She produced photographs of Frank. 'And here he is when he was playing for the Army at Lord's.' It was a formal group. 'Majors and captains and that,' she said. 'Poor Frank,' she laughed. One picture showed Tyson with plenty of hair. He went thin on top after breaking his leg playing for Durham University against the Army. 'Shock does that,' said the taxi-driver. Mrs Tyson said Frank didn't mind about its affecting his appearance – he was a natural sort of boy. 'Quite right,' said the taxi-driver.

We asked if Frank got cross. 'If they sent bumpers at him, he'd do the same. But he never gets vicious with anybody.' 'Never gets nettled, does he?' asked the taxi-driver. Mrs Tyson said no. She was never worried about him. He could look after himself and wasn't dependent on other people. 'He's got push of his own. Education is a good thing. It gives you that independence. It's been a hard struggle, but it's been worth it.' (At the Grammar School, the headmaster, Mr Wren, who had Tyson's record and reports spread out in front of him, said that Mrs Tyson had always worked to help with her son's education after Mr Tyson had died. And Tyson's professional cricket had helped pay for his time at Durham University. He had been a fine boy, a prefect, and had got a good Higher Certificate.)

Mrs Tyson admitted she was a *little* apprehensive about Frank's going to Australia. 'He'd only been in first-class cricket about 12 months, that was the trouble. Our Frank was unheard of, kind of thing. I wasn't too keen on him going. Not enough experience. But Frank was up in arms. You don't like your own getting a slating.'

'How about seeing the local vicar?' remarked the taxi-driver. 'We're Congregational,' said Mrs Tyson. 'Frank was a warden. A big chapel-goer.'

As we were going out we asked Mrs Tyson if she minded all the fame and fuss. 'No, I don't, because I think it's lovely.'

9 January 1955                                              *John Gale*

---

*This is a compare-and-contrast analysis of the two captains in the 1958–59 series between Australia and England. It was written by Michael Davie, who covered the tour after having been Sports Editor of* The Observer, *and who was later voted 'Journalist of the Year'.*

# Peter May and Richie Benaud

'The eyes of the world are on us,' a Melbourne newspaper stated baldly last week. This may be putting the interest in the Second Test between England and Australia a little high, but it is true nevertheless that the attention of a sizeable chunk of the Commonwealth was concentrated last week on the colossal amphitheatre of the Melbourne Cricket Ground, and on the two captains, Peter May and Richie Benaud, who are principally responsible for what happens there.

The strain now on these two young men is as high as almost any kind of public activity can impose. The next few days (the Second Test is followed almost immediately by the Third) will be very tough going indeed, both physically and mentally.

The strain is increased because something more than the fate of the series is felt to be at stake. May, the England captain, plays to win with every nerve in his body, sustained by the belief that his country's prestige is closely involved with the way it performs at sport. He is the kind of fellow who would expect to see any failure by the England cricketers reflected in the price of sterling in Zurich. Benaud, for his part, is the principal gladiator of a nation that tends to assess its international standing in terms of the success of its sporting heroes, and which derives especial satisfaction from humiliating England.

Of the two of them, May at the moment is in the tougher spot: he leads a team which lost the First Test match when it had been expected to win and has virtually lost the Second; he has the crowd against him (though Australian crowds do not always support their own sides); he is having to be the main support of his side's rickety batting, the only sound timber in a house penetrated by white ants.

He is also expected to be as continuously alert off the field as he is on it: since the tour began two months ago he has been publicly berated for spending too much time with his fiancée, for frigidity towards journalists, and for failing to subdue the alleged roistering of his team in its off-hours.

Between Tests, Benaud can retreat into comparative obscurity, but the bloodhounds never leave the trail of the itinerant MCC.

Superficially, the two men are similar. They are about the same age (Benaud is 28, May was 29 last week), the same weight, and the same class (middle middle). May is the world's best batsman; Benaud is the world's best all-rounder. Both are respected by their subordinates. But otherwise they are as dissimilar as their two countries.

Benaud, a smoothly tanned, bright-blue-eyed cove with a complicated Australian profile, is so relaxed that you sometimes feel you want to stir him with a stick to make sure he is still going. He walks with the slow-motion gait of a bushman who is working in a temperature of 120 degrees and is expecting to run out of water. He is gentle, genial and approachable outside, and very single-minded inside. He is thoughtful, mature, a spruce dresser and as clean as the Pacific surf. He has false teeth because his own were smashed by a cricket ball.

May is a textbook contrast. He has a fine-drawn, rather unemphatic face. He is as taut as a wire; he is never still. On the field he is always pulling at his collar, clasping and unclasping his hands or nibbling the side of his thumb. Even if he is not playing, he keeps up an anxious stream of half-involuntary exhortation from the pavilion – 'Well done, Colin!' 'Oh! Back up, Ted!' 'Let her go, Brian!' He hums at breakfast.

Benaud, though of a quiet disposition, is spiritually one of the boys – 'We're all good mates.' May, though he is not exactly shy, has a kind of English frozen-upness about him: to join a hearty cricketers' group at a bar is for him the social equivalent of climbing the Matterhorn. Benaud handles journalists easily; May, not wholly without reason, evidently feels that talking to writers is as unpredictably risky as throwing an egg into an electric fan.

Benaud is not sure about the origin of his name, but believes his great-great-grandfather came to Sydney as captain of a French ship. He spent his early boyhood in the bush, where his father was a schoolmaster, and his earliest memories are of being taken round to country games and watching his father bowl leg-breaks.

Benaud always had a passion for the game; when the family (both Benaud and May have younger brothers who are good cricketers) moved to Sydney before the war, Benaud got into the hierarchical Australian grade system and gradually moved up through the ranks until in 1948 he was picked to play for New South Wales.

Since then he has played in 33 Tests; his career has simultaneously prospered. When he left Parramatta High School at the age of 16 he first worked as clerk, then transferred to the accounts department of the *Sun-Herald* newspaper group, then three years ago switched over to the editorial side, where he now operates as a general reporter and also writes a matey weekly sports column called 'Come in, Spinner!' for the *Sun*. When he travels around playing cricket, he takes his typewriter with him; he produced his column as usual during the First Test, telephoning his copy through from Brisbane before the start of play.

Benaud makes a bit of money on the side by advertising – for instance, the Renault Dauphine. He is married, with two small children, and lives outside Sydney in the respectable city of Parramatta. As a matter of principle he steers clear of politics and religion.

May's career has been rather different, if only because it seems to have had an accidental element missing from Benaud's. His earliest memories are of being bowled at (like W. G. Grace) by his mother on a Surrey tennis court. He went to a prep school in Reading, then to Charterhouse. Alec Bedser, the England bowler and May's great helper, went down to Charterhouse just after May had gone there and was told by George Geary, the school coach, that the 'skinny sort of a kid, tall and willowy', was a future England player.

But if May wanted to be a sportsman at all at that time, he chiefly wanted to be a great footballer, despite his dazzling school cricket career. At Cambridge, where he read history and enjoyed it, he decided that he wanted to be a schoolmaster and nearly became one before a friend of a friend fixed him up with a job at Lloyd's. He first played for England in 1951 and since 1953 has been playing pretty well full time. 'One gets swept along,' he says with his disarming grin.

His formative education among the uncompromising and unforthcoming Surrey professionals has given him their attributes to a marked degree, as it has given him also their manners of speech. To that extent, he expresses a more elaborate personality when batting than when speaking. The total lack of anecdote about him is significant.

Officially May is an amateur but he, like Benaud, frankly makes money out of his cricket. Recently, after he had produced a successful book, his accountant suggested that he should turn himself into Peter May Limited, which he did. This device helps him with tax on, for instance, fees for newspaper articles, and with his income (estimated by a reliable source at not less than £2000 a year) from sponsoring bats, shirts, and boots. He draws the line at advertising goods of which he has no personal experience as a cricketer.

In his spare time – what there is of it – May writes numerous letters, mostly duty ones, and likes reading Trollope and listening to Sinatra and Ella Fitzgerald. He also enjoys driving cars fast – he says it relaxes him, and it is probably the only thing that does. He sleeps nine hours a night, but one imagines he is active even then, moving nightmare fieldsmen and pulling his pyjama collar in his sleep. Since he arrived in Australia he has lost 9 lb.

A former England captain said lately, 'In Australia the ball is hard, the wickets are hard, and the people are hard. And you've got to be hard to beat them.' Both these young men possess a necessary ruthlessness. Both of them are a long way removed from the uncomplicated yokels who used to play on Broadhalfpenny Down when cricket was in its infancy. As May put it the other day: 'This kind of thing isn't exactly *fun*, you know.'

3 January 1959                                          *Michael Davie*

---

*John Arlott, who wrote on cricket and football for* The Observer *before becoming cricket correspondent of* The Guardian, *here tells the story of Basil d'Oliveira's emergence from South Africa. It was written after d'Oliveira's début for England in 1966. The piece ends with a prophetic anticipation of the controversy that was to lead to South Africa's exclusion from international cricket.*

# Basil d'Oliveira

Basil d'Oliveira's first major cricket performance was in 1951, when he was 19. In a match in the Cape, he scored 225 of his side's total of 233 – 100 in 25 minutes, 200 in 65 minutes, with 28 sixes and ten fours – and then retired. A few weeks later he had a bowling analysis, as a leg-spinner, of 9 wickets for 2 runs.

He played in – to use the South African definition – 'non-European cricket' and, as what is there called a 'Cape Coloured', he represented the South African Coloured Cricket Association in racial competition. Within this framework he first appeared for Western Province, in the Sir David Harris tournament, when he was 16.

47

In 1953 he struck 46 runs – 6, 6, 6, 6, 6, 6, 4, 6 – from an eight-ball over. He became captain of his club, province and the representative 'non-European' team.

D'Oliveira first wrote to me in 1958. He wanted to come and play in Lancashire League cricket – was there a chance for him? He now had behind him some good performances in representative matches against the 'Kenyan Asian' sides, including men who had played first-class cricket in Pakistan. But who in England would be impressed by this?

Some good South African cricketers of open mind went to watch him and wrote to say that he was a mighty striker of the ball, a useful bowler who had now switched from leg-breaks, by way of off-spin, to medium-pace 'seam-up' and a brilliant slip who had moved to mid-off.

In 1958 he played in 'friendlies' against white opposition in the Cape and mastered the best bowling brought against him. There was no time to waste: he was now 26. At the best level of play to which he was admitted he was outstandingly successful.

In late 1959 a team of English professionals coaching in South Africa played a representative non-European side: d'Oliveira, playing straight and hitting hard, scored a quick 90 without a chance. This was the last opportunity.

John Kay, who remarkably contrives to be cricket correspondent of the *Manchester Evening News* as well as the eyes and ears of the Lancashire League, persuaded Middleton, his local club, to take a generous risk. They offered the unknown Cape cricketer terms for 1960.

He accepted the offer by cable. Having played virtually all his cricket on matting, he settled for daily practice on turf. Local subscriptions in Cape Town paid his passage to England: he would earn enough to keep himself and pay his fare back. It was make or break in a single season. He arrived modest – and semi-stunned. He was staggered to be allowed to dine on the train with white people. Within a couple of days the Middleton members accepted him, according to a letter in front of me, as 'a nice chap'. They soon recognised him as an extremely capable player.

When he returned to South Africa in September 1960, his own people gave him a riotous public reception. A few days later his son was born. The next spring he was back with his wife. Now he was consciously a professional, but still hungry for cricket – Sunday games, evening matches or any other opportunity; hitting the ball hard; bowling with delight; fielding eagerly anywhere.

Then to Worcestershire, where his basically fine gifts carried him through once more. Last week he played for England on his merits. When the West Indian batsmen threatened to run away with the match, he bowled with superb steadiness. When the English first innings quaked, he batted with fine, undemonstrative aplomb until he was freakishly and unluckily run out. On Monday he shook hands with the Queen of England, who lingered longer in conversation with him than with any other player.

At Worcester, too, they think he is a 'very nice chap'. He is, and the most accomplished all-rounder in English cricket: far too accomplished to be left out of any fully representative English team for South Africa in 1968–69.

26 June 1966                                              *John Arlott*

---

*While representing and captaining England in the 1960s, as an amateur, Ted Dexter contributed a weekly column to* The Observer *entitled 'Dexter Talking'. In 1966 he used this platform to air doubts about the bowling action of the West Indian fast bowler Charlie Griffith. No such furore greeted his in-depth analysis of the West Indian captain on that tour, Garfield Sobers. In retirement Dexter wrote the novel* Testkill *in collaboration with Clifford Makins, the* Observer *Sports Editor of the day.*

# Garfield Sobers

At 29 Gary Sobers has never felt in better nick. This isn't

surprising. The West Indies cricket team he captains is the best in the world and is one-up in a series of five matches with two of them played. He has made a century in each match, bowled as well as any bowler on either side, caught his catches, and captained his side so well that he has almost entirely avoided criticism.

People are saying he is the best all-rounder that ever lived and one of the great players of all time. Is he? And if he is, why can he do it when the rest of us can't?

Sobers has one great advantage: even if you only saw him in the street you could guess he was an athlete. He walks with a straight back, slightly tilted forward, and steel springs in his legs. Because he was born in Barbados he happened to take up cricket; but if he'd been born in Sydney he could now be the world tennis champion; and if he'd been born in San Francisco he'd be earning $70,000 a year pitching for the Giants. He would only have to try a ball game for ten minutes to be on top of it.

He has the champion's drive. It comes from inside him, not from his parents. His father, who was in the Merchant Navy, died at sea when his ship was torpedoed; his mother, left with four boys and two girls, had no choice but to let the children go their own way. By the time he was 13, Sobers was playing against top-class cricketers. Now, suddenly, his ambition was to make the West Indian Test side. To West Indian boys this is the acknowledged passport to fame and freedom.

Today these early longings have borne fruit. His character has matured beautifully. West Indian Test sides used to be volatile and suspect in a crisis; but unlike the West Indians who jump around in the crowd, Sobers nowadays never gets overexcited. He has a deep passion for the game – he can remember the precise details of a shot he played ten years ago.

English bowlers still think they can get him out by bowling outside his off-stump and making him impatient. But though this used to be true, it isn't any longer: he has learned, in his own phrase, 'to govern himself'. But in my view, despite his protestations, I would still rather bowl to him there than I would to Neil Harvey.

It took him six months to decide whether he wanted the West Indies captaincy or not. Sobers never wanted it, and always said he would never take it. Now he thinks the extra responsibility has done him good, though he still shows a trace of anxiety about getting through this tour of England. On Tuesday, two days before this Test started, he drank three whiskies before lunch, and blamed his lack of appetite on the tensions and pressure of Test Cricket, besides his late breakfast.

I have never seen a finer innings than he played in the Lord's game two weeks ago when he personally turned the match upside down, but he still timed the ball badly, sometimes hitting it into the ground. This is a characteristic of his style.

Sobers says he is less worried about hitting into the ground than he is about hitting a catch. He has one hell of a high back-lift and plays the ball on the up, even on English wickets. He likes to see the ball come up off the ground and play it from there. If a ball comes off faster or lower than he expects, then he has to hurry the shot but he catches up with it sooner or later. But the bat is travelling very fast when that happens and the ball still bounces away for runs.

The rumour is that he uses a heavy bat. But in fact he only uses a 2 lb 3 oz.

He never really thought he would get out in that Lord's innings.

When I went out to bat, it was bad. Then Kanhai got out and I didn't like it. He played a bad shot playing forward to a short ball. Had he been in form and cutting, the ball would never have gone to the keeper. Time didn't matter. There was too much time and not enough runs, so I started to get them in a hurry. The wicket began to look like the Kensington wicket in Barbados and I never reckon to get out at Kensington.

Most English wickets are very different from the ones Sobers was raised on. In the West Indies the ball rarely deviates after it has pitched and the only difference between one ball and another is a difference of pace. If a ball swings, it keeps on swinging the same way. There is no question of it straightening off the pitch – though Sobers reminded me that a ball I bowled him did exactly that. A fluke, I assured him, and he had to agree.

So the main problem in Sobers's life has been to adapt his play to foreign conditions. He says:

We West Indians only really learn to play this game once we come to England, and play in the Lancashire League. All these boys in our team – Kanhai, Butcher, Hall, Griffith – have improved their technique by playing over here. When picking the touring side our selectors are always looking for this experience.

When I bat at home now and watch some of the boys hitting everything for four wherever it pitches I wonder what is going on. Butcher and Hunte used to play that way – Pow! Pow! Pow! – until they came to England. When they went back you could see the assurance there. Kanhai took longer to learn. He kept getting out in England and was sorry he had not listened to what people were telling him by the end of his first spell in the League. He came back again and made up for his mistakes.

Despite the experience on English wickets, which could so easily have cramped Sobers's style, he still retains some measure of free strokeplay. He says this is half natural and half studied. When West Indies lost to England at Birmingham in 1963 on a green wicket, with the ball moving around a lot off the pitch, I remember saying to Sobers, 'Better get forward, Gary.' I meant that instead of going back towards his stumps and allowing the ball time and space to move, he'd do better to go out and get nearer the pitch of it.

He told me last week that he's tried to use this method, but he can't. 'I only get my foot there too early, and find myself pushing out at the ball before I know where it is. I must play each ball as it comes and if it moves then I move with it. If it moves too much, too bad.'

This may account for some people saying that the West Indian players play down the line and are not good enough to get a touch when the ball moves. Actually, it is no fluke that the West Indians play and miss a good deal. They don't go as far down the wicket to the ball as English players do, and it may have moved enough by the time it reaches them to pass the bat completely.

But they are also playing late, and the edges go down more often than up.

In 1957 Sobers was in the West Indies team as a bowler and just a useful batsman. He bowled only orthodox left-arm spin then, but within a year things began to change. He felt he could hold his place as a batsman and so could afford to experiment in developing other bowling styles to suit all conditions. He knew his orthodox stuff cut little ice back home, so in the Lancashire League he started to spin it the other way.

'I practised, practised and practised in the nets. You must have a batsman there, not just three stumps, and up in the League they were mostly inferior players who didn't take advantage of a bad ball. I got just the practice I needed, but my spin style is still not so good as I would like.'

Sobers was bowling this style effectively at Test level by 1960. He caught and bowled me, I remember, off a top edge when I tried to work his googly to leg in Trinidad. He never bowled fast in those days in Test cricket, though now it is agreed that his fast bowling is the best of his three styles.

But he was already bowling fast in the League. The professional of the side always opens the bowling in the League whether he bowls fast, slow or indifferent, so he naturally tried bowling fast with the new ball.

Another thing about Sobers and his batting: unlike most English and Australian players, he never ducks out of the way of fast bowling. The reason, he says, is something that happened 12 years ago. He was aged 17, and batting in the West Indies against Fred Trueman, when Trueman was really quick and erratic.

He could see that great players at the other end like Weekes and Walcott, fellows who had spent a lifetime hooking, were ducking out of the way, so when he saw one coming at him particularly short and quick he went down. The ball was still coming at his head so he bent lower, and as he did so brought his hands up and split his head open on the top corner of his bat. He has never ducked since: instead, he hooks, or if he adopts evasive action he never takes his eye off the ball.

Sobers likes to play his shots off balls that pitch on the wicket, because there he can see exactly what he's doing. 'Then I'm still in control, however high it bounces.' He thinks the risk of playing shots increases in proportion to the distance the ball is off the wicket.

In his own phrase, he 'maps the field out every ball', noting exactly where the fielders are placed: 'I hate to hit the ball to the same fellow two or three times; it's a waste of time.' He is different here, too, from some English players. I remember one batsman who had played regularly for England hitting a full toss through the covers and telling me, to my astonishment, that that was the first time he'd ever consciously placed the ball.

No wonder Sobers can manoeuvre the ball. Bradman, we are told, spent his time as a child hitting a tennis ball against a wall with a stump. Sobers told me that, as a boy, when he wanted to enjoy a good hand with the bat he spent time with the grounds-man preparing the wicket. Now, he says, 'I can tell you what a wicket will do most times by the sound of it, when I tap it with a bat and by the way it looks.' He knows the game, literally, from its grass roots.

For me, Sobers must be the best cricketer who has played the modern game. My opinion stems mainly from his ability to bowl various styles successfully in Test cricket. His fast bowling is already the equal of Alan Davidson's, and if you rate Davidson – as you must from his record – in the same class as Lindwall and Miller, Sobers already joins the immortals on the strength of but a third of his total armoury.

A last word on his batting. After talking to him for five hours, I realised he had already reached the same conclusions in regard to techniques on varying wickets in much less time and with far less opportunity than I had.

Ye gods, how I envy him! It was enough for him, it seems, to think of becoming this multiheaded cricketer to achieve it. His body was so obedient to his whim that he didn't really notice. Surely his overall ability is something that no other cricketer in all time has been able to boast?

3 July 1966                                                              *Ted Dexter*

---

*Jack Gregory, of Gregory and McDonald fame, became a recluse, living alone on the coast of New South Wales. He refused to give any interviews after an incident which is explained below. One day, however, David Frith, later editor of* The Cricketer *and* Wisden Cricket Monthly, *drove south from Sydney to see him. Gregory was about to go fishing. But with a little persuasion the author managed this interview, probably the only one that Gregory gave between 1926 and his death in 1973.*

# Jack Gregory

Jack Gregory, the New South Wales and Australian fast bowler who made even Walter Hammond blanch, scorer of the fastest-ever Test century, arguably the greatest of slip fieldsmen, was not discernibly pleased to see me.

He has stolidly resisted interviews for half a century, and my diffident announcement through the fly-screen door that I had driven 200 miles down from Sydney expressly to see him left him quite unmoved. It was a significant moment for me: here at last I beheld the most elusive and evasive of cricket's illustrious living – the massive, dynamic sporting doyen of Australians during the 1920s.

The chief pretext of my call was a small pile of books for the autograph treatment, and as we seated ourselves and commiserated with each other on the humidity, the man who would 'never talk' gradually began to talk.

What had determined him never to write or submit to interviews? The explanation was surprisingly simple. A Sydney newspaperman had cornered him (some physical achievement!) outside the dressing-room and asked if he knew why Charlie Kelleway had been dropped from the Australian side.

'I said, "Blowed if I know!" and next day the paper ran a story: "Gregory cannot understand why Kelleway was dropped!"'

A pity. Gregory's memoirs would have been worth reading. He took only 38 Sheffield Shield wickets, but 85 Test batsmen succumbed to his bouncing dam-buster bowling. He was clearly Australia's major fast bowler between Tibby Cotter and Ray Lindwall, and had his right knee not given way in 1928 he would have played a key role in one further series at least.

'I'm finished, boys,' was his oft-quoted exclamation as he limped from the field. I had put the smell of liniment down to imagination as I climbed up to the house that day. But there was the tube on the table. He saw me peering at it. 'My knee's like a barometer. I had to put some of that stuff on. It's going to rain soon.'

A cartilage had been removed in 1922, when the operation was anything but routine. The treatment served him well until the breakdown. 'That was the First Test played at Brisbane – Bradman's first, my last.'

Did he watch much cricket these days? 'I didn't bother going up for the Rest of the World match [a Rest of the World side toured Australia in place of the South Africans in 1971–72 – Ed.]. Those coves didn't seem to be putting themselves out.' He looked intently at the TV screen through the glasses perched on his slightly retroussé nose.

'By Jove, I like that 50-overs stuff!' he reflected. 'They have to get on with it. I liked to hit hard myself, because I loved the game and I tried to amuse the public. They like to see bright cricket.'

I told him of the restricted bowler's run-up operating in the English Sunday League. 'That would've suited me. I took 12 paces – 15 yards.' I contemplated whether the front-foot law might have set him problems with his famous kangaroo leap.

Ordinarily it would have been time for me to leave, but I bought more time by inquiring after the local activities. 'I fish from the boat – caught six bream yesterday. A friend landed a 9 lb flathead this morning. (Pause.) I play bowls.'

How long had he lived down here? 'My wife died nine years ago, and I stayed with my daughter for a while. I retired early. Thought it was the best thing. The company I belonged to was taken over. The shares were paid out in cash.'

Another silence, and I wondered if a yorker or a bouncer was coming next from this white-haired 77-year-old. There was no material sign about the place that a cricketer lived here. No books, no trophies, no bats or balls.

Emerging from his meditation, he spoke again. 'There was a Gregory in the Australian Test team right up to the time I finished.' (Actually there was an interval of 12 years between bearded Dave and tiny Syd, who himself missed very few Tests in the course of 22 years. The family tradition is nevertheless remarkable.)

Jack, who has a sister aged 98, was one of six children of Charles S. Gregory, one of the mighty brotherhood of seven that included Australia's first Test captain, Dave. The first of the line had emigrated very early in Australia's history. When he was a lad Jack unearthed some family letters dated 1795. His mother was Edinburgh-born, and his middle name is her maiden name, Morrison.

'Plum Warner gave me my chance, you know. It was the name that did it. He found out I was Syd's cousin.'

'Are you sure it wasn't because of your performances?'

'No, I went to England from my artillery outfit in France, and when Warner heard there was a Gregory in the Australian Imperial Forces team, he started the ball rolling for me. I was a batsman then.'

Gregory is not necessarily the first player the uninitiated would choose if asked to name the scorer of the fastest Test century, 119 against South Africa at Johannesburg in 1921–22 – in stunning contrast to C. N. Frank's 152 in eight and a half hours later in the match.

'I didn't know it was a record till my son told me some time later. Seventy-five minutes.'

'Seventy. Jessop's was seventy-five.'

'Yes, well, I just enjoyed batting. Never bothered about records.'

Did he know that his old adversary, Frank Woolley, who made two heroic nineties against him in the 1921 Lord's Test, had married recently? 'Hmm,' he muttered to himself, 'companionship.'

J. M. Gregory, Garbo-like in his autumn years, gives the impression of needing little more than the comfort of Nature's companionship.

8 April 1972                                            *David Frith*

*Ian Peebles, after many years as cricket correspondent of* The Sunday Times, *departed in 1970 in not the most amicable of circumstances and contributed on an occasional basis to* The Guardian *and* The Observer *until his death in 1980. As a wrist-spinner he had taken 923 first-class wickets for Oxford University, Middlesex and England between 1927 and 1948. Here he celebrates the centenary of the birth of the greatest pre-modern bowler.*

# Syd Barnes

On an August day in 1929, a young G. O. Allen was returning from a net at Lord's with a senior professional. Passing under Father Time, he glanced idly at the bowler running up in the middle where MCC were playing Wales, and halted in his tracks. 'Gosh,' he said, 'that's a good action.' His companion looked at him quizzically. 'So it should be,' he said, 'that's Syd Barnes – the greatest of the lot.'

Unlike another great sportsman, Barnes never claimed this title for himself. But his associates, who over a very long active span were many, did so with almost complete unanimity. (Indeed, when Allen saw him at Lord's he was 56 years old, and, having bowled them out a fortnight before, was still hailed by the touring South Africans as the best bowler they had met in England.)

Sydney Francis Barnes was born in Smethwick a hundred years ago next Thursday and lived until he was 94. Heredity, apart from endowing him with splendid physique, gave no promise of his eventual supremacy, for his father alone among his forebears was a cricketer, and a modest one at that.

In his early days Barnes was a fairish fast bowler, less effective than a perfect action would argue. But, in addition to physical attributes, he had a keen and inquiring mind, and soon he knew exactly the end he was seeking. This was no less than the leg-break bowled at fastish pace – a tall order.

Having envisaged all this, Barnes embarked on a period of

experiment until, he told me, it suddenly came to him. It was as though he had penetrated the sound barrier, and from then on it was a matter of refinement and application.

On this superb ball was founded his whole extensive technique, which comprised swing and spin in both directions, allied to every subtlety of flight and pace, all with a complete accuracy of line and length required for each particular ball. Barnes discarded the googly as surplus to his needs, although some say it was at the urgent request of Herbert Strudwick, who said he already had enough to cope with behind the stumps.

It was at the mature age of 27 that Barnes so convinced Archie MacLaren of his quality that he was transported straight from League cricket to the highest, and toughest, school of all – an Australian Test series.

MacLaren's faith was immediately justified, but, a man of spirit himself, he soon discovered that he had happened on a kindred soul. Barnes was a strong character, an individualist and a perfectionist (qualities reflected in his copper-plate handwriting) – not the likeliest mixture to submit to MacLaren's dictatorial form of leadership.

Relations were soon strained to a point epitomised in an old story. Aboard a rickety ship bound for Tasmania on a very stormy sea, a nervous member of the side feared that the ship was about to sink. His captain rallied him with gloomy satisfaction. 'Never mind,' he said. 'If she does, that b——— Barnes will drown along with the rest of us!' Be it said though, that despite an occasional dust-up, this doughty pair never lost a profound respect for each other.

If Barnes was an exacting performer and difficult if mishandled, he was, to a thoughtful captain, an unvarying tower of strength. Early in their friendship, Plum Warner gained his loyalty and affection, and found a tireless ally. When, in Australia, Johnny Douglas jeopardised England's prospects by opening himself instead of with Barnes, it was Plum's diplomacy – and Barnes's instant response to it – that saved a very delicate situation and opened the road to complete success.

A fascinating glimpse of this incident was given me by 'young' Jack Hearne, who walked out behind Barnes and Frank Woolley at Sydney on the morning of the First Test. Seeing Douglas ahead with his sweater slung round his shoulders, Barnes turned to his friend Frank in cold rage. 'What does he think I am?' he asked. 'Bloody change bowler?' It was said that his feelings overwhelmed him throughout the match.

In modesty, I think I could say that I was on particularly good terms with Barnes. On a rainy day during the 1930 Oval Test, Mrs Warner took me to Lord's and introduced me to the great man. An introduction from such a quarter meant that I was received without reserve and, armed with a cricket ball, we spent an hour in the Long Bar, during the course of which I watched enthralled as the Master demonstrated.

It was eight years later that we next met, at the Lord's Test of 1938. Finding that he had no plans for the weekend, I asked him to come to my firm's Sunday match against the Bar Tenders' Guild. He accepted, made the speech of the day and volunteered to umpire, an office he discharged with a care and gravity that sprang from true *politesse de la coeur*.

His record at the highest level is unequalled. In 27 Tests he took 189 wickets in days when there were no minor powers. He was supreme in all circumstances. His great feat at Melbourne, when he took 5 wickets for 6 – including those of world-class left-handers Warren Bardsley and Clem Hill – at the start of the Australian innings, was performed on a bone-hard pitch. Hill said of the over he faced, 'I have never seen the like.'

The most original of all the tributes paid to this prince of bowlers came from that great character, the splendid, confident, but unconceited Charlie Macartney. Dining with him when up at Oxford, I asked him how good Syd Barnes was, and he gave the question due consideration. 'I'll tell you,' he said at length. 'In 1912 I said to the fellas, "I'm going to hit this Barnes for six." ' He paused to give full weight to his point before adding, 'I had to wait until I had made 68.'

15 April 1973                                        *Ian Peebles*

---

*This warm appreciation of Geoff Boycott was written in 1973 when he was still playing for England, before three years' abstinence from Test cricket. The dialogue with the interviewee, caught in good-humoured mood, could hardly have been better captured than by the man who became television's expert on films.*

# Geoffrey Boycott

The ball from David Brown, of Warwickshire, that brought a temporary halt to Geoffrey Boycott's run of mammoth scores inflicted a double indignity upon that great man, for, on its way to damaging his eighth rib, it flicked his glove and then, rebounding lustily from his heart, was caught. Mr Boycott takes up the tale himself . . .

'When I got back to the dressing room one of the Yorkshire lads said, "Did that 'urt thee, captain?" I said, "Aye, it did. But Ah wish it 'ad 'it me straight on t'bloody 'ead or in t'teeth instead." He said, "Tha' wouldn't ha' looked so good wi'out teeth, captain." I said, " 'Appen not, but Ah wouldn't ha' been bloody out, though, would Ah? Ah could ha' got up and got me bloody 'undred." '

This story, recounted in the deliberately exaggerated Yorkshire dialect so brilliantly captured above, tells us two things about Geoffrey Boycott, the first of which we knew already – namely, that he doesn't like getting out.

('Listen,' I said, 'here's the situation: you're batting on a terrible wicket against an extremely fast bowler. Now, be honest, aren't you ever frightened of being hurt?' He looked at me in deep wonderment, as though doubting whether I could be serious. 'The only thing I'm bloody frightened of,' he said, 'is getting out. I don't like getting out, I bloody don't. I like getting hundreds.')

The second, and less familiar, aspect of Boycott's character revealed by that anecdote is that he is a dryly amusing man with a pleasing sense of humour. This comes as a shock to the interviewer meeting him for the first time, because Geoffrey Boycott isn't supposed to have a sense of humour. He's supposed to be a remote, withdrawn man, icy and taciturn, interested exclusively in his own achievements and glory.

It is, I think, because of this widely accepted, though erroneous, image that he often gets considerably more stick and correspondingly less praise than he deserves.

He wasn't the only England player to turn down the tour of India, but he was the one who attracted the adverse publicity. He's the one who gets the blame for the fact that Yorkshire win very few batting points, although, as someone pointed out, 'Just look at the scores – there's Boycott 150 and the rest 70 between 'em.'

Last summer he was much criticised when he declined to play in the last Test against Australia and people implied he was scared of Lillee.

Well, all right, I admit it – I was bloody scared, but not just of Lillee. I was scared of anyone above medium pace right then.

I'd been out for six weeks wi' t'top o' me bloody finger 'anging off [his Yorkshire accent becomes very strong in moments of passion] but nobody mentioned that, did they?

They didn't mention that I wasn't scared of Lillee when I hooked him twice on that rotten pitch at Manchester and hooked him again off his full run in the 'one-day Test'.

He believes himself to be misunderstood by the media and therefore misunderstood by the public at large, and it makes him unhappy. He is not, he insists, the remorselessly dedicated monster he is made out to be. He loves cricket, that's all; that's why he tries so hard.

Nor is he the crazy egomaniac of popular myth and legend. True, he can give you exact details of every innings he has ever played, but he doesn't hurl the statistics about in a boastful way. He uses them, rather, as a defence against those who seek to belittle him.

He's a proud man: proud that he captains Yorkshire ('the leading cricket club in the world') and proud that he plays for his country. He will never tell you that he's a great player, but he knows it all the same – and why not? Only a fool or a churl would deny the fact.

But he feels that the British are ungenerous to their great

players. 'None of 'em's appreciated till he's retired or dead,' he said. Nevertheless, he's not paranoic, doesn't feel himself persecuted and can well understand how his unfortunate image came to exist.

When I started in this game, I must have been a godsend to writers looking for copy. I was a very rare bird in cricket in those days – a young man who didn't smoke and didn't drink, who was shy and introverted and found it difficult to talk to people, who was mad keen on physical fitness and who liked batting so much that he'd go to the nets even when he didn't have to.

Oh, aye, I must have seemed a right crank. And on top of it all, I wore those rimless glasses that made me look like that bloody fellow Himmler.

Still, he says, that was a long time ago and he's changed a bit since.

Okay, I've got a lot of confidence in myself – sometimes. Not always. I need support and encouragement and warmth. I'm a very emotional guy. I'm supposed to be cold and calculating – sphinxlike, they call me, but I'm not like that at all.

I don't show emotion much, but inside, if the crowd is with me, I'm on fire. I play emotionally. In Yorkshire the crowds are fantastic; they really appreciate me, and when I'm batting up there it's tremendous. I want to get runs not just for Yorkshire, not for myself – but for all those people who are willing me on to score more and more.

It isn't just a cricket pitch any more, it's . . . it's like an arena, it's my stage and I'm like an actor and the people have come to see *me* give a performance. I wouldn't swap it for anything.

Indeed he is an emotional man and a friendly one; oversensitive perhaps, and easily hurt, but also engagingly honest and open. He talks with almost boyish fervour of the big moments in his life, like the frightful day when, at 17, he learned he had to wear glasses and thought his chances of a sporting career were over.

In despair he wrote to M. J. K. Smith, that bespectacled rugby and cricket international ('and a marvellous bloke') for reassurance – and got it.

Just to round the story off, when G. Boycott went on his first tour with England, his captain was that same M. J. K. Smith and, just to round the story off even further, M. J. K. Smith couldn't remember the correspondence.

Boycott also talks of the first time he was picked, to his own total astonishment ('I'd never thought I'd be good enough for England') for his first Test, against Australia in 1964.

'I remember nothing of that match,' he said. 'It was like a dream, wonderland. It was only days later that I suddenly woke up to the fact that I'd played for Yorkshire *and* England. Me! I'd played for my country. It were fantastic.'

Actually he does remember one thing, very clearly, about that Test, and he tells it with much relish and amusement.

As I went out to bat in the first innings, Bobby Simpson, the Australian captain, threw the ball to the fast bowler Graham McKenzie and said in a loud voice, 'Hey, Garth, look at this four-eyed cuffer! He can't cuffing bat. Knock those cuffing glasses off him right away.' And I said to myself, ''Ello, Ah thought we'd coom out 'ere for a nice game o' cricket. Ah didn't know it were a bloody war.'

Good bloke, Geoff Boycott. When Illingworth gives up, he should be England's captain. I don't suppose he will be though – too much the pro, too much the 'bloody Yorkshireman' and not enough the gentle amateur that the selectors seem to be seeking as Illy's replacement.

But if Boycott doesn't get the job, I suspect it will be much more England's loss than his.

13 May 1973                                    *Barry Norman*

**4** Until 1972 newspapers were not allowed to photograph action on the field, so their representatives had to be content with what they could find off it. This picture, of Garfield Sobers as he was then, was taken in 1969 by Chris Smith, a Royal Photographic Sports Photographer of the Year before he moved to *The Sunday Times*. Contrast Sobers's facial expression with that of Worrell: not the same inner strength but, as some compensation, he was the most skilful of all-rounders.

**5** 'Chest high, skipper?' 'No, make it head high.' Two great West Indian cricketers, Michael Holding and Clive Lloyd, discuss the finer points at Melbourne during the 1985 Benson and Hedges World Series Championship. It was the last competition in which Lloyd played for West Indies.

*This portrait was born of a conversation, after a day's play, in the bar at Bristol. Arthur Milton, amiable man and admirable Gloucestershire cricketer, had lately become a village postman. Yet he was the last double international to have played cricket and football for England; and he had been one of the 'Brylcreem Boys', although his wife preferred to use the prestigious grease for furniture polish. The author, Michael Carey was later appointed cricket correspondent of* The Daily Telegraph.

# Arthur Milton

When Clement Arthur Milton began his county cricket career, Hammond had just retired, Bradman and Hutton were names to conjure with and the best of Cowdrey, May and Graveney was to come. The era of the sponsor and the dreaded action replay was unborn, crowds flocked to watch good old-fashioned cricket and the sun shone all the time.

Now, 26 years later, with the same enmeshed in intricate one-day regulations, with the players' trade union established and with a new, young Graveney on the Gloucestershire scorecard, Milton bats on, at 46 the oldest and longest serving player in the country.

Only three current batsmen have scored more than his 31,000 runs. He has hit more centuries for Gloucestershire than W. G. Grace, has made 1000 in a season 16 times and – something that now seems a lifetime ago – played for England at football and cricket.

With those talents Milton could name his own price if he were starting today. Sport has not made him particularly wealthy ('except in things I value more than money'), though he was involved in the launch of the inflated personality cult when he was picked to play for England against Austria after only twelve games on the wing for Arsenal.

Even now he cannot comprehend how that happened. 'Finney, the best player I've ever seen, was injured and Matthews was out of favour,' he recalls, 'so they chose me. Me instead of Stan Matthews, I ask you! The fact that I played for Arsenal and that the London Press carried a lot of weight must have had something to do with it.'

It was his only international but it lifted him into the immaculate realm of the Brylcreem Boys along with Denis Compton. Remember how their faces and plastered hair used to greet you from roadside hoardings or from among the razor blades and other bric-a-brac of barbers' shops? They gave him 100 guineas a year and all the Brylcreem he wanted. The money was handy on top of his £17 a week from Arsenal.

Highbury was an awesome place for a young lad from the West Country in those days. It took him some time to become accustomed to going there by tube. Entering the ground for the first time reminded him of a hospital, all clean and clinical and that faint touch of butterflies in the stomach.

Alex James was still on the coaching staff (no one could get the ball off him in six-a-side games) and Tom Whittaker was manager. 'He was really just a good masseur,' says Milton. 'He did well with the players he inherited. When it came to replacing them he wasn't so good. I mean, I played alongside one bloke who couldn't even give me the ball from 10 yards.'

While he was there, a promising young centre-forward called Brian Close joined the staff. He wasn't too bad, Milton remembers, except for a disconcerting habit of heading the ball over the bar from all ranges and angles.

The training staff took Close aside and after a week of learning to head the ball down, he and Milton played in a minor match together. Eventually Milton raced down the wing and crossed, leaving Close with an unguarded goal to aim at. As instructed, he headed the ball firmly down . . . and it *bounced* over the bar.

Milton drifted from football to full-time cricket in 1955. He had started his apprenticeship on the sandy, turning pitches of Bristol, pitches that were so bad that visiting teams used to book hotels for only two nights. It was not until he played abroad that his considerable technique developed.

He made a century in the first of his six Tests and his value to Gloucestershire has been immense, not least as a greyhound tipster. He has made *that* pay, although there was one embarrassing night when he took the entire Yorkshire team to a local stadium, watched a certainty lose and evoked an interesting theory from Fred Trueman on how to improve the dog's performance.

Milton retired a year or two ago, but answered his county's call for help halfway through the season. 'I missed the game like mad, missed the people and the atmosphere – but I didn't tell them,' he confides.

He may finish at the end of this season, if he feels he is no longer making a worthwhile contribution. If he does retire we should all doff our hats to him, not least the journalist who asked him irreverently when Gloucestershire returned to playing at Moreton-in-Marsh if he had played in the last match there in 1912. 'Of course not,' scoffed Milton. 'I was injured.'

2 June 1974                                                        *Michael Carey*

---

*Tony Pawson played for Kent alongside Les Ames and Godfrey Evans, and reported for many days on Alan Knott. Here he compares the modern genius of wicket-keeping with his two Kent and England antecedents, using some words from Knott himself. Not long afterwards Knott stopped giving interviews and maintained a monastic silence through the Kerry Packer and South African 'rebel' controversies in which he became involved. He finished his 95-Test career with 269 dismissals, the most by any England 'keeper, and 4389 runs.*

# Alan Knott

When his benefit match began at Canterbury yesterday, Alan Knott was appropriately sharing the wicket-keeping record of 219

Test dismissals with his Kent predecessor, Godfrey Evans. The sequence of Ames (47 Tests), Evans (91) and Knott (77 to date) has gained Kent a near monopoly of England wicket-keeping since 1931.

Almost every record, good or bad, is held by a Kent 'keeper. Frank Woolley, playing in his last Test against Australia, aged 47, took over the gloves when Ames strained his back and let through a record 37 byes in the second innings. Tony Catt, suffering from sunburn and the mysteries of Wright's spin, conceded 48 byes and 23 leg-byes – making extras top-scorer in a Northamptonshire total of 374. That remains one of the less welcome first-class records.

Is Knott just the product of a tradition stretching back to Huish? Certainly there is no lack of advice and example for Kent wicket-keepers but the Big Three have all been quite distinctive in their approach. That is not just in the inessentials, for instance that Knott began as an off-break bowler in the 2nd XI while Ames finished as occasional leg-spinner in the 1st. It is in the fundamentals of wicket-keeping styles, with each developing the art in different ways.

Leslie Ames brought near perfection to an established method. Like his great Australian counterpart, Oldfield, he was so quietly efficient that you noticed him only when he appealed – and that was usually a polite inquiry rather than a raucous demand. He was the stumper *par excellence* in the golden age of the spinner. With Tich Freeman once exceeding 300 wickets in a season, Ames had an unapproachable 415 stumpings in his career, 52 in one season, 48 in another. In Tests, 23 of his 98 victims were stumped, compared with Knott's 16 out of 219. The death of the spinner has in itself changed wicket-keeping styles.

The modern 'keeper's lot is to that degree made easier, as it is also by better equipment. That great slip-fielder Wally Hammond was once asked when he found it most difficult to concentrate. 'Late in the afternoon of a boiling hot Australian Test day when the stink from the steak in Ames's gloves was unbearable,' was the unexpected reply. Wicket-keepers' hands had no need of steak to protect them by the 'forties, but Evans's technique put new demands on their resources of energy.

Godfrey's ebullience expressed itself in a continuous display of eye-catching acrobatics. 'Just watching him makes me feel tired,' Statham once commented, a tribute indeed from that workhorse of a fast bowler. No one has ever made batsmen so aware of the 'keeper as Evans or done so much for his side's morale. His showmanship and practical skill were ideally combined in standing up to Alec Bedser swinging the new ball late at around Hendrick's pace. It did not bring him many of his 46 Test stumpings but it did make the batsmen feel threatened, Bedser seem even more menacing.

Even ragged fielding was made to look hostile as Godfrey bounded up to take the wide half-volley throw and flourish it one-handed over the stumps. Once, fielding short square leg, I was waiting for a dolly catch as Nottinghamshire's Cyril Poole mishooked. Godfrey had been standing far back but there was a sudden blur of action as a gloved hand snatched the ball from in front of my eyes. 'No confidence in my catching?' I asked acidly. 'Don't get upset. The game was getting dull so I bet Jack Davies a fiver I would be involved in the next wicket.' Godfrey was always involved and cricket with him was never dull.

Knott has something of both Ames and Evans in his style but he too is an original. His keeping is so undemonstrative that its excellence is not always appreciated until a wide catch allows him to display his agility. He stands back to the gentle pace of a Woolmer or a d'Oliveira when his predecessors would have regarded that as a slur on their ability. For Knott it is simply a question of efficiency, of statistical probability. Standing up, a good wicket-keeper *must* miss a number of thick-edge chances since the ball will be diverted too far to stick in correctly positioned gloves. Standing back, such edges will be simple to take. So he stands back, making his own judgements, minimising error, politely ignoring the expert critics still wedded to an earlier fashion.

Before Knott, the one common factor with all great wicket-keepers was that they kept their knees bent and their hands low, staying crouched as long as possible. Knott has developed a unique, straight-legged style.

It was a remark by Keith Andrew which stuck in my mind. He told me that an essential of wicket-keeping was to keep hands and elbows free of obstruction. If you crouch they may brush against your knees and distract you. Then on a pitch at Newark with the ball coming through low, I found that by rising with both legs straight and close together I could take the ball more easily down by my ankles. This stance also helped my general suppleness and the unimpeded lateral movement of my hands. It also means I can have more 'give' in taking the ball as I bring my hands further back towards my legs.

That bestseller, the *MCC Coaching Book*, gives this unequivocal advice about selecting wicket-keepers: 'Of all positions in the field that of wicket-keeper is at once the most important and the most exacting. It can therefore be laid down as an absolute principle in team selection that the best wicket-keeper should always be chosen.'

At Test level there is no such certainty. Batting can be vital to the side's balance. Some of the non-Kent 'keepers of the period, like Paul Gibb and Jim Parks, have been chosen more for their run-getting ability than their wicket-keeping finesse. Knott himself has occasionally held his place in the Test team in preference to that superb 'keeper Bob Taylor by virtue of his superior batting. All wicket-keepers ought to have the eye and agility to be good batsmen, and Kent's Big Three all made the best use of their natural talents.

Ames, a man who might have been selected for batting alone, scored 2434 runs in 72 Test innings for an average of 40.56, hitting eight centuries. Evans had two Test centuries and 2439 runs from 133 innings for an average of 20.49.

Knott has forced himself to be a better bat than Evans. And although never quite in Ames's class he shared one distinction with him. They are the only two wicket-keepers from either country ever to score a century in an England v. Australia Test match [a record subsequently equalled – Ed.].

Knott's 3000 Test runs are something no other regular 'keeper has matched, discounting such batsmen who sometimes kept wicket as Walcott, Hanif and Kanhai. Knott's 3478 runs have come in 119 innings at 32.81. Nor do the figures express the full value of runs so often made under pressure after the top-order batsmen have failed.

It was Knott who first challenged the Indian spinners when Bedi, Chandra and Venkat had the main batsmen struggling. Relying on his sure eye and swift feet he developed a new technique – hitting on the half-volley against the spin. In the textbook that is a sure recipe for disaster. Knott's perfection of timing made it a profitable stroke to a deserted area of the outfield which batsmen were not expected to explore.

Fast bowling gave him more problems.

When I started in the game bouncers were less frequent and more innocuous, just short-pitched balls that flew over one's head. Then John Snow developed this effective form of bouncer that slid the ball up at the chest from a reasonable length, compelling a stroke. As others improved on the method it became difficult for small men like me to 'kill' the ball lifting at the body. So I have had to change my technique. Now I use a more open stance and a different grip with the wrist further round behind the bat handle. This not only makes it easier to fend the bouncer but helps with the best counters like the glance, the hook or the cut.

This is a reversion to the technique that Trevor Bailey used to take the sting out of Lindwall and Miller. In his analysis of the game Knott is always thoughtful and practical, copying in part, inventing in part. It is an approach that will keep his Test records as wicket-keeper-batsman unassailable in our lifetime. He is only just 30, and if the best years are past, there are plenty of good ones ahead.

8 August 1976                                        *Tony Pawson*

---

*Every village club has one – the old faithful who keeps on playing in defiance of opposing bowlers, rheumatism and Anno Domini. David Hunn, a contributor to* Observer Sport *since 1968, offers a gentle sketch of a fellow Sussex man.*

# Denis Stilwell

First cricket match of the year last Sunday and Denis Stilwell began the way he likes to go on. He opened the batting for Petworth Park as usual, made a century, declared immediately (he has been skipper there for 20 years), kept his pads on, stumped one and caught one in successive balls, and was last man out of the clubhouse bar.

His wife, who had done the teas, was on hand to drive him home, which was handy because we had all been anxious to buy him a pint for the ton and he had been just as anxious to return the compliment. The West Sussex afternoon had been long, hot and dry, and being groundsman as well as skipper there was no way, ton or not, that he could leave the bar any sooner.

What a man, this Stilwell! Fifty years old this mid-season, his thirty-third for Petworth Park (in the grounds of Petworth House, home of the Leconfields) and if he tops 1000 runs again it will, he reckons, be the twenty-fifth time.

'Well,' he said, 'there were some wet ones, you know, when you just couldn't get the cricket in.' Last summer was a bit like that, but he managed 1800 runs. The two previous years he was over 2000 – and we're talking about single-innings games with not more than two and a half hours for each side.

Inevitably, way back, he had a trial for Sussex and would dearly love to have been the county's 'keeper, but Jim Parks was persuaded to take it on. 'Not bad either,' says Denis with enormous twinkle, 'not bad, was he?'

He has played cricket for the county 2nd XI, for the Club and Ground, for the Cricket Association; but mostly he has played for Petworth Park. 'Look at it, just look at it,' he said. 'Have you ever seen anything better?' Not often, for sure. A vast green arena, overlooked by the seventeeth-century ancestral mansion, with the divine switchback of the South Downs clear open on the other side and running as far as the eye takes you.

It's a full two-minute walk from pavilion to crease (more when you slouch unhappily out), and at mid-wicket there's a magnificent horse chestnut. 'Four if you hit it, that's the way it's always been. And did you see today, more than 300 runs scored and it was only twice touched?'

A laughing man, Denis Stilwell, a thoroughly happy man, and never more so than when he denies the opposition his wicket. 'Over my dead body, that's how I look at it, over my dead body. There's a bit of Boycott in me, I suppose. Tell you what, anyone gets my wicket cheaply, they're in for a hard time when we play them next. I don't like that. Oh, no I don't. Not a bit.'

Last Sunday, despite their score of 212 for 1 (that one retired, and Stilwell didn't approve of that: 'Retired without being hurt – that's like giving your wicket away. I'll be having a word with him'), the skipper failed to force a win.

'I was surprised,' I said lightly, 'that you didn't take off the pads and bowl them out.' 'I'd 'a' done just that,' he said, 'but I was wearing a new pair of boots, and they weren't half pinching.'

30 April 1978                                                    *David Hunn*

---

*This portrait, of the most famous of women cricketers, was penned by Julie Welch, the first female football corres- pondent to write for a national newspaper. Having been secretary on* The Observer *sports desk for some years, she thought she could write no worse than others, and was duly given the opportunity.*

# Rachael Heyhoe Flint

The first point to make about Rachael Heyhoe Flint is that she genuinely is a terribly nice person. I mention this because people are always asking her what she *really* meant when she said this or that, as if behind that baggy-eyed beaming visage there lurks another, rottener creature who does un-RHF-like things like kicking the family pet and sticking her tongue out at portraits of the Queen.

Some pretty un-RHF-like things have been done to her, of course. In July of last year, she was deprived of her England women's cricket captaincy in one of the breeziest hatchet jobs since Charles I got the bum's rush.

In her new autobiography, which succinctly enough is called *Heyhoe!*, she describes how she was summoned to meet the selectors after a Sunday afternoon game at Halifax.

I remember that hundred-yard stroll so vividly, leaving my friends in the hubbub of the dressing room, though being vaguely aware of mist clinging to the hills to my left and an appalling smell wafting up from the nearby canal, to the moment when I arrived beneath the tennis pavilion balcony, face to face with four suitably solemn expressions.

In case that sounds flippant, it was actually, she says, 'the most wretched moment of my life.' Rachael Heyhoe Flint was given the chop while she was still batting ably, after she had not only popularised women's cricket but made it a sport to be regarded seriously, and within months of her best ever score of 179.

She was given no warning or explanation, merely coldly informed that 'it was a committee decision'. She says she drove home that day across the Pennines on the M62 with the words 'You are no longer captain of England' ringing in her ears.

I was crying, I can't deny it. The only way I could survive the journey home was telling myself that at least I've got the consolations of a smashing son and stepchildren, and a super husband and a lovely house.

In some respects, I literally had no time to feel upset and sad after that. There was a sleepless night, but once the next morning dawned the phone started, and then I was staggered by everyone's kindness. When it happened, I thought I must be a baddie – and then I got these wonderful expressions of support from the public and the Press and MPs, and I knew I couldn't be a baddie after all. The time it really hit me, though,

was when I was typing a letter a few days later; I signed it
England Captain and I had to go and fetch the erasing fluid.

Nevertheless, as Rachael, says, it's an ill wind and all that. 'To be
honest, I've been exceptionally lucky in my life. Really, last year
was the first major setback, but even then the publicity I got was
much more than I hoped or craved for – it gave me a platform to
do other things. I think people have got me into the sporting
mould and think I don't know anything outside sport.' Not a
surprising assumption since she is still an England cricketer and
a county hockey goalkeeper.

The latest Other Thing is her radio work. On the first Monday
in October [1978] she will start as co-presenter of the 'P.M.'
programme on Radio Four – 'I'm thrilled, particularly as I'll be
working with Gordon Clough, who's very experienced and will
probably be helping me through my first nervous days. We've
decided we'll have to have lots of cushions to sit on because
we're both about 5 feet 2 inches. We're calling ourselves the
Poison Dwarf Society.'

The programme involves updating news stories – 'I'm a news
freak, in the evenings I go from channel to channel on the TV, just
hunting for the news' – book interviews, readers' letters, that
kind of thing. She says she prefers working on radio to TV
because it's more relaxed – 'You can have a ghastly expression on
your face trying to think of the next question and grope under
the chair for your notes instead of having to look delightfully
interested.'

She also gets a lot of Will You Come And Speak At invitations –
anything from women's institutes to rugger clubs and stag nights
(the RHF wit is never blue, but can on occasions be a fairly strong
shade of lilac). As well as playing top-class cricket and hockey she
writes for a national newspaper, so she keeps busy, but she
always tries to get back to home base in Wolverhampton every
night, even if it means motoring long distances.

I don't want my son Benjamin to think I'm a burglar. Also I like
to keep the home factor constant for him. My husband Derrick
helps a lot and we've also got a good fairy, Meg, who is a sort of

housekeeper. She can pick Benjamin up from school and get him ready for bed if I'm not back from London.

In the past, I perhaps really should have devoted more time to home and family, but there was always this drive to try to make a success of things, so occasionally private responsibilities took second place. But I hope I'm making it up to them now.

She says she doesn't really get much time for the feminine virtues, she's lousy at knitting and sewing and with cooking it's usually a case of 'What's Tonight's Cremation?' Her great love is fast cars; she's just bought a Ford Mustang. 'It's silver, with a burglar alarm. I feel like a cheap version of Charlie's Angels.'

She is currently mulling over the idea of going into politics, with an eye on the Ministry of Sport.

It's not a daft thought. Obviously I can't go rushing around on a field forever. In ten to fifteen years time, maybe, I'd like to give something back. I am tremendously interested in politics, though possibly very immature politically at the moment. Of course, instead of being an MP I could always try the House of Lords. I've been working on my title. I rather fancy Baroness Flint of Molineaux Football Ground.

24 September 1978                                                    *Julie Welch*

---

*In 1982* The Observer *launched a series called 'The Magic Touch', in which Hugh McIlvanney endeavoured to find out what made great sportsmen tick. He began with Ian Botham. The piece may be somewhat dated by the warm testimony of Peter Roebuck, subsequently the captain of Somerset when Botham had his altercation with the club, over the sacking of Viv Richards and Joel Garner.*

# Ian Botham

When a rapt silence falls over a crowded Glasgow pub and all eyes, bright or bleary, are turned towards some sporting action on television, it is natural to assume that the performers filling the screen will be wearing football shirts, boxing gloves or racing silks. For a man in cricketing whites to hypnotise such an audience into awed admiration is a small miracle. If you should see it happen, as I have, the miracle will almost certainly be called Ian Botham.

Botham, when batting or bowling, even when fielding in the slips, is capable of spreading an excitement that makes fans of people who would normally subscribe to the crude prejudice that cricket is only slightly less boring than watching celery grow or car bumpers rust. His impact has less to do with his technical resources as a player (though these are prodigious) than with the seemingly irresistible vitality that floods everything he does. No one anywhere in contemporary sport more spectacularly channels immense animal vigour and a fierce hunger for winning into an overwhelming effectiveness on the field.

The balls he bowled to take the last five Australian wickets for one run and so win the Fourth Test at Edgbaston, during his historic summer of 1981, were not in themselves wonders of cunning or violence. 'I saw those overs again recently on film and the balls he hit the wickets with weren't doing very much – they were pretty straight,' says Peter Roebuck, a team-mate in the Somerset county side whose deep affection for Botham and intellectual, analytical cast of mind, combine to make him one of the most balanced and informative witnesses on the talent and character of the 26-year-old regarded by many as the greatest English cricketer of the century.

'Yet,' adds Roebuck, 'there was a sense of inevitability about what he did to the Australians that day. He just charged in and made it happen. Had it been anyone else bowling, there would have been nothing to prevent the batsmen hitting those balls. But Botham had grabbed the situation and was shaping the outcome of the match by the sheer force of his personality. You knew that anyone who got in his way would be mown down.'

Remembering the slaughter as we talked in a hotel across the street from Lord's the other day, Botham was inclined to think the Australians had allowed themselves to be mown down too easily. 'They bottled out,' he said simply.

I don't think they could handle it. It was lions and Christians stuff. Suddenly, instead of Lillee running in at Melbourne and 90,000 bloody dingoes yelling, 'Lillee, Lillee, Lillee,' or 'kill, kill, kill' it was me going at them with the crowd roused and urging me on. Perhaps when the guy at the other end with the bat sees you charging in and he knows how determined you are to get rid of him, and he hears all that noise – maybe in that moment he can feel the aggression coming from you. And perhaps it is true that their nerves start twittering a bit more when I am attacking them than they would if it was somebody else.

There is no change in his pleasantly light, relaxed voice as he mentions that last possibility but his physical presence gives the remark a hint of ironic understatement. He is formidably equipped for being hostile on or off the cricket field, even more so than other men of comparable height and weight (6 feet 2 inches and a rather wayward 15 stone).

Apart from the vast thighs that are the basis of his power and the thick, impressive torso, the most striking evidence of the extraordinary strength is in his arms. His biceps are big but that is scarcely remarkable in an athlete of his general build. What is far more significant is the scale of his forearms.

Even at the wrist they seem as wide as a bar on a farm gate and those huge, flexible slabs of bone and muscle make it easier to understand the physical might he has been able to bring to his cricket since the day when, as a 10-year-old, he swung his bat and lifted the ball right over the main building of Milford Junior School in Yeovil and into a distant playground. 'It would have been a six at either Taunton or Lord's,' insists his former games master Richard Hibbitt. Biceps can be developed but those forearms, those wrists, are convincing reminders of the point made by Hibbitt's story – that Botham was born to justify the phrase the late Bill Shankly applied to one of his heroes, born to be 'grisly strong'.

The palpable joy he takes in unleashing his freakish strength is one of the most appealing elements in his play. 'He has much the same approach to cricket as he has to soccer,' says Peter Roebuck, referring to Botham's continuing enthusiasm for a sport in which he showed enough promise to be offered a professional career with Crystal Palace when he was 15.

In soccer he sees himself as a barnstorming centre-forward and he plays cricket that way too. Yet cricket is a game of self-discipline and technical control. I think he is able to give his aggression full rein because technically he is very sound. As a batsman his reproduction of shots is extremely good. He can be confident about letting attacking shots go because he can be pretty sure that he will be able to make the correct strokes.

There are people in the game with similar vigour and drive but they don't have his quality of technique, his mastery of the fundamental principles, and they aren't as enormously strong. When he is ferocious he is usually still playing with great control. He is like an animal hunting. Even when he is smashing bowlers all over the place it's not wild or haphazard. The shots are predetermined to quite a substantial degree.

There is a considerable difference between his batting and that of Viv Richards when both are going well. Richards will play outrageously difficult shots, shots that call for a miraculous eye. In his great innings Viv has the passion of the murderer rather than the cold rationality of the assassin. Despite his polite demeanour, his mild, friendly and chivalrous attitudes – all of which are genuine – Viv is an extremely powerful personality and a very hard man indeed when he wants to be on the field.

Botham hits the ball harder and is a greater batsman technically. But Richards is a tougher person than Botham, who is more naturally open and gregarious.

At the hotel in St John's Wood there was plenty of openness in Botham's response to the suggestion that technically he was superior to the inspired West Indian whose friendship he treasured. 'Yeah, I've been told that, but I point out technically he's got 4000 runs more than I have, and if you count all kinds of cricket about 16,000 more. If you ask what I think of Viv Richards as a batsman, my answer is simple. He is the best in the world and probably the best who ever lived.'

Good judges believe that over the next four or five years Botham himself may have to be recognised as the best batsman in the world, especially as there were persuasive signs in India during the winter that he is learning to subdue his impulsiveness, and to extract essential satisfaction from resisting the temptation of slow bowlers who set out to be negatively aggravating. Making a reputation against fast bowlers is infinitely harder for him than it ever was for Sobers or Richards because he has to face the West Indies' uniquely relentless attack. The season of 1984, when the West Indians tour England, could complete his apotheosis as a batsman. Already his blitz on the record books – scoring 1000 runs and taking 100 wickets in just 21 Test matches by the age of 23 is only a small part of the story – and his utterly decisive contribution to the winning of the Ashes last year have caused him to be bracketed with the very greatest of all-rounders, such as Wilfred Rhodes, Keith Miller and the paragon of his own childhood dreams, Sir Garfield Sobers.

However, though he won't be 27 until November, there are indications that his giant's body may be suffering a gradual loss of flexibility essential to a pace-bowler at the highest level. The kind of performances that intimidated Australia in the Ashes series, the sight of him hurtling towards the crease with the concentrated belligerence that seemed to send a wave of heat ahead of the ball to shrivel the batsman's spirit, may soon become rare.

But, whatever happens to his bowling, we should – if he is spared serious blows to his fitness (such as a recurrence of the back trouble that combined with the strains of the brief and entirely unsuccessful England captaincy to devastate his form between the early summer of 1980 and July of the following year, or a worsening of the weakness in his once-fractured left ankle) – be permitted to savour the full glories of his batting for a handful of seasons more. He may play long enough to pass Geoffrey Boycott's record total of 8114 Test runs. But he will not be borrowing any of the Yorkshireman's methods for the attempt. 'I believe if you are born with a gift you should try to exploit it as naturally as you can,' says Botham.

You should let the talent come through as freely as possible. Obviously I don't want to neglect what I've got. I work to make the most of it but I'm probably the worst practiser in the world. You look at me in the nets and you wouldn't think I was a player. I just slog. I'm not really interested. To me Geoffrey Boycott made himself into the batsman he is. You only have to listen to him talk. 'Is my knee bending right? Is my elbow right?' No good asking me about those bloody things.

He smiles with the last sentence and his face, large and attractive under the sandy hair that descends into curls around the neck, looks considerably more boyish than it does when he is putting the frighteners on opponents. Above the thick moustache, the nose is long and has been reshaped but not grossly disfigured by being broken a number of times, in keeping with a tendency to court hazard and collect scars that has been conspicuous since boyhood.

His appetite for risk is represented now by the flying lessons he is taking, the aerobatics he did lately as a passenger with the Red Arrows, and by driving his car at alarming speeds, using even his rustic pursuits of fishing and shooting as excuses for exhausting, break-neck journeys between Somerset, the cottage he shares with his wife and two young children in South Humberside and his favourite rivers in Scotland. He would like to set up a fish-farming business in Scotland when he retires from playing but his innate restlessness may be a complication.

Peter Roebuck again:

Ian tries to take his abilities in the game and everything else in his life right to the very edge. For him if something is not done to excess it's hardly worth doing.

And through it all he is, basically, a very nice and generous man who puts tremendous store by loyalty. I don't think anyone who really knows Ian Botham dislikes him. He's a man's man. When he gets a few drinks he can be a bit silly. He can be mistaken for a lovable oaf at times but that is well wide of the mark. He's quite bright, bright but not calculating. He can be persuasive as well as assertive and domineering in an argument. And he brings a marvellous spirit to his cricket, a real life-force. That wonderful back-handed sweep shot he plays in a way that no one else, not even Viv Richards, can equal says a lot about his attitude to the game.

I've seen him send the ball over the boundary with one bounce using the back-handed sweep. That's more than great talent. There's something roguish about it, a genuine joy in his power and capacity for the outrageous. The nerve that allows him to believe so profoundly in his gifts is a magnificent thing.

Botham's friends can see no deeper flaws in him than can be traced to a vitality which often appears to compare with that of ordinary men as Niagara does with a bathroom tap. 'It usually makes him terrific company but if things go wrong it can involve him in punch-ups,' says one admirer, 'especially as he has a taste for the kind of down-to-earth drinking companions you find in public bars rather than cocktail lounges.'

He is pestered by loud-mouths who want to make themselves look big at the big man's expense, and ignoring all the provocations is difficult for someone who is vehement on the subject of cowardice. In the course of being found not guilty of an assault charge in a Grimsby Court not long ago, Botham agreed that kicking a man on the ground would be an act of a coward and added, 'That is one thing I am not.'

Up in those Glasgow pubs they have never had any doubt.

26 September 1982                                    *Hugh McIlvanney*

---

*The meeting between the finest batsman and sports writer of their period took place one Monday in Manchester. Recognising the importance of the occasion, Nature held up play now and then – Viv Richards scoring a century between the showers – to allow time for the interview. A sympathetic chord must have been struck in Richards by the similarity between his late, great Scottish friend, 'Jock' McCombe, and Hugh McIlvanney. The author, in turn, found the character of Richards similar in power to that of Joe Frazier, Muhammad Ali and Lester Piggott. During an unrecorded part of the conversation Richards made the statement: 'Helmets are unfair – to bowlers.'*

# Viv Richards

It was a time for going against the tide. While more than 50,000 of the country's most committed football supporters flooded towards one Old Trafford, magnetised by Manchester United's leadership of the First Division, about 1500 of us straggled willingly into the neighbouring premises of the same name to watch Lancashire and Somerset play a bit of cricket.

Our choice, last Monday afternoon, was much less eccentric than it may have appeared. Vivian Richards was due to bat and that is something he is capable of doing better than anyone else on the planet.

The setting – spectators scattered in chilled, huddled handfuls around acres of seating under stubbornly threatening clouds – was scarcely calculated to galvanise the spirit. But greatness does not require a quorum. When he came to the crease, his juices were flowing and the tiny audience was treated to one of the most memorable experiences in the whole of contemporary sport: a bravura (i.e. characteristic) century by Viv Richards.

It is unnecessary to report that many of the shots that took the recently appointed captain of West Indies beyond a hundred for the sixth time this season (he scored a seventh century three days later to strengthen his position at the top of the batting averages) were breathtaking. Some of the 11 fours in his 120 clattered into the boards almost before the bowler's arm had completed its motion and more than one of his five sixes soared away from a swing of the bat so fluid and flawlessly timed, so outrageously relaxed, that the power imparted seemed slightly eerie.

Yet neither the glittering details of a single innings nor the cumulative wonders he has fed into the record books during the long decade of his pre-eminence in cricket can adequately explain the full effect that Richards at his best has on those fortunate enough to be on hand as witnesses.

Of course, a dramatic physical presence is part of it. A man standing an inch under 6 feet and weighing upwards of 13 stone might be expected to look bulkily, perhaps ponderously solid, but in him grace is as basic as breathing. Just watching him walk slowly to the wicket can be more of a thrill than seeing other famous sportsmen at the height of their performances.

His demeanour at such moments has been described as insouciant but regal might be nearer the mark. The downward curve of the fine nose, the level gaze, the wide, expressive mouth within the handsome beard – all combine to indicate that if he ever went after the role of an emperor, the price of the second-favourite at the audition would be 33–1 and drifting.

Still, even when his looks, his sense of theatre and his dazzling technical brilliance are taken into account, the extent to which Richards can electrify his audiences, the way he can stir responses only rarely touched by sport, remains extraordinary. Maybe the best attempt we can make at identifying the extra factor involved is to suggest that he is a remarkable example of a man able to channel a great deal of a large and intense nature into the playing of a game.

All great sportsmen, once in the arena, make statements about themselves but few achieve the eloquence, the vehemence or the depth of declaration that comes from Richards. When he is in action, you have the feeling that you are being addressed by a big spirit and had better pay attention.

The potency of his aura certainly does not diminish at close quarters. One distinguished cricket writer admits to being enfeebled by extreme nervousness at the mere approach of Richards, even when the Antiguan's mood is obviously benign. It's not just that he exudes the kind of challenging strength that makes the contrived machismo of other athletes come across like the currency of a primary school playground. His capacity to make those around him crave his approval is out of all proportion to his own remarkable prowess.

When Ian Botham, with whom he has sustained a long and genuinely deep friendship rooted in mutual affection, admiration and spontaneous rapport, said that he did not seriously consider playing cricket in South Africa because he wouldn't have been able to look Richards in the eye, the chances are that Botham was speaking literally.

Richards does not vociferously condemn those who have been part of compromising expeditions to Mr Botha's *laager*, insisting that each individual must answer to his own conscience. As West Indian captain, he has carefully stayed quiet on the Graham Gooch case and its threat to England's winter tour of the islands, refusing to be drawn when his friend Lester Bird, the Antiguan Foreign Minister, articulated the possibility that Gooch's attitudes would make him unacceptable as a tourist.

The definite impression is that if last week's avowal by Gooch of strong opposition to apartheid clears the way for the Essex man to visit the West Indies, that will please Richards, for it did not take the events of Thursday and Friday at The Oval [Gooch made 196 and David Gower 157 against Australia] to place Gooch and Gower at the head of his personal rankings of outstanding English batsmen. And when he and his team go into battle on their own turf, they don't want any favours in the shape of weakened opposition.

His consistent view is that cricketers who have been drawn from the rest of the world to entertain in South Africa, especially fellow West Indians who have yielded to the blandishments and financial lures, have been systematically 'used'.

'Knowing what the South Africans really think of our people, do you imagine they would offer us that sort of money if everything was right with them?'

His face darkens and he shakes his head in dismissal of the ludicrous thought. Then, suddenly, the frown is swept away by an irresistible smile, the kind that might register on a light metre at a range of 100 yards. 'Of course, our talents are worth more than they could ever pay – but it's not appreciation of our worth that makes them dangle that money in front of us.'

The fact that his century on Monday was followed by a relentless drip of frustration in the field throughout Tuesday as

Lancashire progressed to a comfortable victory might have made complications for an interviewer.

But he was as courteous as he was fascinating and the ultimate effect on a scribbler with a fair amount of mileage on the clock was a profound sense of having been privileged to keep such company. Boxing, and a shared respect for the pride and dignity Joe Frazier brought to that rough old pursuit, gave us a good start.

When I first toured India and Pakistan with the West Indies in 1974–75, I remember that in supporting Frazier against Ali I was outnumbered about 17–1 but I didn't mind. Ali was great but Joe, with his big disadvantages in height and reach, had to be very brave and very special to do what he did. I believe in people who put all their heart into what they do and Joe was like that. I used to feel, 'Here's my man, going out to do a job, to give it his best shot.' They might beat him but they could not break him.

The empathy with Frazier, which has combined with a noticeable facial resemblance to give Richards a series of dressing-room nicknames that are variations of Smokin' Joe, has a first-hand basis. In his teens Richards boxed for his neighbourhood in St John's, Antigua, competing with boys from surrounding districts.

'I still spar a lot at the local gym when I go home to Antigua. It gets rid of my frustrations and it helps me to keep fit. I swim too. We have a lot of wonderful beaches. I hate jogging or running for miles, so I like to swim or go to the gym. I believe in burning up the little bit of energy I do possess. Hitting the heavy bag is comforting.'

His aggression has not always found such innocuous outlets. As a young footballer (he actually preferred that game until an ultimatum from a Leeward Islands cricket official abruptly clarified his thinking) his rumbustious activities in the back four caused him to be known as The Bull.

'I was inclined to take things into my own hands, to go for a little bit of physical stuff,' he says, grinning at the memory. Looking across at the relaxed sprawl of his wide-shouldered body, in which what he calls his beef is kept hard and flexible by a daily programme of exercise that includes about 70 sit-ups and 40 press-ups, it was easy to sympathise with The Bull's opponents.

At that moment, dressed in the whites that always heighten his glow of fitness, with an unextravagant glint of gold on one finger of his right hand, at the wrist and at his neck, he was the picture of a successful young athlete at ease with the world. But his fierce pride in himself and his people can release an element in his personality that is positively volcanic.

'I don't stand rubbish from no one,' he said quietly on Tuesday.

A man has to approach me the right way, then I think I can be fair and decent to anybody. But don't come and put rubbish on me, man. I won't stand that shit from no one. I have lost my cool on numerous occasions and I haven't always regretted it. I was not sorry for what I did on the last West Indies tour of Australia.

There was a bad taste about that series. People like Geoff Lawson were behaving like school kids. There were racist remarks and some of our guys were badly hurt. It couldn't go on. Eventually Allan Border was involved and Graeme Wood and Steve Rixon, though Geoff Lawson was at the centre of it. In the last Test at Sydney in January somebody said something to me and I totally went wild. I said, 'No use we talk about it here in the game. After the match we can sort this out.'

I was waving and making a lot of rude gestures and some nasty words came out. I took plenty of stick from the Australian crowd and the Press but I felt better afterwards. I had to make them aware that we are not idiots. The trouble was serious. We were just waiting for one Australian to get out of hand again and everything would have turned loose. That's how bad the guys felt.

His anger then was thoroughly understandable but less explosive natures are alarmed by the scale of the rage that can be detonated by the conviction that he has been given out unjustly. It led to him being banned for two years as a teenager in Antigua and while on tour in India as vice-captain of West Indies in 1983 what he did to a dressing room instantly became a legend.

'I didn't get any runs in the first match and I wanted desperately to do much better in New Delhi,' he recalled. 'I was going really well until this ridiculous decision put me out. When I got back to the dressing room all the lunches were laid out and I chucked the bat and the first pot it hit had curried mutton in it, or something like that. All hell turned loose.'

In spite of the serious implications that attended the outburst, he cannot remain solemn when he remembers the curry-splattered scene. The rich voice breaks into a staccato laugh.

However, there is no doubt that captaincy of his country will make him more than ever determined to offer the right example in vital areas.

I always want to behave the way a man should, not to do anything cheap. It is true that in the West Indies you're expected to be more than just an exceptional player. You're expected to present yourself in a particular way, the way you have known since you were a kid in the islands, with the natural panache that means so much in a place where the cricket is so important.

His people, he convinces you, could never settle for any mathematical representation of greatness in a cricketer. True heroes like Sobers and Worrell had to fill the mind with glorious memories. The Richards career, brimming though it is with stunning statistics, will surely survive in the end as a parade of unforgettable images.

He has his own varied pantheon of heroes, from Nelson Mandela to Frank Worrell to Bob Marley, and he is as loyal to the ideals they embody for him as he is to those nearer to his everyday experience who have an affinity with the emotional essence of his nature.

Botham is one, and another was Peter McCombe from Airdrie who befriended Richards in the lonely early days at Somerset and had become as trusted as a brother by the time he died of a heart attack in Antigua last year.

Richards says he would never disown a friend and will

certainly never turn his back on the many men who grew up with him and are now Rastafarians. 'These people are a lot cleaner in their hearts than most who criticise them, and they are and always will be part of me. I believe totally in a friend.'

He believes also in his obligations to the mass of ordinary West Indians in this country. 'So many of them work in lowly jobs and when we do well on the field they can walk a little taller, and hold their heads up. Whether I'm batting, bowling or fielding, I cannot feel satisfied unless I give every ounce to try and make them proud of me.'

For some time the wonderful eyes that he reveres as the greatest of his God-given gifts have been susceptible to inflammation from a condition akin to cataracts. He bathes them religiously with an assortment of lotions and balms to keep the problem in check.

Vivian Richards, now 33, long ago realised that he had to do a great deal more than look out for himself and his family.

1 September 1985                                    *Hugh McIlvanney*

# PART 3

# *Matches*

*The Old Trafford Test of 1902 saw the closest finish in Test cricket up to that point, and the match had already been graced by the first Test century before lunch, by Victor Trumper, on the opening day. On the third and final day England were set 124 to win. They failed dramatically, but the drama is something not conveyed in this agency report, typical of the style of the day.*

# Fred Tate's Match

## England v. Australia, Fourth Test, 1902

The Fourth Test match, which produced some remarkable cricket, ended at Manchester yesterday after an exciting finish in a win for the Australians by 3 runs. Having previously been successful in the game at Sheffield the Australians have now won the rubber. The result is all the more disappointing to English-men as on Friday evening the England XI, after a splendid fight, had pulled round a game which appeared to be well nigh hopeless. The position at the close of the second day's play was that Australia with 8 wickets down in their second innings for 86 were only 122 runs on, Jackson and Braund by their batting, and Lockwood by a splendid piece of bowling, having completely altered the aspect of affairs. Had there been no change in the conditions, the chances were that England would have won the match comfortably, but as it happened rain fell heavily during Friday night. The wicket was so soft that the game could not be proceeded with until an hour after the appointed time, and then, under the influence of sunshine, became difficult. The last two Australian wickets went down for the addition of one run, and England were left with 124 runs to get to win. An encouraging start was made by MacLaren and Palairet, the pair scoring 36 before lunch without loss. They were parted at 44, and then, with Trumble and Saunders bowling, finally matters began to go somewhat badly with England, and Tyldesley, who made a few hits, left at 68, and four runs later MacLaren, who played finely, was dismissed. Ranjitsinhji, who could do little more than keep in, was leg-before at 92, and with five runs added Abel, who showed fair form, was bowled. Still, with a hundred on the board and five wickets left the chances appeared to be all in favour of England. However, a great change occurred shortly afterwards, Jackson, Braund, Lockwood, and Lilley being dismissed. Then, with the score standing at 116 for 9 wickets, rain stopped play for 40 minutes, and on continuing Tate hit a four. However, at 120 Tate was bowled, and Australia were left the winners of a remarkable match by 3 runs. Trumble took 10 wickets in the match for 128, but Lockwood with 11 for 76 had the best record.

27 July 1902                                                           *Agency*

*Scores:* Australia 299 (Trumper 104, Lockwood 6–48) and 86 (Lockwood 5–28); England 262 (Jackson 128) and 120 (Trumble 6–53). Australia won by 3 runs.

---

*The Lord's Test of 1921 ended in defeat for England by 8 wickets. In analysing at some length England's second heavy defeat of the series, and their seventh in succession at Australian hands, the anonymous author calls on much classical allusion and lays the blame squarely on professional batsmen and their methods. So did the selectors, even though Woolley (F. E.) scored 95 and 93, and Dipper (A. E.) 11 and 40 in this, his only Test match. (It should be added that Dipper's rustic Gloucestershire habit of stopping the ball with his boot contributed to his downfall.)*

# The Darkest Hour

## England v. Australia, Second Test, 1921

Saturday 11 June was a fateful day for English cricket; it brought to Lord's the largest and the most intelligently critical crowd that the ground had ever seen; it saw the chosen XI of our country thoroughly outclassed in all three departments of the game, and yet it left one with the feeling that this was, indeed, the darkest hour, and that the dawn was at hand. By the end of that day a real conviction was spreading in the cricket world that, though the Australians were admittedly and comfortably our superiors, there was no reason at all why we should not put up against them a far better fight than we had up to date, provided that we had the courage to face facts and set our house in order in accordance with them. This impression was strengthened on the Monday when for a time we thoroughly held our own, and especially when Woolley and Dipper were together at the wicket. Woolley in both innings, and Dipper and Mr Tennyson in the second, all showed that our opponents' attack was far from being the irresistible avalanche that it has at times been painted.

We lost the game beyond recall in the first four hours, when on the most beautiful wicket I have ever seen at Lord's our batsmen failed through sheer bad batting. Watching that dismal performance one was inevitably reminded of an article written by that great judge of the game, Lord Harris, which was first published in the 1910 *Wisden*, and which was re-embodied in his recently published book, *A Few Short Runs*. In it Lord Harris makes a frontal attack on the general method of modern batting, its predisposition towards the two-eyed stance and the back stroke, played almost entirely with the right hand, and with both legs pointing down the wicket. This 'development' of batting was inaugurated, largely under the influence of the Jam Sahib's example [Ranjitsinhji's], and primarily to deal with the new threat of the swerving ball. It is hardly too much to say that it has vitiated, and still vitiates, the whole body of first-class batting, and especially is this true of our professionals. It led directly to several of the major disasters on Saturday; had Dipper kept his left shoulder up and played down, instead of across, the line of the ball, he would have found no difficulty in forcing just square of mid-on the almost vulgar resemblance of a long hop with which Mr McDonald bowled him. Hendren was bowled playing a very crooked and right-handed back stroke to a ball which Mr Lionel Palairet would have driven like a bullet to the off-boundary, while a bowing acquaintance with a straight bat, guided by the left hand, would have saved both Parkin and Strudwick from their rather ignominious exits. But it is not merely that this vicious habit has impaired our defence; it has also undermined our attack, for the initial movement it involves immobilises the batsmen from any possibility of driving in front of the wicket or cutting behind it. On the Saturday morning before lunch the length of the Australian fast bowlers was really generous. Mr MacLaren and Mr Jackson would have revelled in the luxury of the overpitched ball and no man out, and yet during those two hours not three balls were driven to the boundary between mid-on and cover point.

Mr Evans will have been written down as one of the failures of the match, and so far as figures go it will be true, and yet the contrast of his style with that of most of his predecessors was so marked as to be almost a shock. Even when he missed the ball he looked more of a cricketer than some others when they hit it; one felt instinctively that if in practice and in form he could play an innings of which no one else on the side, except Woolley, was capable against the fast bowling.

But there are signs that the high price at which we are buying our lesson is not being paid in vain. Already Mr MacLaren and Mr H. K. Foster have in print thrown the great weight of their authority most unmistakably upon the right side, and all over the Pavilion at Lord's on Saturday one heard members – and most of them experienced and playing cricketers – reiterating their belief that our batting methods had got to be recast and the left shoulder and the straight bat come into its own again.

This counter-revolution may take some years; it is difficult, almost impossible, for a man to alter methods which are ten years ingrained. The future lies with the young cricketers of today and the misfortune is that they have so few sound models to copy. It may, I think, be taken as certain that the public schools will labour on the right lines, but under present-day conditions it seems inevitable that the professional should outweigh the amateur element in first-class cricket. It is the professionals who are the worst offenders in batting method, and it is the professional nursery at the county ground that is the crucial point of reform.

**6** Viv Richards dominates – the bowling and the relationship – during the Old Trafford one-day international of 1984, when Richards scored 189* out of 272 for 9 by West Indies. On Ian Botham's face is uncertainty; not on that of Richards, and it may be this psychological mastery that accounts for Botham's relatively poor record against West Indies. The photographer, Adrian Murrell, emphasises the importance of the background. 'In international cricket it's best to have a packed crowd behind. If there are only two men and a dog in the background, it detracts even from the most exciting picture.'

**7** Geoffrey Boycott animatedly defends during the innings at New Delhi in 1981–82 which gave him the world Test record aggregate, beating Sobers's 8032 runs. Batting first on an all-too-perfect pitch Boycott scored 105 in 7 hours 20 minutes. By an uncalculated irony, the photographer Adrian Murrell has captured India's Srikkanth in the background, the most dashing Test opener of recent times.

**8, 9** David Gower (below) carves through the covers during his century at Perth in the Second Test of England's 1986–87 tour. The sun was shining on him again, and even Australia's 'keeper Tim Zoehrer is for once speechless. 'Effortlessly carves', some might say, but the photograph above helps to put the record straight. The ball has no doubt been driven so late that it would have broken anybody else's wrists, while the sinews of his left forearm are writ large with effort.

The professional batsman's primary consideration is defence, and it is at this that the modern overemphasis of back play and right-hand methods is directed; the trouble is that against the mediocre bowling of present-day county cricket their tactics are relatively successful, and enough bad balls are bowled to enable the batsmen to proceed sedately on their scoring way. But against Mr McDonald's fast break-backs and Mr Gregory's bumping deliveries they break down as defence, while against any bowlers who can maintain a length approximate to Mr Armstrong's they inhibit altogether the capacity to score. It is almost ludicrous to contemplate what would happen if a Shaw and an Attewell suddenly appeared at opposite ends of the wicket and proceeded to bowl off-theory of their normal unimpeachable length.

Two down and three to play is not an enviable position, and the selectors have, for Leeds, a more difficult task than ever. We cannot yet forgo altogether the hope of recovering the Ashes, and so cannot regard the next match as the first of three invaluable trial games for English cricketers of the future. On the other hand, it would be idle to pretend any great confidence in our ability to beat Australia in all the next three games. Saturday, the 11th, was a dreadful day for the selectors; they gambled, and most of their horses were 'left at the post'; but we may be glad that they are all three men of courage, and we may hope that they will take heart of grace from the Monday and continue in their policy of enterprise.

What, then, are the immediate needs of our XI at which that enterprise may legitimately be directed? The first is of confidence, the second is, to use a time-honoured, but now perhaps forgotten, phrase of 'an upright and manly style' of batting, the third is of bowlers who will bowl a length and make the ball come quick off the pitch, the fourth and last of fielders who will stop and run and throw.

What then of the first? Moral [*sic*] is a very real, if elusive, factor in success, and somehow we have got to shake ourselves free of the inevitably rather gloomy associations connected with our recent meetings with the Australians.

The Romans used to demand of their generals three main qualities: *virtus*, *constantia*, and *felicitas*. No one who knows Mr Douglas will question his stoutness of heart, his batting record for the last eighteen months proves his consistency and resolution, but as an English captain he has been neither successful nor lucky – and the Latin word has this double significance. It would be no reflection upon him if the selectors looked to a new captain for inspirations and a fresh start. It is, in light of this season's events, a pity that Mr Warner is not still playing; he would, as captain, command the fullest confidence, and would as likely as not make runs; but failing Mr Warner, there is Mr Fry. He had a bad match against Lancashire, but good judges who saw him play in other games thought his batting within at least measurable length of his best standard. He has already captained this country to success in the Triangular Tournament of 1912; he has a striking personality on which an XI naturally focuses, and no one, without exception, has studied the game more deeply. Mr Douglas would, we feel sure, gladly play under him, and the change might, in fact, add to his value as an individual cricketer.

Now as to batting: if Hobbs and Hearne are fit and in form, our strength is automatically increased 30 per cent; the fast bowlers will not pitch the ball up to Hobbs with impunity, and Hearne will never be caught playing back with a crooked bat. They, with Woolley, and possibly Dipper, who has the great merit of batting in the same style for a Test match as he does for an ordinary county fixture, will form a fine nucleus. To this we want to add two or three batsmen who can attack as well as defend, who will drive the fast bowlers if given the opportunity, who can field – this is our fourth need – and, above all, who *possunt quia posse videntur*. Personally we would always play George Gunn – at his best one of the few real batting geniuses – a man who plays fast bowlers as if they were slow-medium, and who believes in himself. Of other candidates there are Mr Tennyson, whose natural confidence will have been increased by last Monday and Tuesday, and Mr P. R. Johnson, whose method is exactly that demanded by fast bowlers on fast wickets, and then there are the 'Varsity cricketers. Is it really too late to avoid the deplorable clash between the Third Test and the University match? Could not Eton and Harrow play on the Monday and Tuesday and the 'Varsities on the last three days of the week? It is no secret that the Australians were really impressed by the form of Mr Hubert Ashton, Mr Chapman and Mr Jardine; the two first are glorious fieldsmen whose very presence on the ground would galvanise the rest of the XI. Mr Chapman, they say, fishes for the off-ball, but so did Woolley at Lord's, and Mr Ashton has already driven Mr McDonald to the boundary nearly as often as the entire English XI at Lord's.

The bowling is the hardest nut to crack; it is to be hoped that the selectors will keep a very sharp eye on the Midland and Northern Leagues; if Barnes can still bowl well, he ought to play; he has bowled Australia out often before, and, what is more, the Australians will remember it. Cook is another possibility; he is not young, but he probably bowls a better length than any English bowler, and up north he can generally get something out of the wicket. If the wicket is hard, Mr J. C. White might be given a trial, for he can really make the ball come in quick from the pitch, and with their predilection for, if wonderful use of, the cross-bat, this is more than anything else likely to find the Australians at fault.

But whatever happens, let us have no Jeremiahs about our cricket, still less ill-tempered criticism of the selectors, the captain, the players. We have had long periods of failure before, we are having one now, and shall have them again, but we have also had long periods of success and, if we cannot beat our friends this year, we will at least learn our lesson from them and be grateful to them for teaching it to us.

19 June 1921                                    *A Special Correspondent*

*Scores:* England 187 (Woolley 95) and 283 (Woolley 93, Tennyson 74*); Australia 342 (Bardsley 88) and 131 for 2 wickets. Australia won by 8 wickets.

---

*The Third Test of the 1926 series was made famous by Charles Macartney hitting a century before lunch, the second batsman to do so, after Victor Trumper. England had asked Australia to bat after winning the toss, an uncommon decision in those times: England had done it only four times before, as had Australia, in Test matches against each other, and six of those games had ended in defeat for the adventurous captain. The game is described here by Donald Knight. As a Malvern schoolboy Knight had played for Surrey before the First World War, gone on to Oxford, and was rated the equal of Hobbs in 1919. But in 1920 he became a schoolmaster at Westminster, and was hit on the head while fielding at short-leg. His elegant batting was thought never to have been the same again, although he played twice for England against Australia in 1921. In all first-class cricket Knight scored 6231 runs at an average of 30.*

# Macartney's Century Before Lunch

## England v. Australia, Third Test, 1926

Once again, as at Lord's, the sun shone out on the ground, and we feared it was to prove a very deceitful luminary on this occasion. Carr won the toss, having previously taken out Sutcliffe with him to inspect the wicket, and he boldly put his opponents in. We then heard that Root, Larwood, and Parker had been left out, and that Macaulay and Geary had found favour with the Selection Committee. This, in the case of the two former, I submit was a correct policy, as it was essential, in my opinion, to change the weapons in our armament from what they were at Lord's, if only to give the Australians some fresh problems to face.

It seemed a pity, nevertheless, in view of Carr's policy of sending his opponents in, to dispense with the services of Parker, who seemed to be the very bowler the situation demanded. Also Geary has great similitude of pace to Macaulay. One can but commiserate with Carr in the unfortunate circumstances which dogged both himself and the English side during the next two hours.

The start of the game was unforgettable. Tate sent the first ball down, and Bardsley was gloriously taken low down in the slips by

Sutcliffe. What wonderful contrasts this great game of cricket affords in that a man who defied the cream of English bowling for seven hours, can, only a fortnight later, play an innings lasting one second. For the moment Carr's policy was justifying itself, and anything seemed possible for England after such a shattering start as the Australians had experienced.

In comes the perky little Macartney, and then comes the great turning point in our fortunes. Off the fifth ball of Tate's first over he was missed by Carr at third slip. The ball went swiftly to the skipper's left-hand side. He got two hands to it, but, alas, out it bounced, a difficult catch but one which he would have accepted more often than not. Cricket is full of regrets, but think what might have happened with Bardsley and Macartney dismissed in the very first over. And the sun obliterated itself, never to appear again throughout the whole of the day, and the wicket, instead of rapidly degenerating into a gluepot, simply proceeded to play dead and easy.

Then Macartney began to play one of the most marvellous innings it has ever been my privilege to witness. His timing was simply perfection, and he started at once to paste every one of the sorely tried bowlers to every direction of the field. His innings at Lord's was a great one, but this was a hundred times finer. With his side sent in to bat, with his captain dismissed the first ball of the match, and with the English bowlers nerved to supreme endeavour by the sensational start, he proceeded to hit every single ball plumb in the middle of the bat and, moreover, to produce every single scoring stroke that the game possesses. It was brilliant, dazzling, and almost bordered on the uncanny.

Macaulay was quickly knocked off his length. One fears he does not possess the equable temperament requisite for Test matches. Woodfull played beautifully as well, and with his bat looking like a brick wall, successfully kept our bowlers at bay while the marvellous genius at the other end helped himself in what way he liked. The dazzling drive through the covers, the graceful leg glide, and the neat late cut were all alike made with a sureness of execution that almost beggars description. He reached his hundred in almost exactly 100 minutes, amidst such a roar of appreciation as I have never heard on a cricket field. By lunch-time these two batsmen, in two short hours, had completely revolutionised the whole aspect of the game, and the score stood at 153 for 1, with Macartney not out 112. What a wonderful proportion! He scored his hundred out of 132.

Our bowlers had been made to appear like schoolboys, not because they themselves had bowled so badly, but owing to the superlative genius and skill of a tiny little man only just 5 feet 5 inches in height. Our fielding before lunch had not been up to the standard set at Lord's, there being several cases of careless overthrows. Carr had once more been brilliant in his pick-ups near the wicket, and had done his very best to retrieve in some small measure his disastrous mistake in the first over.

The wicket was playing ridiculously slowly and easily, and the sun steadfastly refused to make its presence felt and thus enable Tate and Kilner to get some bite out of the pitch. In fact, so easy was the wicket playing that the batsmen appeared to make run-getting a matter like shelling peas. After lunch Woodfull quickly reached his 50, which he completed in two hours and a quarter.

At last the long partnership was ended, after the two had been associated for 2 hours and 50 minutes, having put on 235 runs – not bad going for a side put in to bat by the opposing captain. Just as the record partnership for Australia in Test matches was being approached – I refer to the 243 put on by Clem Hill and Hartigan at Adelaide in 1907–8 for the eighth wicket – Macartney appeared to get under one of his beautiful slash off-drives, and his great innings, perhaps one of the greatest of all time, was brought to its close by an easy catch made by Hendren at mid-off, Macaulay being the bowler. Macartney's 151 was scored in 2 hours and 50 minutes.

In my opinion it must rank with the very greatest efforts of either Victor Trumper or Ranjitsinhji's. To those fortunate enough to have witnessed it, his innings will bring ineffaceable memories. Strokes were played which, alas, seem to be vetoed from the game now, and the great batsman, by his miraculous (I do not consider that too strong a word) display, did much in these wonderful two hours to show the rising generation to what heights the true art of batsmanship can rise. We thank you for showing us once again that the glorious strokes of the game are not quite extinct. Let us all try to bat like Macartney; at least to hold him up in our mind as our ideal, and then once more shall we revive the glories of the days that are past.

Soon after Macartney's dismissal Andrews stepped in front of a straight ball from Kilner, and with our bowlers heartened by their success, things looked a little bit more cheerful. Macaulay, in particular, seemed to start bowling much better. Woodfull at last got his first hundred in Test cricket, after batting 3 hours and 35 minutes, but in doing so he was very nearly caught and bowled by Kilner, who flung himself at full length on the ground. Australia owe him their best thanks for his imperturbable and rock-like defence, a great innings in its way. Geary then missed Richardson at first slip, our second dropped catch in the present series of matches. We had a clean slate at Lord's except, of course, for chances at the wicket. At tea the score stood at 334 for 3, Richardson having completely obtained the measure of the bowling. This partnership for the third wicket had completed our discomfiture for the day, and the last gleam of hope of getting our opponents out for a reasonable score, which we entertained for a brief moment after Andrews' departure, had now vanished. Geary's missed catch was the death-blow to those hopes.

After that the game proceeded amidst an ever-deepening gloom, both of the weather and of the mind. The score was slowly advanced to 366, with Richardson not out 70, and Woodfull not out 134. The cricket, compared with the dazzling glories of the morning and first hour of the afternoon, seemed to me very featureless. At this stage the rain came down in a steady drizzle, and play was abandoned.

11 July 1926                                          *D. J. Knight*

### AUSTRALIA – First Innings

| | |
|---|---|
| W. Bardsley c Sutcliffe b Tate | 0 |
| W. M. Woodfull not out | 134 |
| C. G. Macartney c Hendren b Macaulay | 151 |
| T. J. E. Andrews lbw b Kilner | 4 |
| A. J. Richardson not out | 70 |
| Extras | 7 |
| Total (3 wickets) | 366 |

Fall of wickets: 1–0; 2–235; 3–249

To bat: J. M. Gregory, J. M. Taylor, J. Ryder, W. A. Oldfield, C. V. Grimmett, and A. A. Mailey.

ENGLAND: A. W. Carr (captain), A. P. F. Chapman, Hobbs, Woolley, Sutcliffe, Tate, Hendren, Strudwick, Kilner, Macaulay, Geary.

*Final scores:* Australia 494 (Woodfull 141, Macartney 151, Richardson 100); England 294 (Macaulay 76, Grimmett 5 for 88) and 254 for 3 wickets (Hobbs 88, Sutcliffe 94). Match drawn.

---

*Cricket correspondent for* The Observer *in 1938, Douglas Jardine here reports on a routine day in the 'Varsity match of that year and laments the falling standard of university cricket. Its decline, both in the quality of players and quantity of spectators, has evidently been as long as the Decline of English Cricket itself. The following season Jardine went over to* The Daily Telegraph *and was replaced by Robertson-Glasgow.*

# The Hundredth 'Varsity Match

## Oxford v. Cambridge, 1938

The Oxford captain began the hundredth match between the two Universities by winning the toss. It was high time Oxford did win the toss in this contest. A careful record is kept of such things in the Boat Race, where admittedly the toss may be important, but scarcely more so than at Lord's. An old Cambridge captain would have it that it was the first time in nine years, but could not substantiate this.

The hundredth match also saw a new departure made by the Saturday start to the match; but the result, though a slight improvement on recent years, did not produce the large gate hoped for among those whose memories carry back to the yester years of pre-war days.

It is sad to see the University match so ill-attended. The lack of championship points at stake may account for the decline of such games as Gentlemen v. Players at The Oval, apart from the lack of quality in the sides in recent years; but the ladies, curiously enough, must bear some of the blame at Lord's for the decline in popularity of the 'Varsity match. If top hats and tail coats were *de rigueur* as of yore, and these things depend upon the ladies, the crowds would be infinitely more numerous.

Before a ball was bowled it was generally known that both sides were lamentably short of bowling of quality and variety. Batting takes wickets as well as bowling, as Surrey have proved for years, hence the importance of the toss.

It was, however, generally anticipated that Friday's heavy shower would give bowlers the chance of showing their abilities in the first hour's play. But it was not to be, or else the ability was signally lacking.

Rees-Davies started from the Nursery end with a replica of the field to which McCormick bowled for Australia in the Test match. Two gullies, two slips, and two square legs, with their attendant third man and long leg, do not leave much margin of error, and the spectator as well as the batsman is left wondering just for what the bowler is going to bowl. Eleven men are not enough to cover both sides of the wicket with fieldsmen either for wicket-taking or run-saving purposes.

Dixon and Walford opened quietly but confidently, the former being content to leave the lion's share of the scoring to his partner. At the end of the first hour the score was 45, and almost immediately afterwards Walford was out caught at long leg for 34 valuable runs – he might have been out in the same manner earlier but for the fieldsman being unable to pick up the ball early enough in the queer light often associated with Lord's.

It had been a quiet but efficient start – with rain appearing imminent Oxford might have been tempted to go for the runs while the going was good – but steady was the order of the day, and by and large the policy was made to pay. Lomas had an agonising half hour before he broke his duck – a tribute to some steady bowling and keen and accurate fielding.

Yardley changed his meagre bowling judiciously, but he might have been well advised to give Hewan the benefit of the slope to help his break at the start instead of bowling him originally from the Nursery end. Even from that end the bowler found he could turn the ball sufficiently to bowl round the wicket.

All eyes were on Gibb behind the wickets in view of all that has been said of his possibilities as a substitute for Ames. Candour compels one to admit that he had an unsatisfactory day – in common with some of the spectators, he appeared almost surprised when his bowlers occasionally managed to beat the bat. Rain held up play once for a quarter of an hour and would have done so again in almost any other match.

After lunch, Dixon and Lomas went on to consolidate the good start until at 156 Dixon only half got hold of a ball from Hewan, which turned from leg, and was caught at square leg off the splice for an invaluable 73. Though not brisk, he never encouraged the bowlers, and Cambridge supporters must have been heartily relieved to see his departure. Kimpton, who followed him, comes in the category of match winners rather than match savers – the position could scarcely have been better prepared for him.

The day's play can best be divided between before and after tea. Before tea the early Oxford batsmen entrenched a position in true Yorkshire style which the north countrymen would not have failed to turn into an impregnable one. The policy was sound enough and be it said with regret that throughout a fair amount of the success which attended it was due to some far from worthy fielding.

Cricket is the chanciest game in the world – as far as batting and bowling are concerned, but ground fielding in the University match should be a certainty, and the poorer the bowling the better the fielding should prove itself.

After tea 3 wickets fell in rapid succession for only 6 runs. Kimpton has never showed his true form this year, and lately the strain of keeping wicket has appeared too much for his true batting form. Grover got one of the best balls of the innings, and Lomas, after surviving his trying start and showing the best batting form of the innings, was caught at mid-off off the least admirable stroke he played. Much may be excused to a Freshman in the 'nineties in his first University match – and Lomas should be a thorn in Cambridge sides for some years to come.

106

Eggar raised hopes that he might repeat Lomas's triumph over a harassing start – he was over twenty minutes at the wicket before scoring – which in the state of the game was hardly warrantable. Having survived it, however, he was most unnecessarily run out off a run which no tactful midshipman would have attempted to steal from a full and bearded admiral standing at old-fashioned point.

The sun shone when Cambridge began batting. Gibb and Carris avoided all risks, but when Macindoe changed to the Pavilion end he made a ball go straight through and Carris was lbw. Stumps were then pulled up with the score 18 for 1 wicket, Cambridge being 299 behind.

3 July 1938                                                 *D. R. Jardine*

*Score:* Oxford 317 (Lomas 94, Hewan 6–91); Cambridge 18 for 1.

---

*During the summer of 1938 Charles Macartney provided 'the visitors' point of view' in his Comments for* The Observer. *In the First Test he had praised Charlie Barnett's century as being of 'such high quality that it must rank with the best played in Test cricket, and is undoubtedly the finest I have seen since arriving in England this year'. In the Fourth, Australia took a 1–0 lead that meant they retained the Ashes. In reviewing the reasons why, the 'Governor-General' advocates aggressive batting methods – and in this case, at least, it cannot be said that he was a journalist who couldn't practise what he preached.*

# Pusillanimous Batting

## England v. Australia, Fourth Test, 1938

Australia, by winning the Fourth Test at Leeds, has retained the

Ashes of international cricket for another two years, and England must now wait until her representatives visit Australia before she can wrest the title from her opponents. While the visitors will fight to a finish at The Oval in order definitely to win the rubber, the position now occupied will enable them to play their natural game free of any great strain, since they know that the laurels are theirs . . .

The Fourth Test match provided one of the most interesting and exciting games seen for a considerable time, the dominating factor throughout being the wicket. The pitch at Headingley was of a character that would always render unnecessary any extension of time for Test matches in England. At no time was it dangerous as far as physical injury is concerned, and as long as that is the case, then the preparation has been quite sufficient. But it was a wicket that brought the bowler on even terms with the batsman – something that has been wanting for a long time.

For years now everything has been done with an eye to the batsman, and unless the quality bowler is encouraged by the possibility of receiving a fair reward for his labours, no one can blame him for giving up the thankless task in disgust. The Fourth Test wicket was one that called for both batting and bowling skill, supported by such a field that every chance counted full value. The bowling and fielding on the whole performed admirably, but, excepting in isolated cases, the batting was found wanting.

To some extent the overprepared pitches are responsible for such batting failures. When a pitch like that of Headingley is encountered, and the opposition attack contains sustained accuracy and controlled spin, the batting is temporarily perplexed by the amount of resource required to circumvent it. Were more Test wickets like that at Leeds presented to the players, it would not be long before more skilful cricketers would be seen, and certainly more bowlers of the true spin class, essential for the uplift of the game.

Before criticising the methods employed by the English batsmen during the recent Leeds Test, it is only fair to say that England probably would have been much better fortified had Hutton and Ames been available for action. They would certainly have strengthened the department that was the sole cause of defeat. I have nothing but admiration for Price's wicket-keeping, which was almost flawless, but Ames would have lent that confidence and assurance to the batting that England so sorely needed. However, I am convinced that England lost the Test at Leeds by their false batting policy as demonstrated on the first day.

In their second innings, when their batting again failed against Australia's spin attack, there was a mite of excuse – the wicket then was revealing signs of wear and tear, and perceptibly assisting the spin-bowlers. But in the first innings, having first use of a wicket that must then be at its very best, whatever the quality, and knowing that the crumbling process would take place more rapidly than usual, their primary objective should have been runs, and runs made quickly, but with discretion. Such runs can only be compiled by the adoption of certain methods – aggression, enterprise, and footwork.

England possessed batsmen fully capable of employing these tactics, but they were not forthcoming. Instead, they adopted defensive tactics which absolutely played into the hands of such bowlers as O'Reilly and Fleetwood-Smith, who asked for nothing better. These bowlers were thus enabled to force matters without fear of punishment, and furthermore, the field were never pressed as they should have been in a Test match. Much too frequently did the cream of England's batsmen play a stroke which was neither forward nor back – uncertain for defensive purposes, impossible for run-making. What more could the heart of a bowler like O'Reilly desire!

When one remembers Barnett's brilliant innings at Nottingham, one wonders why such magnificent strokeplay should be suddenly extinguished. A stroke-player of the calibre of Edrich, one of the finest young and aggressive batsmen England has produced for years, should never be forced perpetually back on his wicket. Compton, another stroke-maker, who should rank high in the near future, was bowled with his feet not 6 inches from the stumps. Hardstaff, too, a batsman naturally gifted with powerful strokes if he would only use his feet, will never counteract the wiles of an O'Reilly by the methods he employs.

I repeat that the one and only way to foil a spin attack is by quick footwork, aggression, and the spirit of adventure. If the batsman gets out in the process, he at least has the satisfaction of knowing that he got out doing the right thing. I am not blaming England because they lost, but I am convinced that had the right tactics been observed in the first innings, they would have won – another hundred runs, perhaps even fifty, would have done the job. England has the players, but they are on the wrong lines.

Let the purely defensive defend, but for heaven's sake let the stroke-players produce the strokes! There is room in a properly chosen side for all, and if they do their work according to their ability, they will at least not be caught at silly point when they should have been caught on the boundary.

31 July 1938                                                    *C. G. Macartney*

*Scores:* England 223 (O'Reilly 5–66) and 123 (O'Reilly 5–56); Australia 242 (Bradman 103) and 107 for 5 wickets. Australia won by 5 wickets.

---

*The Oval Test of 1938 remains one of the most remarkable of Test matches. The game was televised: 'the pictures from the pavilion end of The Oval were the best yet seen in sports television' according to* The Observer. *Above all, the Test was notable for Len Hutton's score of 364. Here is D. R. Jardine's report of the first day's play in which Hutton scored 160 of them.*

# Hutton's Record-breaking Innings

## England v. Australia, Fifth Test, 1938

England made a brilliant start to the Fifth and final Test match against Australia, which was started at The Oval yesterday, and will be played to a finish. W. R. Hammond again won the toss – the fourth time in succession – and although Edrich was out with

110

29 scored, being O'Reilly's hundredth wicket in Test matches against England, Hutton and Leyland proceeded to build up a formidable total and were undefeated at the end of the day, having added 318 for the second wicket, thus beating the record of 188, which Sutcliffe and Hammond set up at Sydney in 1932–3.

Australia were without the services of E. L. McCormick, their fast bowler, and Bradman had to rely mostly on O'Reilly and Fleetwood-Smith, who could get little assistance from the wicket.

Any early surprises provided at The Oval were due to the selectors on both sides. Both took their gambles, and be it said at once that the palm for courageous gambling must be awarded to Australia. Mathematically the odds on winning the toss must always be even, but human nature must necessarily fancy its chance of winning the toss at least once in four. It may be guessed that the Australian team was picked on some such assumption. It was not to be, and once more England had choice of innings. There is only one choice on one of Martin's guaranteed guileless Oval wickets. With or without neuritis McCormick's omission should be regretted against a side of even strong county class on such a wicket faced with only three regular bowlers.

It must be very many years since any international side had a less impressive opening pair than Waite and McCabe. So much for the Australian gamble on the toss, or, put another way, Australia's dependence upon O'Reilly throughout, coupled with the hope of at least two inspired spells from Fleetwood-Smith.

In the First Test match at Brisbane in 1928 England took a similar gamble, with only three bowlers. It was a brilliant success but Larwood, Tate and White were the bowlers, and despite its success it was wisely never again attempted. Really strong sides should not have to gamble in this manner.

England's gamble did not need to be quite so barefacedly obvious. In the first place, by contrast, the fast attack was preferred to the slow, rightly it may thus early be submitted on an Oval wicket. But this apart, the selection of Edrich in preference to Fagg must have surprised more than merely Kentish supporters.

While it is sound policy to disturb the batting as little as possible when ringing the changes on the bowling, Fagg might well ask what more he could have done to command a place, while, on record or experience, Barnett should rank handsomely in front of Edrich. The ways of selection committees are sufficiently difficult and mysterious, but a solid phalanx of five Yorkshiremen at least ensures a gratifying sufficiency of skilled determination.

It was a slow but steady start, the singularly inoffensive bowling being backed up and bolstered by some really admirable fielding upon an extremely bumpy outfield. After half an hour O'Reilly came on, and one felt that now the match was really beginning.

But this fresh start was the end of Edrich, who furnished O'Reilly with his hundredth wicket in Test matches against England. O'Reilly is the sixth of his countrymen to do this – the late Hugh Trumble heading the list with 141 wickets. Edrich was out to a half-hearted stroke.

Meanwhile, Hutton had been batting adequately, but after the manner of one rather short of batting practice, though determined to rectify this. It was the same with Leyland. The wicket was taking no spin. Indeed, the nearest approach to wicket-taking deliveries were two full-pitchers from Fleetwood-Smith, off the first of which Barnett missed an anything but difficult chance of stumping Hutton with the score at 91. A little later Leyland was all at sea with a similar ball which appeared to dip in the air.

The score at lunch was 89 for 1, but before tea the English record for the second wicket, previously held by Sutcliffe and Hammond with 188 in Sydney in 1932, had been handsomely surpassed. Hutton completed a hundred, marred only by the chance of stumping mentioned. Leyland generously nursed his partner into three figures just as the new ball at 200 was due.

However satisfactory a great score may be, it scarcely produces sufficient incidents to make up an enlivening day's cricket unless the rate of scoring be phenomenal. There was nothing phenomenal in the pace at which Hutton and Leyland made their runs, but their great stand – and 'great' accurately describes it – paved the way for England's mastery. Throughout there was a heartening sense of mastery about the batting – workmanlike mastery.

Both scores mounted close together, save for half an hour whilst Leyland toiled in the nineties and Hutton forged ahead despite the new ball. When each had made a hundred, Hutton had hit eleven fours to Leyland's ten.

The Australian bowling, anything but strong, was made to look almost club-like save when O'Reilly was on or when Fleetwood-Smith got a very occasional ball into the wicket-keeper's hands. A great – perhaps the greatest – English bowler of all time, when asked what he thought of the Australian change of bowling, described it as 'merely a way of passing the time', and one may be sure that in Australia the captain of the fielding side would not have lacked for advice from the crowd to put both umpires and the clock on.

Throughout the day the ground was never full. The start of football, and tales of the queues waiting, may have accounted for this, and another 5000 could have been admitted easily to watch a record-breaking day.

Just after the 300 had gone up Leyland should have run himself out by yards, but the bowler in pardonable anxiety to recollect what the fall of a wicket felt like, broke the wicket before the ball was in his hands. Before this the running between the wickets had been refreshingly good and enterprising. A word of praise is also due to the Australian fielding which on a bumpy ground and throughout a disheartening day's play never faltered and never flagged.

Bar accidents and rain Australia should make a lot of runs when it is her turn to bat – the wicket too may last surprisingly well. Yet England could have hardly done more to consolidate the twin advantages of winning the toss and catching their opponents short of bowling.

To lose after such a start would be a cricketing freak of the first water. But one may pause to think that a wicket, or wickets, which reduces the world's present best bowler to such impotence, also constitutes a cricketing freak, or freaks, hardly conducive to the best interests of the game.

It was officially announced last night that 12,999 people paid for admission yesterday, and that members and others present numbered 3,500, making a total attendance of 16,499.

21 August 1938                                         *D. R. Jardine*

ENGLAND – First Innings

| | |
|---|---:|
| Hutton not out | 160 |
| Edrich lbw b O'Reilly | 12 |
| Leyland not out | 156 |
| Extras | 19 |
| Total (1 wkt) | 347 |

To bat: W. R. Hammond, Paynter, Compton, Hardstaff, Wood, Verity, K. Farnes, Bowes.

AUSTRALIA: D. G. Bradman, S. J. McCabe, C. L. Badcock, S. Barnes, B. A. Barnett, W. A. Brown, J. H. Fingleton, L. O'B. Fleetwood-Smith, A. L. Hassett, W. J. O'Reilly and M. G. Waite.

| | O | M | R | W |
|---|---|---|---|---|
| Waite | 33 | 5 | 62 | 0 |
| McCabe | 17 | 4 | 45 | 0 |
| O'Reilly | 35 | 10 | 79 | 1 |
| Fleetwood-Smith | 35 | 3 | 121 | 0 |
| Barnes | 11 | 2 | 21 | 0 |

Byes 5, leg-byes 9, wides 1 (Waite), no-balls 4 (O'Reilly)

*Final scores:* England 903 for 7 wickets declared (Hutton 364, Leyland 187, Hardstaff 169*); Australia 201 (Bowes 5–49) and 123. England won by an innings and 579 runs.

---

*Jack Fingleton covered the first post-war Ashes series for* The Observer. *Here he describes – presumably without great relish, as Don Bradman was not his best friend – The Don's comeback in the First Test at Brisbane. Sometimes peppery, ultimately salty, Fingleton returned eventually to* The Observer *after a long period with* The Sunday Times.

# Bradman's Comeback

## England v. Australia, Brisbane, 1946–47

Mark it down immediately as a bad two days for English cricket. Nothing on earth, it seems, but a flash of Bradman generosity or boldness in declaring the innings closed some time early on Monday, can stop Australia, now 595 for 5, topping the best Australian score of 729 for 6 made at Lord's in 1930. I must admit I am in a perfect whirl of facts and figures and broken records at present.

I do not quite know whether to dwell at length on the Bradman incident, over the disputed catch by Ikin when 28 on Friday, or try to assess just what Gibb, as wicket-keeper, cost England, with Hassett missed at 40 and McCool missed when 1, both catches; but I do know this. There were long periods in the game today when McCool was playing as if on a picnic or Sunday-school match. He so belaboured the England attack that the last thing I thought I was watching was a traditional Test game between England and Australia.

It was a Gilbertian situation that a man, who ostensibly was chosen as Australia's number one slow bowler, is now on the verge of joining the immortals with a Test century in his first game.

Let these following facts be clearly stated, and then see where we can move from there. Bedser lost much strength yesterday through stomach illness, and is deserving of high credit for a grand physical effort made today when still feeling unwell. Voce, who, because he has the same unusual name, must surely be some relation to the man who was here in 1932, toiled as hard for a few overs as his advancing age and aldermanic girth and the hot sun would allow him. Wright spun a good one every now and then, but not very often; and Edrich took the stumps of the man who was beginning to bare record-breaking fangs once again.

It is not sufficient to say that the England bowling was weak. We always knew that, but once again today we saw any vestige of bowling hostility robbed, negated and aborted by a 22-yard stretch of rolled, rerolled, and concrete-like preparation which goes by the name of a wicket. It is high time that many fossilised old gentlemen who walk this earth as cricket legislators were clamped on hard and made to say with one voice, 'Give us a new order in cricket. Underprepared wickets, like that at Leeds in 1938, give bowlers some chance of life – or off goes your head.'

I try to look at these games now with unjaundiced eyes – as one who, too late, learnt the lesson of one's own dreary negative ways in the days of cricket effort, and believes that cricket can do much now to make up for the good things of life of which the war and its aftermath robbed us. But overprepared wickets are the damnation of the game, and I fully believe that had the coin come down Hammond's way England tonight might well be 595 for 5. Which is but another way of saying that too much hinges on the toss.

But enough moralising. To the game, gentlemen! Bradman had a glint in his eyes this morning, which suggested to me that he had Hutton's record at the back of his mind. The spirit was willing, but the flesh weak, though today Bradman was much more confident than yesterday, and played two strokes reminiscent of the old bowler killer. In desperation Voce tried to bowl the only bumper so far of the match, but it was a poor flicker of what he once served up, and Bradman ended its career first bounce to the mid-on pickets – a Bradman shot of the old days.

Yesterday, in an hour, Bradman made more streaky strokes than in his whole career formerly. His batting lacked certainty. His feet, once so twinkling, came forward hesitantly. Englishmen aver that he was caught when 28 by Ikin. Others on the field were just as vehement that he was not. I give no opinion. The pavilion is too far away to be dogmatic on such split decisions. He played back defensively in the ball's last 2 yards to him from the pitch and I noticed Bradman's bat waver uncertainly.

Hassett was most un-Hassett-like in his first Test century in which he denied his art and culture. It was a real bulldog innings, but I loved every moment of the brilliant innings by Miller. His driving was glorious and never have I seen a better hit in a Test than his six over long-on.

Let's draw a veil over Gibb's misses. I have dealt with his doubtful wicket-keeping ability many times, but Hammond and

Bedser also spilt catches – simple ones, too. It seems to me now that England's best chance is to play for a draw. And there is plenty of good Yorkshire and Lancashire spirit in this side for that.

Wright was the pick of the bowlers, but Bedser was splendid yesterday. And as if to pile on the agony England presented 20 no-balls to Australia. As I wrote previously, not at all two happy days for English cricket, but the ground fielding of Washbrook, Ikin, Compton, Yardley and Hutton was simply superb.

1 December 1946 *J. H. Fingleton*

### AUSTRALIA – First Innings

| | |
|---|---|
| S. Barnes c Bedser b Wright | 31 |
| A. Morris c Hammond b Bedser | 2 |
| D. G. Bradman b Edrich | 187 |
| A. L. Hassett c Yardley b Bedser | 128 |
| K. R. Miller lbw b Wright | 79 |
| C. McCool not out | 92 |
| I. Johnson not out | 47 |
| Extras | 29 |
| Total (5 wickets) | 595 |

To bat: R. Lindwall, D. Tallon, G. Tribe and E. Toshack.

Fall of wickets: 1–9; 2–46; 3–322; 4–428; 5–465

| | O | M | R | W |
|---|---|---|---|---|
| Voce | 28 | 9 | 92 | 0 |
| Bedser | 37 | 3 | 150 | 2 |
| Wright | 37 | 4 | 135 | 2 |
| Edrich | 23 | 2 | 96 | 1 |
| Yardley | 13 | 1 | 47 | 0 |
| Ikin | 2 | 0 | 24 | 0 |
| Compton | 6 | 0 | 20 | 0 |

*Final scores:* Australia 645 (Wright 5–167); England 141 (Miller 7–60) and 172 (Toshack 6–82). Australia won by an innings and 332 runs.

*In this report, Michael Davie describes a practice game at an empty Melbourne Cricket Ground in 1958–59. Not only does he say that the day was very hot, he also manages to convey what it was like to be there in the intense heat.*

# A Hot and Futile Day

## Victoria v. MCC, 1958–59

MCC are slumped in a sweating daze tonight after five and a half hours in the field of one of the hottest and most pointless first-class cricket matches yet played.

One or two of them, including Cowdrey, who captained the side, have been sick since the close of play.

It was not a day for anything at all, except sitting in a cold bath up to the neck, which is how some Melbourne inhabitants spent it. The temperature was just nicking 100 when Cowdrey lost the toss to the Victorian captain. By lunch it was 104, and during the afternoon it reached 108.5, the hottest day in Melbourne for seven years. The tarred roads of the city were like putty.

Hassett, the former Australian captain, thinks it went even higher, basing his estimate on the known fact that when he has had two cold beers and is still thirsty the temperature is invariably 109 in the shade – that is, with his hat on.

The vast cricket ground amphitheatre was like a boiler-room. In the middle it was possibly ten degrees higher than the weather bureau reading.

When play began, there were as many spectators present as if it were the third day of a Leicestershire v. Hampshire fixture at Snibston. Most of them lurked in the shade of the enormous concrete stands, but throughout the day some 60 madmen sat in the sun, which was white rather than yellow, with their shirts off.

The heat made them exceptionally derisive. The players also had to put up with a searing north wind from the Australian interior, a wind that tonight is pushing ten very big bush-fires across the State of Victoria.

Yesterday the Victorian opener Colin McDonald, who hurt his

leg during the last Test match and is not, therefore, playing here, gave his opinion that MCC ought to finish this game in two days, as the Victorians' batting is so weak.

But only a magician could have got wickets today. Apart from the heat, the wicket was something like an old-fashioned Australian shirt front: shaved, uniform, and giving a very even bounce.

In the morning, especially, the few batsmen who have any strokes in this State side were cutting and driving in a way that would have got them into trouble on almost any other wicket MCC have so far met on the tour. Crompton was the best to watch, a tall, black-headed left-hander.

At lunch Victoria had managed 77 for 2, and MCC's bowlers were already looking as if they were ready for oblivion. The members' menu offered pea soup and sippets, followed by pork sausages and apple sponge.

Peebles (Middlesex and England) said he once played in a Test in South Africa with the temperature at 107. Hassett said his limit would have been about 105 or 106.

Someone said South Australia once travelled by train the 1100 miles between Adelaide and Sydney, arrived half an hour before the start, lost the toss and fielded for two days at 104.

Bowes (Yorkshire and England) said he had played in Brisbane when it was 115. The *Daily Mail*, wearing a heavy, green tweed coat, ordered himself a hot meat pie and a cup of tea, and said it was well known that the humidity in Durban was worse than anywhere in the world.

After lunch the game dragged on, Cowdrey trying to split up the bowling equitably. When Crompton was out, Maddocks came in, and the *Sydney Morning Herald* murmured about Maddocks and Englishmen going out in the midday sun.

One wondered which MCC bowler would collapse first from exhaustion, and it was, not surprisingly, the slow spinner Mortimore. He does not look strong.

After he had bowled very well for 17 overs, and had even managed to take two wickets in two balls, he doubled up and was sick. He asked to go on bowling. Eleven runs were hit off his nineteenth over, then he bowled another and went off the field.

Later Tyson apparently folded, too. He had had a spell of six overs, none of them, understandably, very good, and he walked off towards the pavilion gate with his canvas hat on the side of his head as if he were a drover who had just hit town after days on the stock route. Then he seemed to collect himself and stayed in the pavilion shade at third man.

Dexter bowled a lot, but rarely to his field. When he had an off-side field he bowled on the leg, and *vice versa*.

Drinks came out every half an hour. The *Evening Standard* said it was as bad as India: the test was whether your hair got hot. The *Times of India* said he could not understand why Australians complained about Indian temperatures. Perhaps they had too much hospitality from Indian princes.

The Englishman, or Yorkshireman, who came best out of the day in the spectators' eyes was undoubtedly Trueman. He gave the impression that he was enjoying the cricket. Whenever Cowdrey asked him to bowl he went almost flat out – sometimes absolutely flat out.

When he fielded forward short leg he put one foot on the wicket, made the crowd howl and subsequently established an actor's rapport with the men under the stands, making them shout at will when he moved his feet.

Loader, today at least, did not look like a bowler who might replace Trueman in the next Test at the end of the month. Subba Row, in his first game since his injury, wore a protective bandage round his hand, and must have lost weight after some brave runs to the boundary.

The day's takings were $A748. It is to be hoped that not too much of MCC's share has to go on doctors' bills.

17 January 1959                                    *Michael Davie*

VICTORIA – First Innings

| | |
|---|---:|
| W. Lawry b Dexter | 24 |
| A. Aylett c Watson b Loader | 2 |
| N. Crompton c Mortimore b Trueman | 73 |
| J. Shaw not out | 93 |
| L. Maddocks b Mortimore | 21 |
| I. Huntington b Mortimore | 0 |
| J. Potter not out | 47 |
| Extras (b 4, l-b 6) | 10 |
| Total (5 wkts) | 270 |

Fall of wickets: 1–4; 2–59; 3–130; 4–191; 5–191

Bowling (to date) – Trueman 10, 0, 36, 1; Loader 9, 2, 41, 1; Tyson 10, 1, 29, 0; Mortimore 20, 2, 72, 2; Dexter 14, 0, 66, 1; Cowdrey 2, 0, 16, 0.

*Final scores:* Victoria 286 (Trueman 5–42) and 180; MCC 313 (Watson 141) and 156 for 1 wicket. MCC won by nine wickets.

---

*Clement Freud wrote about cricket and other sports for* The Observer *from 1956 to 1964. He then transferred to the colour magazine and numerous other activities, becoming Liberal MP for Isle of Ely in 1973.*

# An Island in the Sun

## Hampshire v. Gloucestershire, 1959

Its pitch as green as man's endeavour with a hosepipe can achieve against the elements, the island's premier cricket ground was ringed with deck-chairs occupied by holiday-makers in shirtsleeves sucking ice creams, toffee apples and local rock. Clearly it was a day for winning the toss, a feat Ingleby-Mackenzie duly achieved.

With a feeling of nostalgia we again saw those Sussex stalwarts, Jim Parks and John Langridge, walk out to the wicket together. Their ages now total 105; they wear caps and coats and stand as umpires, but it was good to see them together again.

Hampshire, in this, their one offshore fixture of the year, made heavy weather of the first innings, and on a goodish fast wicket on which Emmett used six bowlers they were very largely responsible for their own downfall. Of the recognised batsmen, Marshall, for whom cricket on an island in the sun should be second nature, stroked the ball into second slip's hands. Horton, accept-

121

ing a straight full toss with his left pad, and Ingleby-Mackenzie, whose attempt at a hook was caught at backward slip, left the arena as a result of their own folly.

Gray batted beautifully until he played on to his wicket a ball that kept low, and Flood, having employed each of his favourite strokes – past mid-on for four and over mid-on for six – paid the penalty for not using his feet to the spinners. This left the new Hampshire man, Baldry, and the old Hampshire man, Harrison, to knock a semblance of respectability into the home team's total.

Baldry's was an innings in three stages. Facing Milton, who bowled to him as one bowls to a friend, he hit him as one hits an enemy for ten runs in his first over. He then batted out 50 minutes before lunch for two singles, returned after lunch with 30 runs in as many minutes, and settled down to selecting the right ball to hit to the boundary. When he was bowled by Allen it was through an error of selection; his 60 included 11 fours.

Harrison had scored with some judiciously driven fours, and after Baldry's departure he carried on to reach 64, his highest innings for two years. He could hardly have chosen a better day for this, and when home rule comes to the Isle of Wight he will doubtless be recognised for it.

In an impressive first-wicket stand, Young always looked the better of Gloucestershire's openers, and his 54 contributed largely to the score of 83 for one at the close.

18 July 1959                                                  *Clement Freud*

*Final scores:* Hampshire 229 and 133 (Horton 54*); Gloucester-shire 233 and 131 for no wicket (Young 72*, Milton 56*). Gloucs won by ten wickets.

---

*The West Indian tour has always been the most difficult tour for English journalists to report for one simple reason: the time difference, which varies between four and five hours behind GMT. Accordingly, the style has to be 'run of play', such as is to be found in evening newspapers: that is, the story is a straight chronicle, beginning at the start of play and ending at the close. An introduction of a few paragraphs, composed at the end, is then placed at the head of the report to summarise the day. In this account of the riot-torn Trinidad Test, the 'intro' clearly ends after the fourth paragraph. Being behind the clock, and with a separate news story to write on the riot, the correspondent had no way of avoiding this abrupt change of gear.*

# The Trinidad Riot

## West Indies v. England, Second Test, 1960

This was the most dramatic day in the history of Test cricket. The play alone would have placed it high, for England in an amazing reversal of form and probability, swept away the major West Indian batting. Ninety-eight runs for 8 wickets on such a pitch is utter rout.

Then one of the greatest crowds ever gathered at a sporting event in the West Indies – some 30,000 people – began the pitiful, shameful rioting which thrust cricket scores into the background of human, and humane, thought.

It is now becoming a serious question whether the match will be able to continue, and the series as a whole must be considered in jeopardy. If play is resumed on Monday, May will certainly have the right to enforce the follow-on but he probably will decide that England shall bat again.

The scenes coincided with a run-out decision against Charan Singh, a local player, included for his bowling but a negligible batsman. Indeed, before his dismissal it was clear that West Indies – 284 behind England's first innings of 382 – would be liable to follow on.

It was immediately obvious this morning that whatever else Hall and Watson had done with their speed – and their bouncers – they had put Trueman and Statham on their mettle.

The two Englishmen kept the ball well up, varying their pace, and every now and then whipping in a really quick one. This was the intelligent tactic in the circumstances.

Statham, in his second over, removed Hunte, who pushed forward on the leg stump. The ball skidded off bat and pad to Trueman at backward short leg. Kanhai tried to drive a swinging full toss from Trueman three overs later, missed and was lbw.

Now this vast excitable crowd, like a spilled paint-box under the saman trees, was properly humming. Sobers drove his first ball firmly to cover and the relief was audible. He tried then to crack a slightly wider one, the ball flying off the edge at decapitatory pace to third slip.

May shot out a hand, the ball went almost vertically up and Barrington at first slip stood under it, caught it, and threw it as high as the tulip tree. Not even Olivier before his Agincourt speech achieved so total a silence as lasted while that ball was in the air.

The bowlers stuck to it marvellously. Some of the green essences of youth seemed to well up in both, and Solomon time after time was left groping at Statham. The first hour produced 18 runs; three bouncers, as opposed to a round 15 by Hall and Watson during the comparable period, had been bowled.

Worrell, too, was beaten off the seam more than once. Pullar, at forward short leg, made three staggering stops in a row off hard drives. Trueman's field at this stage was four short legs, four slips and only cover point in front of the wicket on the off-side. Statham's was roughly the same.

Ten minutes before lunch May gave Barrington a turn at Statham's end. Solomon slashed the last ball of his first over hard to Allen at cover and called. Worrell sent him back and Solomon, caught on the turn, was beautifully thrown out. He had batted two hours for 23.

Worrell now flung his bat at a ball well up to him from Trueman, got a thickish edge and Swetman scooped the ball up an inch from the ground. West Indies were 45 for 5. Trueman's figures were eight overs, five maidens, 12 runs, three wickets. It had been a fabulous morning's cricket.

It was a fitting sequel to England's innings. Whether one looks at that with a batsman's or a bowler's eye, it remains a notable re-covery. At 57 for 3 the masts had been shot away, the stern holed.

Up to that point, and again later, Hall and Watson were as quick as anything I have ever seen. They have long arms, loose slinging actions, and enough height to bang the ball down without demonstrably striving for lift. They bowled more than a fair share of bouncers.

But it was not the palpable bouncer that made batting the hazardous job it was. Rather was it the constant attack to the extent of three or four balls an over just short of a length. The batsman was committed to a stroke, usually fending away off the back foot, and the ball flew steeply up at him from all angles.

From time to time a forward short leg and two backward were brought in to the picture. Nobody could possibly have forced the batting, for it was scarcely ever possible to get on to the front foot.

Hall's stamina was astonishing. On Thursday evening he was as fast as he had been at noon. On Friday morning he was quicker still. Watson, though less quick, has a nasty, jerky action that had the ball coming through at varying heights.

Would the English fast bowlers reply in kind? The answer to that depended on May's restraining influence on the energies of Trueman and Statham, and on the pitch itself.

May had to strike a nice balance between allowing Trueman his head and seeming to encourage retaliation out of pure spite, between making plain that the pace is not all on one side and banking up those fires of resentment that may already be burning. In this connection many passages quoted from English newspapers, and often torn from their context, appear grossly exaggerated to most Trinidadians.

Pirate ladders were hoisted during lunch at strategic points outside the ground; admittance for the nippy was possible at ten cents a climb. The more orthodox rushed the gates or swarmed up the trees, which quickly became festooned with blue trousers.

The afternoon was almost devoid of incident. Barrington bowled 12 overs of leg-spinners for three runs and he will never do that again. Illingworth, taking over from Trueman after Alexander had turned him twice to the fine-leg boundary, bowled seven overs for eight runs. Butcher was an hour over three runs.

At 65 Statham came back at Trueman's end and Butcher gave a

sharp chance to Trueman at backward short leg. He had been hurried all the time by the quick bowlers and soon, shuffling back to Statham, he was lbw.

May used Trueman and Allen after tea, Trueman bowling into a shifting wind. Alexander, who had batted stout-heartedly for over two hours without much trouble, suddenly left one alone on the off-stump from Trueman and was lbw.

Four runs later Ramadhin called Singh for a sharp single to cover. The return from Dexter was quick to the top of the stumps and Singh was run out. Now came the bottles, first in gentle jabs from the back then in heavy showers from all corners of the ground.

Suddenly, after an hour of frenzy and animation, it was all over bar the shouting. The hospital cases were removed, the sirens of the ambulances died away. The flocks of white pigeons which habitually circle the ground at this time of day took the late sun on their wings as they dipped against the hills.

Out of an incident too trivial to provide any possible excuse came this dangerous and sadly shaming business. What the consequences will be no one yet can say.

30 January 1960                                                                                   *Alan Ross*

*Final scores:* England 382 (Barrington 121, Dexter 77, Smith 108) and 230 for 9 wickets declared; West Indies 112 (Trueman 5–35) and 244 (Kanhai 110). England won by 256 runs.

---

*After the West Indian tour of Australia in 1960–61, which did so much to revive interest in Test cricket, Frank Worrell was signed by Christopher Brasher, the Sports Editor of* The Observer *as he was then, to give his lucid comments on the 1961 fight for the Ashes. As a captain and commentator Worrell tended to favour the status quo: it shows here in his comments about David Allen's removal from the attack during the decisive Test at Old Trafford. Sir Frank Worrell died in 1967.*

# May's Sweeping Reverse

## England v. Australia, Fourth Test, 1961

Wherever one has travelled in the last few days it has been impossible to escape the post-mortems on the Fourth Test. The consensus of opinion seems to be that the Australians were lucky to have won the game after being outplayed by England for 25 of the 30 hours. I must confess that I agree with these views.

I thought that England made two crucial tactical errors, one by the captain, the other by Close. The first was when Peter May got cold feet immediately Davidson decided to chance his arm against Allen and scored 20 fortuitous runs off one over. Allen had begun the day by capturing the wickets of Benaud and Mackay. He had also caused both McKenzie and Davidson more concern than any other bowler. Better for Allen to have bought Davidson's wicket, giving England extra time to get the runs, rather than to have brought back the pace-bowlers on an unresponsive wicket. This only gave the Australians opportunity to settle down. Their 98 runs played a crucial part in the victory.

Subsequently Dexter's great innings of 76 put England abreast of the clock and it needed only the customary grafting of the recognised batsmen, May, Close, Barrington, Murray and Allen.

Alas, May was bowled around his legs by Richie Benaud attempting a pull. But it was an excusable shot. The first thought that enters a batsman's mind when facing a right-arm leg-spinner bowling around the wicket is that if a ball is pitched on or outside the leg stump then it can be hit. Furthermore Benaud did not have a boundary fielder behind square leg. Unfortunately the ball hit a bootmark and turned virtually at right-angles to find May's leg stump. Although the pull is not particularly a shot one associates with Peter May, it was a terrible piece of luck.

Benaud bowled better than I have ever seen him bowl before, and his going around the wicket was a third vital factor on this extraordinary final day. His accuracy and direction from both sides of the wicket were fantastic. It appeared that he bowled around the wicket to the left-handers to exploit the rough spots made by the bowlers' boots and he stayed there to immobilise

Dexter, who is generally less ferocious to a good length ball on the on-side.

With Dexter gone the Australians' confidence appeared to rise tremendously, so much so that even Mackay, with his short-of-a-length medium-pace bowling, commanded an unnatural amount of respect.

Then came Close's performance. His tactics were totally incomprehensible, the technique that of a captain giving his leg slips practice on the eve of a Test match. A more unorthodox exhibition will surely never again be seen in Test cricket. This was the turning point of the game.

It has been argued that Close was acting under instructions; if he were, I am sure May could not have demanded quite such a degree of cross-bat. Many cricket enthusiasts, in fact, have been trying to discover what instructions, if any, were given to the England players in the second innings. I am of the opinion that after Dexter had set the tempo no instructions should have been necessary to this team of experienced professional cricketers. Similar situations are frequently encountered in county cricket and are capably dealt with. All the players must have been aware that the occasion demanded careful selection of balls to be hit, plus a sharp eye for the singles.

A final point is that the left-handers in this series have been at a tremendous disadvantage because of bootmarks on the pitch. The man mainly responsible is Trueman, who has a tendency to run quite straight after delivering the ball. Unless Trueman can develop the ability to run off the wicket he will be a thorn in his own side's batting for some time to come. England have more left-handers than any other country.

6 August 1961                                          *Frank Worrell*

*Scores:* Australia 190 (Statham 5–53) and 432 (Lawry 102); England 367 (May 95) and 201 (Benaud 6–70). Australia won by 54 runs.

**10** Sunil Gavaskar batting for the Indians v. Surrey in 1986 at The Oval. It was on this ground in 1979 that he scored 221 against England. Of that innings Sir Len Hutton wrote in *The Observer*: 'I have seen many double centuries in Test cricket but this superb innings by Gavaskar could well be the greatest of all time, taking into consideration his team's hopeless position at the start of their final innings. At the very least, it can be bracketed with Stan McCabe's 232 at Trent Bridge and Walter Hammond's double century at Lord's, both in 1938, which were truly the innings that only great batsmen can play.'

**11**   Rachael Heyhoe Flint swings to leg at La Manga in Spain. The trip was arranged after the England Women's tour of the West Indies had been cancelled for political reasons.

**12**   And for my next trick . . . Mike Brearley ponders what next to pluck out of the bag in the year of his return to the England captaincy, 1981. In 1972–73 he contributed two despatches to *The Observer* on England's tour of the subcontinent, before departing to other company. The picture was taken by Eamonn McCabe, frequent winner of the Royal Photographic Sports Photographer of the Year award.

*This was the last Test match in England to end in three days
and Australians, even now, cannot be convinced that the
Headingley pitch was not 'fixed' in order to assist England
to retain the Ashes. The match-winning bowler was Derek
Underwood, who happened to have been brought back for
the game.*

# Underwood's Revenge

## England v. Australia, Fourth Test, 1972

England made sure of keeping the Ashes when they beat Australia
at Headingley by nine wickets to lead 2–1 in the series with only
The Oval Test to come. The victory stemmed from Illingworth's
and Snow's courageous partnership and Underwood's lethal
bowling on a pitch ideally suited to him.

The decisive factor undoubtedly was the wicket, which played
to our strength and Australian weakness. If it were never as bad as
the Australian batting made it look, it was still not fit for a five-day
Test.

How well Underwood took the opportunity. He is a unique
bowler, spinning the ball at close to medium pace and quite
deadly when it bites. On so slow a surface the ordinary spinner
*could* be played with patience, but Underwood's extra speed
gave the batsmen little chance to adjust. Ten for 82 was his best
match performance against Australia.

At the day's start Illingworth was intent on stretching England's
lead and ensuring that his bowlers did not face a full day in the
field.

Despite the rough patches on the pitch, Mallett and Inverarity
got so little turn that Mallett was soon bowling over the wicket.
So innocuous did they look that Lillee was quickly brought on.
Arnold played him impeccably, but Illingworth was beaten by
one that moved back into him. His 57 runs had decisively altered
the balance of the game, the innings a model of courage,
concentration and technical competence.

A lead of 117 put England in a commanding position in a match in which the batsmen were apprehensively attuned to low scoring. A good start was essential if Australia were to make a fight of it.

Stackpole, cheerfully belligerent as always, glanced the first ball to the boundary. In the same over Edwards tried to emulate him, but this time the glide was too fine. Knott knelt to take the catch as if in gratitude for so welcome an offering.

Edwards clearly was no exception to first-class cricket's law that it keeps everyone's head small. At Trent Bridge he had made a masterly 170 not out. Here he had lasted three balls in the match.

Edwards had been unlucky but there was nothing fortunate about Arnold's next wicket. A perfect outswinger drew Ian Chappell forward on the line of the off stump to clip the edge of the bat and give Knott the easiest of catches. The whole England team seemed to be high in the air, their arms upflung, their appeals an exuberant chant of triumph rather than a query.

Clearly there was a little more pace and bounce in the wicket, making strokes easier against the quicker bowlers. Greg Chappell was soon forcing Snow off his legs and driving Arnold confidently through extra cover.

These elegant shots seemed to indicate that the Australians might regain their poise. Underwood's first over shattered that illusion. No sooner did he drop the ball short than Chappell, usually so orthodox, played a nightmare stroke, contravening every rule in the book. His mistimed slash against the spin lofted the ball into d'Oliveira's hands at mid-on.

Stackpole is the gamest of cricketers, his determined batting often the foundation of an Australian score. Once more he battled purposefully, stretching right forward to kill the spin, or sweeping fiercely when Underwood deviated outside the leg stump.

With his crouching stance and tubby figure, the only feline quality about Stackpole is the number of lives he gets – nine already in this series. This time he rode his luck too hard, sweeping ever more riskily until he missed a straight one. That was 51 for 4, and long odds against Australia lasting the afternoon.

Sheahan alone made a fight of it and it was good to see this handsome player having some success. His temperament has been suspect in the past, but this time there was as much to admire in his concentration as in his technique. He has the long reach to play right forward and the patience to wait for the right ball to hit.

The unhappy Walters was always ill at ease, his anxiety showing in a foolish call for Parfitt's misfield, which so nearly ended in a run out. Out of form and out of luck, he was soon caught at slip off a brutal ball that whipped across the width of the wicket. Marsh swung fiercely at one wide on the leg-side for Knott to take a fine catch despite the distraction of the flashing bat.

Inverarity, so tenacious in the first innings, nicked his first ball on to his pads for Illingworth to take a simple catch at silly point. Mallett and Sheahan added 24 with little sign of stress until Illingworth, switching to Underwood's end, at last beat Mallett's solid forward stroke.

Lillee and Sheahan gathered runs with some ease until Underwood was brought back to bowl Lillee. Massie had yet to score in a Test match, but he was now the leading light in the highest stand of the innings. Of the 25 added for the last wicket, he made a gay 18, including two thumping fours off Illingworth and a soaring six from Underwood. When Illingworth bowled him, England were left with just 20 runs to win, which they achieved with nine wickets to spare.

30 July 1972                                                    *Tony Pawson*

*Scores:* Australia 146 (Stackpole 52, Underwood 4–37) and 136 (Underwood 6–45); England 263 (Illingworth 57, Mallett 5–114) and 21–1. England won by 9 wickets.

---

*Christopher Wordsworth went to prep school around the corner from Lord's and well remembers Patsy Hendren hooking and cutting. Ever since, the short, explosive batsman has stirred him most, such as Kanhai in this Benson and Hedges zonal match. Besides covering cricket and rugby for* The Observer *since 1961, the author is a book reviewer for the literary pages, as befits a descendant of the poet. With his genetic gift he first coined the phrase, of a bibulous Sports Editor: 'a legend in his own lunch-time'.*

# Majesty

## Northamptonshire v. Warwickshire, 1975

Northamptonshire's battery of seamers plus the wiles of Bedi had a sobering effect on Warwickshire in the heavy atmosphere at Northampton, but they were forced to bow in the end to the genius of one small elderly man with grey hair and a suspect knee.

Kanhai's unbeaten 102 out of 250 won this match last year; yesterday he went one better and although Northamptonshire bravely maintained the challenge, the writing was on the wall once Mushtaq had gone and they finally fell short by 28 runs in the last over, the precise number that Kanhai savaged from the last over of his innings.

Kanhai had first to construct the Warwickshire innings, on shaky foundations before his great demolition act. Here are his statistics and it would be *lèse-majesté* not to give them pride of place. His unbeaten 119 came in 116 minutes out of 174 in the 34 overs he was at the crease. Seventy-six came in boundaries, eight vast sixes, in an arc between long-on and mid-wicket, and seven fours.

Near the end he hit Watts clean out of the ground, but that was only a pale crescendo to the final over which yielded 4, 6, 4, 2, 6, 6. Sarfraz was the luckless bowler who provided the feast and, fresh from his 5 for 53 that destroyed Somerset on Friday, it cost him an analysis of 1 for 78. Such is one-day life in tiger country!

Warwickshire won the toss: Jameson dealt out some punishment without looking at ease and judging by the way Amiss was playing and missing, it looked as though the confrontation between arguably the best bowling and the best batting in the country might be a low-scoring affair.

Jameson lofted his fourth four over the very short leg-side boundary and was caught next ball sparring at Sarfraz at 40. Kallicharran, adjusting his strokes deftly to the conditions, but calling for runs like a potential suicide, lost an out-of-touch Amiss in the twenty-first over, bowled by Bedi to a defensive prod. At 93, Kallicharran was bowled driving disrespectfully at one of Cottam's best cutters and there was growing cause for concern when at 116 in the thirty-seventh over Cottam pounced on Smith's slow dab and hit the stumps.

Kanhai's first boundary earned the fielder Sarfraz a glare of some malevolence from his captain and he proceeded to lay the keel with Murray as a sound partner before opening that gloriously leg-side onslaught with eight overs left. Dye did his economic best but another soaring six brought up his century and the 200 that had looked a remote target, as he continued on his murderous and refulgent way.

Northamptonshire well knew that they had no such divine flail and therefore had to maintain a good tempo throughout. Cook soon pulled a full toss into square-leg's lap but Mushtaq, ebullient, and Virgin, solidly impregnable, kept them well in the hunt until Mushtaq was out at 92 in the twenty-ninth over.

When Virgin followed five overs later, caught off the meat at the second attempt by Kanhai at mid-on, Watts and Steele played confidently enough to make a target of six per over still seem feasible but the wickets seeped away to intelligent bowling by Brown and Hemmings, Watts playing for the spin to one that went with Hemmings's arm, Steele, after two brave sixes, to a well-judged swirling catch, and some hurly-burly from Sarfraz and Bedi brought down the curtain.

11 May 1975            *Christopher Wordsworth*

*Scores:* Warwickshire 239 for 6 wkts off 55 overs (Kanhai 119*); Northamptonshire 211 off 54.2 overs (Virgin 46, Brown 3–28, Hemmings 3–39). Warwickshire won by 28 runs.

*This was luck. I flew to New Delhi one Friday in October 1983, and the next day – the opening day of the Second Test between India and West Indies – Sunil Gavaskar equalled Sir Donald Bradman's record of 29 Test centuries. As he never looks at the scoreboard, Gavaskar did not know he had done it until his partner came down the pitch to congratulate him. Afterwards he modestly said that no one could properly equal Bradman's feat, except by making 29 Test centuries in 52 Tests.*

# Gavaskar Equals Bradman

## India v. West Indies, Second Test, 1983–84

They stand together now, the 'boy from Bowral' in the Australian bush, Sir Donald Bradman, and the guru of Indian batsmanship, Sunil Gavaskar. In Delhi yesterday, with a scintillating innings against West Indies, Gavaskar equalled the world record of 29 Test centuries that Bradman has held for over a generation.

At the best of times comparisons are odious, and all the more so when they are made in India's capital at the end of a long hot summer. For a start, how can the opening batsman for one of the weaker countries in the modern era be compared with Australia's no. 3 who batted after Woodfull and Ponsford in the days of yore and spin?

Both giants of the crease are small men. Perhaps, if a conclusion has to be reached, the supporters of either side might agree that the difference between them is the same metaphorically as it is literally: that Gavaskar, at 5 feet 5½ inches, falls marginally but perceptibly short of Bradman at 5 feet 6¾ inches.

However, by happy coincidence or design, Gavaskar drew level with 'The Don' by means of an innings that was Bradman-esque. He thrashed West Indies' four fast bowlers as Graham Gooch has done, and almost no one else. His hundred yesterday was one of the fastest recorded in Test cricket in terms of balls received – 94 in his case. For contrast, Ian Botham's two epic centuries in 1981 against Australia came off 86 and 87 deliveries.

Gavaskar reached his Nirvana with a drive for four through mid-wicket, much as Geoff Boycott did when he scored his triumphal hundredth hundred at Headingley. But dhotis and sandals were flung into the air yesterday afternoon, scattering kitehawks into the bright sunlight, not flat caps as in Leeds. As Gavaskar acknowledged the applause of the thousands present, and of tens or hundreds of millions not present, Viv Richards strolled up from slip to shake his hand, getting to know the man he has to beat.

Gavaskar had to play the exorcist as well. The West Indian fast bowlers, led by Malcolm Marshall, gave India a thorough working-over during their innings victory in the First Test of this series. It was Gavaskar's duty to lead the riposte; and counter-attack he did too, from the first over after Kapil Dev had won the toss, quickly hooking Marshall for four and six.

This was the young, attacking Gavaskar born again, not the careworn defender weighed down by the frailties of his colleagues and the responsibility of captaincy which he held for so long. He was helped by the pitch, of course. Delhi's groundsman works for a brewery and knows how to concoct something flat.

So Gavaskar achieved it in style, hard though it may be to define exactly what his style is. He favours neither off-side nor leg, front foot nor back. To watch him practise of an evening in the Brabourne Stadium in Bombay, the Lord's of India, where members recline in basket chairs around the boundary safe from the city's din, is to be reminded of the old photograph of WG practising in a net in his garden. Both are at home, and monumentally assured. Perhaps it is best to say that, if all living things in India are incarnations, Gavaskar is technical orthodoxy made flesh.

The Indian has taken 166 Test innings to make his 29 centuries (only 13 of them in India), against Bradman's 80. It should be borne in mind, though, that Gavaskar has never had the chance to bat against India's gentle bowling (Bradman did and scored four centuries). Nor did 'The Don' have to face a four-man pace attack, except once, whereas yesterday was but one of many occasions when Gavaskar has had to do so.

Gavaskar reached his fifty off 37 balls, giving his only chance *en route* to the 'keeper Dujon off a mishook. He slowed down in his fifties, attained the solid base camp of 62 by lunch, and set off briskly afterwards for the summit.

There was one nervous moment when Holding appealed for lbw but umpire Gothoskar was unmoved (in fact only five Indian umpires have ever been moved to give him lbw – and five abroad). Then Marshall tried to ruffle him with three bouncers from round the wicket: the first was hooked high and safe for four, the second along the ground to the squarer of two long legs, and the third straight between them to tumultuous shouts.

Soon it was his record-equalling century. He doffed the white hat that is his trademark, now fitted with a Brearley-type skull-protector inside. It was only the thirty-fifth over of the innings. Having pulled Larry Gomes for a second six, he was bowled off-stump by his arm ball for 121, made off 128 balls in 224 minutes. It was his twelfth Test century against West Indies – Bradman's preference was for England, against whom he made 19.

More records are sure to go Gavaskar's way. He now has 8017 Test runs. Sobers scored 8032; Boycott has 8114. By the time Yorkshire's special meeting is convened on 3 December, Boycott is likely to have been knocked off that pedestal too by the insatiable Indian.

30 October 1983                                           *Scyld Berry*

*Final scores:* India 464 (Gavaskar 121, Vengsarkar 159) and 233;
West Indies 384 (Lloyd 103, Kapil Dev 6–77) and 120 for 2 wickets.
Match drawn.

---

*Anyone, it is said, can write about an eventful day's cricket. The test comes when there is nothing to write about, and here is a brilliant example of how to do it: 1.2 overs bowled, yet the correspondent has produced this vignette, replete with wit. Mike Selvey took up cricket writing in 1984, after playing for Middlesex and captaining Glamorgan.*

# A Trivial Pursuit

## Northamptonshire v. Indians, 1986

The Indian touring team, after a little interlude across the Irish Sea at Downpatrick, have arrived in Northampton, which hardly seems like treading the road to Nirvana. By all accounts, they had a close call against the Irishmen, lulled, no doubt, as touring teams in the past have been, by silver tongues, matchless hospitality and the black stuff.

Now they are in search of some rather more serious practice in preparation for the First Test next week and they can hardly have been best pleased by the curtain of drizzle which hung across the county ground.

They have lost substantial time in each of their four three-day games to date and although a delayed start was possible, it was all too brief, eight balls to be exact, as the players were driven from the field and the sponsors into their marquee – a larger structure, incidentally, than the new football stand at the far end of the ground.

There was time, however, for one of those believe-it-or-not débuts that might crop up in Trivial Pursuit ten years hence. The Indians had won the toss and had elected to keep all but their opening batsmen, Srikkanth and Gavaskar, in the warmth of the dressing room.

It was the second over that produced the interest. Northants had given a début to a 19-year-old left-arm seamer, Gareth Smith, a Geordie in the best Northants tradition. He was required to bowl to Sunil Gavaskar, the most prolific batsman in Test history – a daunting prospect.

It was more daunting still after one ball, which Gavaskar had smacked crisply over mid-on's head for four. I know exactly how Smith must have felt – the first ball I ever bowled to the little master, when we were both schoolboys, went over the stand at square leg for six.

Smith's recovery exceeded my own. The next ball was bang on a length and slanted across, tempting Gavaskar to drive, finding the edge and Waterton, the wicket-keeper who was also making his Northants début, took the catch.

And so to Trivial Pursuit. Which other Northants fast bowler, who made his début against the Indians, also took a wicket second ball, the first having gone for four. The answer, as you well know, is Frank Tyson and the catcher that day was Brian Reynolds, who just happened to be on the ground yesterday.

Oh, come on, I know Tyson wasn't left-handed, but it's not a bad effort.

1 June 1986                                                                 *Mike Selvey*

*Final scores:* Indians 301 for 5 wickets declared (Amarnath 101, Azharuddin 100*); Northants 118 (Kapil Dev 5–35) and 239 for 4 wickets. Match drawn.

PART 4

# *Occasional Pieces*

*Percy Fender commented on the 1930 series between England and Australia for* The Observer. *Renowned as having one of the most acute of cricketing brains, Fender here brings it to bear on the problem of Don Bradman, who had changed the face of Test cricket by scoring 8, 131, 254, 1 and 334 in the first three Tests of the series. Fender's solution is not 'Bodyline' but is characteristically ingenious. The bowler he advocates to 'solve' Bradman is not a fast bowler at all, but Tom Goddard of Gloucestershire, who had but one season of off-spinning behind him after converting from medium pace. And although not selected in the original twelve, Goddard played in the following Test, when his figures were 32.1 overs, 14 maidens, 49 runs, 2 wickets. He was dropped for the next Test, when Bradman hit 232.*

# How to Deal With Bradman

With the Fourth Test less than a week ahead, and the score all square, it is interesting to review the position and collate the facts, in an effort to note what has been seen and learned, and what corollaries may be drawn from the facts. The first point is that the only Test which has been played throughout without interference from rain was won easily by Australia. The second is that the results which Australia have so far obtained have been so very largely connected with the performances of two players that our attention is naturally focused almost entirely upon them. Bradman and Grimmett have been the outstanding influences in the Tests so far, to such an extent that England may well be forgiven for feeling that if these two can be subdued, the Fourth or Fifth may be won. England's best chance, of course, is to win the Fourth, because by so doing she will prevent the last being played under conditions which cannot but favour Australia. It is natural that our visitors will fancy their chances more in an unlimited match, and England can prevent her from playing under such conditions by winning at Manchester. So far in Tests I think that it may be fairly said of the players who have represented England that they have dealt with all the Australian batsmen, except Bradman, in a manner consistent with the positions of those batsmen, and that Bradman is their great problem. The problem of the selectors is to provide players who will subdue Bradman and cope successfully with Grimmett.

After the Leeds game, I think there is reasonable hope that the six English batsmen who played there are the best of whom we know for the latter purpose. Of the six, and judging from the ringside, I thought that the two who had most difficulty with Grimmett were Hobbs and Sutcliffe, and we need not worry a great deal about their ability in this respect, for they have wonderful records against him. We cannot allow our faith to be shaken in the slightest by one uncomfortable match. Now that Hammond has found his form, and Chapman, Leyland, and Duleepsinhji have demonstrated theirs, I do not think that we need look further.

So far as Bradman is concerned, it is a very different problem. Up to date, England bowlers have shown that they can keep all other Australian batsmen within limits commensurate with their positions in the batting order, but what of their efforts with Bradman? Tate stands first in this matter, for in Australia, on the shirt-front wickets, he bowled 296 balls to him for 119 runs, and got him out twice. So far in this series he has got him out three times for 165 runs, off 314 balls, and no other English bowler can approach that. In any case, Tate is as essential to the bowling strength of England today as it is possible to imagine any bowler being. Larwood never got Bradman out in Australia, nor has he done so in this series, but England cannot go into the field without a fast bowler, and no other bowler would be good enough but Larwood, with the possible exception of Essex's Nichols.

Geary did well against Bradman in Australia, where he bowled 174 balls to him for 77 runs, and got him out twice, but at Leeds the batsman took 56 runs off 88 balls bowled to him by Geary without losing his wicket to him. Apart from that I was rather disappointed with Geary's bowling in the Third Test, even after making allowances for the very easy nature of the wicket on the first day. I thought that he would under such conditions have bowled a better length uniformly than he did. I feel that while such facts and figures as those above may be interesting, and in some cases encouraging, one will have to look along other lines for any solution to the problem of the way in which to control the wonderful Australian automaton.

With this in my mind, I have carefully studied him when at the wicket, and there are some very interesting things to note. I calculate that he has made about 45 per cent of his runs by his now famous hook shot. Another 25 per cent has come from his late cut, and the remainder from his defensive back stroke which guides the ball towards long leg or deep third man. Bradman very seldom drives straight, though when he has done so, his manner of making the stroke has left no doubt about his ability to use it when he wishes.

The above are approximate percentages, but they are not far short of the mark in actual figures. Working along these lines, in an attempt to control such a prolific run-getter, one naturally seeks a bowler who will provide him with the fewest possible opportunities of making his regular shots, and the maximum necessity for playing other shots to get runs.

There is one bowler who bowls in such a manner that, theoretically, neither the hook nor the late cut can be made to him. Tom Goddard may not have great figures this year but he certainly has regular methods. He bowls good-length, medium-paced, off-spinners, with plenty of 'bite' and some variation of pace. No one is more consistent in sticking to his normal plan, and that plan is one which seems to me to offer fewer chances to Bradman for playing his natural game than do the plans of any other bowler in the country.

Goddard bowls rather too fast through the air for Bradman to be able to 'get to' him, and too good a length to pull without risk, and his field is one to which he bowls religiously, and which covers all Bradman's normal strokes except the late cut. As Goddard bowls at the stumps nearly all the time, and his only variation of direction is occasionally towards the leg-side, I doubt if Bradman would care to risk that cut very often, and even if Goddard's length did sometimes enable him to get in his hook shot, he would seldom get more than one for it with Goddard's field.

Another point not without its significance is that Bradman's normal defensive stroke is just the one which Goddard is always trying to get batsmen to make, for he has shown, time and again, that he can make the ball spin up off the bat for his short legs, no matter how good the wicket, and he can be deadly on a bad wicket. I personally have great faith in Goddard, and in this case his methods particularly recommend themselves to me for the controlling of Bradman. Goddard has played only one game in higher circles than county cricket, and then he did a fine performance at Lord's last year in the Test trial when he and Robins got rid very cheaply of the side which had just returned from Australia with the Ashes.

Where direct attack has failed, as is now the case with Bradman, a trial might well be given to a method which has strong claims to answering the need, at least in theory, and Goddard would never bowl badly, no matter what the results of his efforts to control Bradman. When an outstanding personality or genius appears in the field, and all the best among our bowlers have tried without sufficient success to tame him, there is nothing left beyond analysis of the methods of that genius and an attempt to use something dictated by the result of reasoning. I feel convinced that something new will have to be introduced to Bradman, and that the best way of selecting that 'something new' is to seek it along the lines of theory.

20 July 1930                                             *P. G. H. Fender*

---

*During the winter of 1932–33 Neville Cardus came into the* Observer *offices of a Saturday to write discursive commentaries on the Bodyline series, supplementing the scanter agency reports. At first he followed the 'official' line: that the type of bowling by Harold Larwood and Bill Voce in Australia was nothing new, that leg theory was old hat and harmless, that the Australians were squealing. This problem of 'misinformation' arose from the lack of eye-witness accounts: only three journalists from England covered the tour, and for one reason or another none could present a clear enough picture of the unprecented methods D. R. Jardine was using. The first piece selected here was written, following the First Test, in this state of semi-darkness. By the time of Cardus's end-of-tour review the issues had been clarified, thanks to letters and newspaper reports from Australia which had made the sea voyage to England.*

*It may be reassuring to note that Cardus, even then, tended to be a praiser of times past. He thought an England team containing Sutcliffe, Hammond, Jardine, Larwood, Verity and Voce, and an Australian team including Woodfull, Ponsford, Bradman, McCabe, Oldfield, Grimmett and O'Reilly, were not fit to compare with the previous generation. 'There is much mediocrity in the ranks of both sides,' he wrote. 'I doubt if there are two England players who would have got anywhere near the England XI of 1902 or 1905'; 'and I suppose it will be admitted on all sides that the present Australian XI is the worst batting side that ever wore pads in a Test match.'*

# Bodyline

## I

A politician who was a picturesque person, one of the forerunners of the Socialist–Labour movement, once referred to those 'magnolia-scented liars, the writers for the daily Press'. Without endorsing this vituperative description it may legitimately be said that the ultra-modern journalist, with his passion for the sensational and his daily search for a *tour de force*, or stunt, certainly gives free rein to imagination, and when he pours out his eloquence on such a subject as cricket he is sorely taxed, but from his point of view, and for those who are not imbued with the spirit of cricket, he has succeeded. Cricket does not lend itself as a game to this treatment, but the Test matches between England and Australia have provided these gentlemen for some

145

years with subjects and 'stories' for those who say, with George
Meredith, 'ink is my opinion and the pen my nigger'.

They have seriously helped to make Test matches a business.
The public mind has been inflamed. To such an extent is this true
that the 'gates' have become material. The revenue has become
more important than the cricket. Test matches, not as games of
cricket, have become as solemnly or as foolishly discussed as a
policy involving national welfare. The matches rank as business
affairs, just as much as big boxing, spectacular football, and world
championships at golf, lawn tennis, and the like. It is said that
Australia is looking forward to recoup the Board of Control and
the State associations for the considerable losses sustained by
them over the Tests played during the recent visits of West Indian
and South African teams to their country. The present rubber
will, it is hoped, provide handsome profits and England will, of
course, take her share of the favourable balance. We recognise
that this is true.

A Test match is no longer a game, for money enters into it.
Years ago a great England captain was sympathised with because
a fine English bowler was unable to play owing to injury. He
replied, 'What does it matter? After all this match is only a game.'
We cannot sincerely say the same nowadays. The game has been
magnified into a momentous event. The Australian Press has
become excited because England has now overseas a platoon of
fast bowlers who have been characterised as 'the pernicious body
battering attack', employing a style 'utterly foreign to true cricket'
and 'an alarming danger'. If speed be legitimate to get out
Bradman and nine others, the number of bowlers of this kind is
immaterial. To rely so much upon one type may yet prove a
weakness.

Surely Australia has no right to dictate to her opponents the
character of bowling they must employ. The authorities have
never taken up such a position. No one, certainly no responsible
critic, argued that Australia should not have sent Gregory and
McDonald to England in 1921. If Australia had possessed a third
fast bowler equal to either of them, he would certainly have been
brought over. Gregory and McDonald swept English batsmen
aside, and the Motherland never reached a total of 300 until
Australia had won the rubber. The English players, unaccus-

tomed to fast bowling for years, were, as a whole, slow in movement and scared. Some of them recalled Gregory with the Imperial Forces team, and did not hail his return with joy. These are plain facts. But they did not squeal, nor did commentators talk about 'body battering', even after Nottingham in 1921.

Someone has even advocated that Bradman should not be exposed to the risk of being hurt. This is a poor compliment to Bradman, who has repudiated such a childish cry, for he is still the man who did as he liked with the bowling of Allen and Larwood in 1930 and was much more vulnerable when facing spin or swerve than any other kind of ball. Of course, Jardine is unmoved. He says truly that exactly the same type of attack has been tried times without number from village cricket to Tests – the only difference being that the field is placed differently. He would not be fit to lead England if he lost sleep wondering whether he should continue as he has begun. His task is to construct a team; not to consider the question from any aspect save that of legitimate success.

When the Gentlemen had the two fastest bowlers in England – W. Brearley and N. A. Knox – did they hesitate to pit them against the Players and win? Did not one of the Players say that it was impossible to dodge them with one at each end? Speed is an argument, especially before a batsman has become accustomed to his surroundings. Maybe some of the friends of the Australians fear that the ball will 'fly' to an intimidating height. There is here an insinuation that the bowler has with malice aforethought tried to bruise the body of the batsman. That would not be tolerated by MCC, Jardine, or any other captain who placed the game above the prize.

During many decades have we not seen fast bowlers send down balls which are peril-laden? At Lord's in 1896, when Richardson and Jones were the speed men, a famous war correspondent expatiated on the danger which the batsmen faced. Quite, but a manly out-of-door game that is without the possibility of peril or mishap would be an insipid infantile recreation. Read Adam Lindsay Gordon, the Australian poet and sportsman. Does anyone believe that Spofforth, Jones, Cotter, McDonald, and Gregory troubled about the position of the batsmen? F. R. Foster, A. Jaques and Root were fond of this leg-stump attack with fieldsmen clustered near the striker.

Does any fast bowler worry about his opponent? He does not try, if he be a man, to lay out his adversary and see him carried to the dressing-room. There have been very few serious accidents at cricket. Happily they are very rare indeed, and that should be because the batsman has a weapon not only to hit the ball and protect the wicket but to guard himself. In *The Jubilee Book of Cricket* Prince Ranjitsinhji writes that 'anyone who wishes to make a player must make up his mind to stand his ground, trusting to his bat to defend his body. It is wonderful what a useful shield that narrow strip of willow can be if properly manipulated.' A county player who received the ball on his legs complained of 'hard luck'. A hard-bitten Scotsman who was near him rejoined, 'What do they give thee a bat for?'

All this twaddle about 'shock' bowlers and the preservation of Bradman by his omission amounts to mere babble, for the batsman who moves away from the ball generally 'walks into it'. Note where Ranjitsinhji tells a player to stand his ground. In the Manchester Test match of 1896 Jones at his fastest made the ball rise face high, but Ranjitsinhji never moved away. He got straight in front of the balls, deflected them to leg, and even cut some of them. 'Ranji' told Lilley that he did fail to establish contact once. 'I felt,' he added, 'some blood trickling down my neck, and I found that the ball had split the soft part of my ear.' Again, when Cotter was 'bumping' the ball in the Nottingham Test of 1905, A. C. MacLaren, F. S. Jackson, and J. T. Tyldesley never jumped about through fear. And the crowd hooted Cotter. That was quite unnecessary as he was providing runs. Folks forget that the ball pitched about mid-wicket should be punished. McCabe is a brilliant example of one who faced this 'alarming danger' with confidence and success. During the last cricket season in England batsmen were not terrified by this 'body battering' brigade. So much of this anguish about 'shock' bowlers is mere blather to batsmen who are in the highest class, and ought to be, if they are worthy of a place in any Test match.

18 December 1932                    *Neville Cardus*

# Bodyline

## II

When the English team left these shores last autumn, our hopes and prayers went with them – especially our prayers – but not our unbounded confidence. We had seen the players in action every day during the season of 1932, and though we all knew of the beneficial effects of a sea voyage, none of us expected sun and ozone to transform good cricketers into great cricketers.

Larwood, in particular, was 'suspect'; we doubted his stamina. We had seen him more or less impotent in the Trial match at Old Trafford, and also during the Duleepsinhji–Pataudi stand at Lord's in the Gentlemen v. Players match; on these occasions he was unable to get the ball higher than the stumps, and he languished. When Bowes was rushed into the England side at the last minute, there were people who saw in this a vote of no confidence in Larwood. Again, the question was asked, 'Why *four* fast bowlers?' It really did seem a strange notion. Years ago, an England XI could have chosen Lockwood, Kortright, Richardson and Mold – four of the swiftest bowlers that ever lived. But in those days the general idea was that one fast bowler was ample for a Test match combination.

We did not know what we were talking about last September when we questioned the composition of Jardine's attack. We were in the dark. For a deep strategy had been connived to bring about the downfall of Bradman and Woodfull. It was, as Smee might have said, a sort of a compliment to these two great batsmen. To cope with genius, you must put forth special and uncommon measures. The fast leg-theory attack had been tried at Trent Bridge – and also, in a mild way, at Kennington Oval, last August. Not everybody who saw it admired it – but it was a likely specific for the Australians, the very thing to solve the Bradman dilemma.

The cricketer who is always scoring double centuries is a pest to the game; he must be done something with, as the Brothers Cheeryble said of Tom Linkinwater. Fast leg-theory has won England the rubber; as Hobbs has said – and he ought to know all about fast leg-theory – it was the strange method and wonderful

149

accuracy of Larwood that reduced Bradman's average from over 100 to a respectable 50 or so.

We have all praised Larwood's achievement. Yet for many of us it has been a mystery how he 'did it', and also how Verity and O'Reilly managed to spin the ball on the second day of a great match on an Australian wicket. For years and years the Australian turf in good weather has been all against the rising fast ball and the slow bowler's spin. Even McDonald could not bump the ball breast high in Australia; and Cecil Parkin, the cleverest spin-bowler of our time, was reduced by Australian turf into a more or less up-and-down bowler. It has usually needed the wrist and the fingers of a Mailey to break the ball at Sydney, Adelaide and Melbourne in recent years. Last summer, when H. W. Taylor, the great South African batsman, told me we could win the rubber this time, by means of a concerted plan based on fast bowling, I replied that the Australian wickets in the past have invariably broken the hearts of fast bowlers. Obviously he knew a secret; he was playing in Test matches in Australia last winter.

The truth has been revealed in an article by Mr J. W. Trumble, which recently appeared in the Melbourne *Argus*. Australian wickets today are not what they were: different soil is used in preparing them. The new turf does not 'produce the polished glossy surface developed by the old Bulli and Merri Creek soil. The ball now gets a grip on the ground. This enables the spin-bowler to turn the ball, and also enables the fast bowler to "lift" more than formerly.' Australian turf nowadays is full of 'bounce' at the beginning of a match; then, after a constant pounding away by a fast bowler, the soil becomes loose – and then the spin-bowler comes in. If it is a fair question – did H. W. Taylor let our Intelligence Department know that our fast bowlers would find it easier to bump the ball in Australia this winter than in England last summer? Anyhow, the plan of campaign was worked out skilfully; and a strong man was put in charge of it, a captain of cricket with an iron will and a superb disregard of the noise of the Australian crowd.

Jardine's determination was needed to carry out the new fast bowling experiment; had he been a weak man, all the energy of Larwood might have proved as vain a thing as it did in 1930.

150

It is true that Allen, who did *not* bowl leg-theory, took 21 wickets in the Test matches. It is true, too, that Larwood was always hitting the stumps. But it was the leg-theory which unsettled the mind of Bradman, and compelled him to readjust his machine. The point I am trying to make is that on the old reliable Australian turf Larwood and Voce would have toiled in vain to bump the ball much higher than the batsman's hip. The rubber has been won by a perfect blending of executive and strategical forces; an Intelligence Department must have got to work early in the day, else why the four fast bowler 'brainwave' last autumn? Surely it was not merely a gamble? Larwood and Jardine did the rest, backed up, of course, by capable all-round assistants.

There seems yet some difference of opinion in this country about the way our fast bowlers have exploited leg-theory. Our esteemed and beloved editor of *Wisden* writes of fast leg-theory as a method of play which has often been practised in the past by Australian as well as by English bowlers. For my part, I have never heard of fast leg-theory being exploited in a Test match until this present series. And by fast leg-theory, I mean the sort of bowling described by reliable writers in the Australian newspapers in their accounts of the methods of Larwood and Voce. The Sydney *Referee* denies the English view that 'there is nothing new in this kind of bowling'. The *Referee* says: 'It is new. It has never before been practised in a Test match between England and Australia ... Gregory and McDonald never bowled a body attack with a packed leg-side field ... The fact is that the present English "shock" bowler is deliberately bumping short balls.' Again, the *Referee* says: 'Nobody objects to fast bowling and nobody objects to legitimate leg-theory, but the Larwood–Voce attack is a planned attack by means of short-pitched kicking balls aimed at the batsman, with a leg-field.'

Hobbs has gone so far as to suggest that Bradman has been reluctant to take chances with the fast leg-theory attack for fear of getting hurt and damaging his career. 'So he took no risk of injury – and in view of his slight physique I do not blame him.' I am not discussing this leg-theory in any vein of moral indignation. I am simply attempting to get at the real cause of Australia's defeat, and at the cause of Bradman's transformation into an ordinarily great batsman. Some day it will be necessary for somebody to write a dispassionate history of the 1932–33 Test matches.

Have Bradman, Woodfull and thousands of Australian lovers of the game, not all of them 'squealers' and 'hooligans', been the victims all winter of an optical delusion? And, of course, I am not belittling the achievement of Larwood. A bowler needs unfailing accuracy and a brilliant pace to pitch anywhere near the leg-side and not suffer punishment.

Bradman is reported to have fallen from grace because his average has fallen. His strokeplay has plainly been dazzling. Yet such is the modern conception of batsmanship that a cricketer is supposed to be playing badly if he takes a chance and cracks the ball in the manner of J. T. Tyldesley. Bradman was the only Australian, I gather, really to counter-attack Larwood. He moved away to the leg-side and hit the ball audaciously to the unpro-tected off-side. As a consequence of this piece of superb re-source, even his best friends accuse him of recklessness; indeed, they say he 'ran away'. But how on earth is any batsman going to tackle fast leg-side bowling (to a crowded leg trap) unless he hits it to the off? And how can you hit leg bowling to the off-side unless you do move away and get on the proper side of it for the stroke?

Against Larwood Bradman was beginning to reveal his genius in a more gallant light than it has ever been seen before: given a few more innings he might have mastered it. And for all his pains and imagination he is called 'reckless'. J. T. Tyldesley would be banned from modern Test cricket, evidently.

Nobody will deny that the better side won the rubber, even in Australia, where, despite the 'rumpus' about the fast bowling, the newspapers have, on the whole, been fair and generous to the English cricketers. Paynter has won high praise for his fielding and batsmanship; Verity is already acclaimed the successor to Rhodes as a slow left-handed bowler who can bat. The reputa-tions of Sutcliffe and Hammond have lost nothing of lustre. Both countries, though, are likely soon to want an amount of new blood; Australia, indeed, want it at once. More than anything else, they want all-round players. The Australian 'tail-end' in this rubber has been long enough to wag the dog clean off the field.

5 March 1933                                    *Neville Cardus*

*The aeroplane altered the cricket tour for ever. Whereas touring had been a slow, friendship-building exercise in the days of shipboard travel, it became a whistle-stop, jet-set business. In this dispatch from aboard the ship which took the England team to Australia in 1954–55, Alan Ross captures the pace of the old life.*

# At Sea With Hutton's Team

Aboard ss *Orsova*

We are on the last lap now, having exchanged the classical blues of the Mediterranean for the deeper heat-beaten blue of the Indian Ocean.

Cricket has once again become a reality as well as a topic of conversation, a fact brought nearer by the rain squalls we ran into last night which transformed the spilling skies around the ship into a grey opaque tank of mist, a passable imitation of Old Trafford on a Test match afternoon.

However, the blue is back now and the flying fish skidding away from our bows are our only ocean companions. The eating, sleeping, and sunning rituals of this voyage, with their gentle saturnalia of fancy dress balls, cabarets and competitions, have been interrupted twice for brief cricketing interludes – Hutton's press conference and MCC's few hours' practice against Ceylon at Colombo.

The press conference was an informal affair, at which Hutton and Mr Geoffrey Howard, the manager, went to some pains to establish the right kind of liaison and to make plain their desire for full co-operation with the travelling correspondents. Considering the varying requirements of the latter, this is not quite as easy as it may seem. However, Hutton and his manager are both men of great natural charm and there is every indication that this will be a smooth and enjoyable tour.

Whether charm will be enough to make of this party of 18 gifted but unusually vulnerable players a team in the stricter sense of the word remains to be seen. At this same conference

Hutton, perhaps unwisely, raised the matter of bumpers. He committed himself to the sentiment that despite England having at last a handful of bowlers well able to make the spryest of Australian batsmen keep a weather eye open for things other than runs, he would rather not win the Tests at all than see them degenerate into bouncing contests.

This completely honourable desire might have been better unexpressed at this stage. We are relying largely on pace, and to offer an opinion as to how many bumpers an over are or are not within the spirit of the game seems asking for trouble.

I hope Hutton will see that none of his fast bowlers intentionally bowls a single ball that does not demand a stroke – and not for protective reasons either. They are a great waste of time.

The Colombo match, as is customary, was drawn. The heat on this banana and frangipani fringed ground was intense, and the only refreshment coconut milk. The wicket, prepared by a squad of groundsmen in dhotis of brilliant pink and peacock blue, was fast and true and a moderate game was notable for a fine innings by Cowdrey and for some splendid driving by F. C. de Saram, an Oxford blue of 20 years ago who captained Ceylon. De Saram, keeping his head well down, hit Wardle high and hard to the untenanted deep and picked him beautifully off his toes. Before the war most counties had a couple of amateurs at least who batted like this, but so rare are they now that Wardle must have thought himself faced by some strange species newly risen from the sea.

For a friendly or any other match far too many short, wasteful balls were bowled by MCC. Statham was the best of the English bowlers, but when he and Tyson are bowling together the tempo becomes funereal beyond all possibilities of enjoyment. Another noticeable thing was that each time a batsman put the bat to Tyson at all, even if the ball went only a few feet, there was a run: the wicket-keeper has no earthly chance of getting up to the stumps and both wickets are left deserted.

It is quite evident already that there are going to be too many players for comfort. Hutton will need great tact to keep 18 cricketers usefully occupied. It is also going to need the wisdom of Solomon to choose the best Test side, for if the strongest attack is played, the batting and fielding will hardly bear contemplation.

One hopes some good use can be made of McConnon, for he is one of the few who can hold a catch near the bat. He has, however, always bowled round the wicket for Glamorgan and I understand this practice has never been successful in Australia. Hutton, talking idly the other day at the swimming pool, told me that from a batsman's point of view it is not when an off-spinner is turning the ball that he is a problem in Australia but when he floats it away straight on past the off stump.

Early this morning we crossed the Equator, so now we sail under the ceiling of the Southern Cross.

3 October 1954                                                    *Alan Ross*

---

*When the traditional system of county cricket was ailing in the 1960s, many blueprints for reform were put forward. Among the most revolutionary, and persuasive, was this one by the Australian opening batsman Colin McDonald. He had just retired from Test cricket, after scoring 3109 runs at an average of 39 (and 11,375 in all first-class cricket), and after three tours of England. By late 1961 he was working in the London office of an insurance brokers' firm.*

# The 'Sixties Malaise

As an Australian I have little right to criticise suggestions made or actions taken to alter this country's system of county cricket. I would therefore ask that my comments be regarded purely as those of a cricket lover and from one who has a great regard and respect for MCC.

I would agree with that body that the time has come for action to keep first-class cricket a popular spectator sport, but I am not at all sure that the plans scheduled for 1963 will have the desired effect.

The revised fixtures and competition still mean that at least as much cricket will be played as at present and by far the larger amount of it will be of the same unsatisfactory variety. The one-day competition will be relatively minor, and even if large crowds attend – and I am sceptical of this – the overall effect on county treasurers will not be much changed.

I think much more drastic action is necessary. I suggest that the whole framework of first-class cricket needs altering.

Cricket is a national sport and the county game should therefore have two objects. One should be to provide the best possible cricket for the player and spectator, and the other is to make a county place the goal for every cricketer in the country. At present, I humbly submit it does neither.

Cricketers who play six and sometimes seven days a week cannot possibly retain their keenness for the game. Under such circumstances it is inevitable that most games become dreary affairs with players waiting only for 6.30. This is especially so when players are under annual contracts with their clubs and their bread and butter depends on good figures at the end of a season. The most negative batsman or the most defensive bowler may well be – and, in fact, often is – the most successful under these conditions.

The second sad aspect of the system is that many of the best cricketers in the country decide that county cricket is not a career for them, go off to safer employment, and are lost for ever from first-class cricket. Alterations to the laws of cricket will not remove these basic faults from the system.

I would propose: (1) That there should be no such things as county cricket clubs, but that a cricket association from each county or designated area should elect selectors to pick the county team from clubs in the area; (2) That there should be no full-time professional players, but that players are paid an allowance per game to compensate for loss of salary from their normal employment; (3) That the number of first-class counties is drastically reduced – I would suggest no more than eight; (4) That each county or area would play only one first-class game each fortnight and where possible on Saturday, Sunday and Monday.

An offshoot of this suggestion, which may perhaps avoid many declarations now necessary in county cricket, is to spread the games over four days. MCC may need to arrange extra matches to cater for the special needs of London, but this should not be hard.

My first proposal is the vital one – and consequently the most difficult. It involves a complete change in control and would be most unpopular with many able and enthusiastic administrators. It also leaves unsolved the problem of a county cricket ground and the responsibility for its upkeep, but the advantages outweigh these minor snags.

Fewer games would open the county competition to all players, for it would be a hard employer indeed who would not allow eight or nine unpaid days off each season. Some would fall during holidays anyway. Only a player picked for Test matches and tours would have a serious time-off problem.

The elimination of the professional under contract and the reduction in the number of games would remove a big financial burden from cricket and create greater keenness among players. Once the overheads are reduced, it no longer becomes necessary to have large attendances but, as the cricket would probably improve, more people would attend anyway.

I've no doubt that many of you think that I am attempting to impose the Australian system on England. To some extent this is true because I do believe it to be a better one. It is far less dependent upon the financial rewards that come from large crowds. Each State has only to finance about seven games per season and it is far simpler to average a high attendance over a few games than over the many which are played by each county in this country.

Certainly Australian overheads are spread over fewer matches but, as a counter to this, Test match profits are distributed to fewer sources.

It has been said that even Australian cricket was failing two years ago, but its demise was not thought of and a conscious effort on the part of non-professional Australian cricketers and the brilliant West Indian tour has, within two years, brought a lot of money to the six State associations.

I say this with no feeling of smugness as our system evolved purely from the geographical nature of our continent. Nevertheless, public and player interest is high in Australia and from a population one-fifth that of England's we can produce a team to match England. The West Indian system is similar and they too compete well against all-comers. England has nothing to fear internationally by the changes I have suggested.

31 December 1961 *Colin McDonald*

---

*After his first-class career Frank Tyson settled in the land where he had risen to fame by taking 28 wickets for 20 runs each, helping Len Hutton to win back the Ashes. He became a French teacher in Melbourne and reported on cricket in Australia for* The Observer *through the 'sixties, before being appointed Director of Coaching in Victoria. Hailed as the fastest of all bowlers on his tour of triumph, Tyson could not be better qualified to discuss the major controversy of that period.*

# On Throwing

The recent refusal of the Australian Norman O'Neill to play in the same match as controversial West Indian fast bowler Charlie Griffith only goes to prove that all the world hates a thrower – even if he is only a man under suspicion. There are those, of course, who feel that the decision of O'Neill not to travel to England for the Rest of the World game is based either on personal motives or on that sentiment once expressed by a doyen among batsmen that some play pace-bowling better than others but no one likes it. Since, however, O'Neill and Griffith were to have played on the same side, we may discount the latter reason and assume that the Australian does in fact have some compunction about playing in the same game as a man whose action may be said to fall into the category of the illegal.

Since the term 'unfair action' implies intent, I think this accusation is not one to be levelled: almost invariably the wanderers from the straight and unbent elbow are completely unaware of their aberration. If Griffith does throw, let's admit now that he possesses weapons not to be found in the armoury of the more orthodox bowler. In the first instance, the additional hinge of the elbow increases the field of wrist movement and facilitates cut off the pitch. A more frightening aspect of the thrown delivery is that it invariably seems to rise at a steeper angle after it has pitched: Peter Loader's bouncer, for instance, a delivery which was always viewed with suspicion, appeared to have an ascent rate which roughly approximated to that of Gemini Four.

But perhaps most dangerous of all, as far as batsmen are concerned, is that the flailing action of the elbow permits of speeds which have no relation to the pace of the bowler's approach or the velocity of his arm swing. With little or no perceptible change in his arm action, the thrower can undercut a tantalisingly slower ball or give it the full benefit of his straightening arm and hurl it down.

If the bowler throws only the occasional delivery then his range of pace and the consequent confusion of the batsman are all the more increased. Imagine that you are a batsman who has been at the wicket for an hour and is completely at ease against a range of medium-fast bowling. You are assessing the quickness of each bowler by his run-up and the full swing of his arm. Suddenly one of the bowlers curtails the arc of his arm by a full quarter of a segment, and whilst the subsequent delivery may be only a little if any faster than the previous balls, it leaves the hand a fraction earlier than expected and as a result catches the batsman in the middle of his back-lift.

This is the time sequence which upsets the natural stroke-players: this was the fate of May and Cowdrey in 1958–59 when they faced Meckiff and Slater. It was the inability of such keen-eyed players as O'Neill and Thomas to pick up Griffith's line of flight that first led me to suspect the West Indian's action even from a distance of 10,000 miles. Too often, when the batsmen were well established, the wicket placid and the bowlers tired, Griffith suddenly pulled a yorker out of the bag – a yorker twice as fast as the preceding deliveries and proportionately as accurate.

Bill Lawry's exploits against Trueman, Statham and Pollock of South Africa have proved him a fearless and accomplished hooker. Griffith is one of the few bowlers ever to have caught the Australian opener embarrassingly, even dangerously, early in his shot. If we discount for the moment such weighty opinions as those of Barrington and Dexter, what more indications are required to show that Griffith, unlike Caesar's wife, is not above suspicion and that O'Neill's protest is justified and does not spring from pique? In the classic mould of the throwers, Griffith's run-up is deliberate and ponderous for his ultimate speed.

21 March 1965                                                     *Frank Tyson*

---

*Arthur Fagg, in an unprecedented action, threatened to stop umpiring during the Second Test of 1973 between England and West Indies at Edgbaston. In fact he missed one over on the third morning and only resumed after receiving some reassurance from the management of the West Indian team – their captain, Rohan Kanhai, having shown annoyance at a decision by Fagg. Frank Lee, the writer here, umpired in 29 Tests, having scored over 15,000 runs in his career with Somerset.*

# On Umpiring

The action of umpire Arthur Fagg in retiring from the Second Test at Edgbaston, if only briefly, may have served one desirable purpose. Nobody can now doubt that umpires have to endure terrific pressures in the blaze of modern publicity, that some players trade on that fact, and that the tendency must be stamped out.

Any top-class umpire expects during his career to handle controversial incidents; now these rank as national disputes. The eyes and the ears of the world are riveted on every Test match. Think of the boiling-point controversy of the chuckers, Ian Meckiff of Australia and Geoff Griffin of South Africa.

The onus and the obloquy of drumming such fine fellows out of the game fell upon reluctant umpires. Although the captains backed their bowlers up to the hilt at the time, they had in the end to admit that the umpire's verdict of 'guilty' was absolutely justified.

Umpires don't like the spotlight played on them, and I found myself involved in a really unpleasant affair when I called Griffin eleven times for throwing at Lord's in 1960. With the Test over early, an exhibition game was started and Syd Buller no-balled him as well. More embarrassing still, after four such calls Griffin's captain, Jackie McGlew, advised him to finish the over bowling underarm. I was not informed and was therefore by law forced to no-ball him for not telling the umpire, who would in turn tell the batsman, of a change of delivery.

Shortly afterwards came the unwelcome news that an objection had been made to Syd Buller and he took no further part in Test matches that season, a decision I felt most damaging to the cause of umpiring.

The toughest Test matches I have experienced were with the Australians in 1953. Feeling ran high, and after four drawn games the Fifth was won by England at The Oval. Harry Baldwin and I umpired in the Second Test at Lord's, which reached a climax on the fifth day when England, with five wickets down, were saved by Willie Watson and Trevor Bailey, who batted nearly all day.

I received so many appeals that I began to wonder whether my ears were deceiving me. One Australian bowler, after an appeal for lbw was turned down, slowly looked me up and down, sniffing with contempt. He apologised when his colleagues told him that the batsman had edged the ball on to his pad.

Umpiring in the Fourth Test of that series at Leeds I found even more nerve-wracking, and wondered what it must feel like to be 'punch drunk'. I was on my own one evening during that match and went to a cinema to relax from the stresses of the day. Just after taking my seat, Pathé News came on and started with 'The

Leeds Test'. That was just too much for me to endure. I got up and walked out.

Everything, of course, does not end on the dismal side. With Frank Chester ill, I was called in to umpire in the final Test at The Oval with Dai Davies. I expected more pressure than ever, only to find it a most pleasant match.

I gave Godfrey Evans run out, a decision he disliked, but during the winter Godfrey generously came to me in a restaurant and commented: 'Frank, I thought you would like to know that I have seen a photograph of that run out at The Oval, and I was out.'

Again, during that final Test Keith Miller gave me a horse called My Lady for my brother Harry to back each way. After tea Keith told me that the horse had come second at 100–6.

Later, bowling at my end, he and the whole Australian side appealed for an lbw decision. I showed myself unimpressed. Keith, shaking his fist, remarked, 'My Lady, 100–6! I'll give you no more so-and-so tips for your brother Harry.' So next time you watch from the ringside a supposed 'angry scene', don't be too sure the crowd can rightly read what's going on in the middle.

My early Tests were made easier, too, by the New Zealand tourists, who were a genial lot and much enjoyed their cricket. At Old Trafford Tom Burtt, the New Zealand left-arm bowler, after many lbw appeals to Chester, politely inquired, 'Is there any chance if I appeal this time?' Chester, in my opinion the greatest umpire ever, replied with equal courtesy, 'I'm afraid not.'

Let me give one instance of how strict are the demands on an umpire's concentration for six hours a day. It happened during Laker's match at Old Trafford in 1956, when Jim took 19 Australian wickets. We had endured all manner of fanciful appeals, including one by Ian Johnson, the Aussie captain, against the sawdust. When Jim got his final leg-before, the Aussie batsmen shook him by the hand.

Giving Jim his sweater, I inquired about the congratulations, and was amazed when he replied that it was his tenth victim at my end. And I was amused when I later read that Tony Lock had held back with his bowling to enable Jim to reach his world record, especially after hearing Lock's frustrated language during that time.

What, then, is the cure for umpiring ills? Well, players make matters much harder than they need by showing ill-feeling. The answer is that captains can and should curb these trouble-makers.

First-class umpires realise players' frustrations because of their own previous experience of playing and make due allowance for the odd display of temper. Players should return such consideration in kind.

19 August 1973                                                         *Frank Lee*

---

*This was surely the definitive piece on the revolution brought about by the Australian businessman Kerry Packer. It appeared, not in the sports pages, but in the 'Notebook' column which had been taken over by Michael Davie.*

# The Packer Revolution

I get the impression from my non-sporting acquaintances that they are missing a lot of entertainment, and some social enlightenment, by their failure to follow the Packer cricket case, now in the High Court and likely to be there for ever.

On the surface, it is just a case about cricket, or, as some think, the whole future of the national game. But there is more under the surface than that.

Formally, what is happening is that Mr Kerry Packer, the Australian TV tycoon who looks like the man in a stocking mask, is suing the Test and County Cricket Board and the International Cricket Conference for banning his players. Packer signed up (secretly: an extraordinary coup) 32 top-class cricketers to play in a series of 'super-Tests' to be staged by himself. The authorities replied by banning them from county and Test cricket. 'Lock-out!' cries Packer. 'Self-protection,' reply the Authorities.

They feel understandably threatened. They fear the Packer enterprise will wreck the existing game by (a) stealing its revenue and (b) creaming off the best players as fast as they are produced by the present system.

There could be no greater contrast between two groups than between the Authorities and the Packer men. You sense, at once, a different view not only of cricket but of life itself. The Authorities come into court in sober dark suits. The Packer men are a riot of colour: Packer in pale blue with a multicoloured tie; Richie Benaud, the former Australian captain now working for Packer, in a polychromatic costume with crocodile shoes; a Packer partner in primrose yellow; another fellow in orange leather.

Packer's base is Sydney, where American influence is strong. You do not need to talk for very long to the friendly Packerites to realise that it is no accident that they are dressed as if for a TV studio in Burbank, Los Angeles, rather than the Committee Room at Lord's. There is a spiritual gulf.

They reminded me, the Packer people, of a highbrow piece I read recently in the *New York Review of Books*. The piece was called 'The Corruption of Sports' and the writer went back over the history of sports with particular reference to the classic work, *Homo Ludens*, by Professor J. Huizinga, a study of the 'play' element in culture.

Huizinga, who published his book in 1938, saw the history of civilisation in terms of the steady decline of 'play'. The NYR writer developed the thesis with reference to the impact on sport of television. Television distorts sport, he argued, changing its very nature. The whole point of sport – or 'play' – is that it should be pointless – an escape from reality (though it is, of course, deeply serious). Once sport is put into the service of some ulterior purpose – profit-making, or the sale of products – it becomes degraded.

I didn't swallow the thesis whole, but I kept being reminded of it as I listened to the case in court. It is full of talk of deals, contracts, what this one was earning in 1965, accountants, tax liabilities and tax avoidance schemes. Mr Packer referred to the recent England v Australia Test series as 'the product'. It was a long way from Huizinga's notion of useless play as a primary human need.

However, the men in the dark suits do in fact think in Huizinga-like terms. Cricket to them is in some sense, as one of them remarked to me, stumbling over the words, 'about, well, it's about the human spirit'. He was embarrassed to be using such a high-flown phrase; but he meant it. Packer he obviously regarded as a monster from outer space, a destroyer of tradition and ritual.

Packer, it is true, does look a shade forbidding. One of his own lawyers described him to me as 'the sort of man you wouldn't want to meet on a dark night'. But he spent two and a half days in the witness box, and even under extended cross-examination from a very clever opposing QC had plenty of time for his shots. He impressed me as a smart man and by no means an ogre, especially if you are on his team. He must also have impressed the cricketers he has hired. Derek Underwood, the England bowler, met him for the first time at the Dorchester Hotel and signed up with him the same night.

The Authorities seem to have been slow to realise what they were up against. They thought they were dealing with a bruiser. They appear to have underestimated both his attraction for the players – who plainly trust him personally as well as his money – and his readiness to fight vastly expensive court cases to get his way (he has a few cases in progress in Australia, as well).

People used to make the same mistake with his father, Sir Frank Packer, who built up a newspaper empire – now sold – as well as the TV. They saw a fellow who looked like a retired boxer, which he was, and thought his brain would match his manner and appearance, which it did not. He was tough as well as shrewd and sometimes ruthless, so Kerry Packer grew up in a hard school.

Packer got into this dispute because he wanted to make money out of putting cricket on his television network. He tried and failed to buy the exclusive rights to televise Test matches in Australia. So, thwarted, he bought up the best players and said he would stage his own matches. He may have been moved by pique; he was certainly moved by the model of American television.

Sums unimaginable by British TV are paid by the American networks for the right to televise sport. Packer knows (or thinks he knows) that cricket is underpriced. He says he laid out

£3,500,000 on buying up players and grounds for his super-Tests. That sounds a lot of money, but it would probably cost him more to make programmes to fill the same amount of time. If he can really attract a mass TV audience to his Tests, and find commercial sponsors, who produce the serious money, and sell off TV rights to stations outside his own network range, then the profits could be very high. His father was a gambler, and so is he.

To make the profits, of course, he must first convince potential sponsors that he can deliver a mass audience. His agents even now in Australia are selling the Tests: there might be one sponsor for each Test, or one sponsor for all six Tests. I talked to his partner, Mr John Cornell, who explained what they have in mind.

The super-Tests are to be given American-style TV treatment. The assumption seems to be, no doubt wisely, that the games themselves, televised in a quite BBC-like manner, could not be guaranteed to hold a mass audience. The television coverage must therefore 'give the viewer a better than ringside seat', as Mr Cornell put it. He meant, I think, that it must be made more exciting to the viewer than to the actual spectator on the ground.

Technology can do the trick: eight cameras instead of the usual five; microphones sunk into the wicket (perhaps at the stumps, Richie Benaud told me) to pick up the thump of the bowler's feet and insults traded with the umpire; a 42-inch zoom lens to show the 'sweat and tension'; split screens; golf buggies taking out the drinks to speed things up; interviews with batsmen and possibly umpires. Mr Cornell loves that zoom lens idea – 'wouldn't you like to see the expression on an umpire's face when he gives his decision?'

He might have been supplying material for a supporting footnote for the thesis of the 'Corruption of Sports' article: that TV turns sport, which used to be for the participants, into a spectacle for a mass audience who have to be fed with sensations extraneous to the sport itself in order to hold their attention, and keep them alert for the ads.

As Mr Cornell left me, I thought of the ways that sport has been changed by television: world heavyweight fights staged in the middle of the night, the worst time for fighters but the best time for the TV satellite; cross-country athletes running around race-tracks, jumping artifical hedges, because cameras cannot follow them across real country; baseball pitchers no longer batting because they bore the viewers.

These days, whether a particular sport flourishes or declines largely depends on its suitability for TV. Tennis is easy for the engineers to televise; requires only two players, is staged in a small arena, and lasts a convenient time, one to three hours, so tennis has become the most lavishly sponsored and richest sport. Golf needs scaffolding for the cameras, but golf, too, makes great television, so golf is nearly as rich. Show jumping can be televised at night under floodlights; so it flourishes, too. With swimming you film mainly water, so swimming is hard up. The gap between rich and poor sports has never been so wide, thanks to sponsors and TV.

A point obvious in the High Court was that – as the 'Corruption' writer noted – the sportsman has ceased to be a hero.

To achieve heroic status, the hero must put something ahead of his own personal interests. But the former England captain, Tony Greig, and the cricketers who appeared in the witness box last week have all put their own interests first. The evidence of Alan Knott, the England wicket-keeper, was full of mentions of Jersey and the Isle of Man, where he has a deal with a Packer company that, Knott has been told, hires out entertainers. Like any other entertainer, Knott has gone where the money is.

Likewise Underwood, the England bowler. He bowls like a god, but talks like a civil servant. How many Test wickets had he taken? 'I think it is in the vicinity of 270.' Only two cricketers have ever taken more; did he not want to exceed those records? 'It has been an ambition of mine for some years, I confess.' But he sacrificed this ambition, ruling himself out of the coming England tour of Pakistan in order to play for Packer; the attraction, he candidly explained, was 'the financial reimbursement'.

The decisions of both Knott and Underwood are perfectly reasonable and respectable of course; but unheroic.

9 October 1977                                          *Michael Davie*

*Before England's 1977–78 tour of Pakistan, I visited a town
beside the Indus which had once been involved in the
heaviest defeat of all time. It was difficult at first to find
anyone who remembered it or, at any rate, who would
speak about it. Eventually I tracked down one of the
opening bowlers, and through an interpreter he spoke of the
match, with what appeared to be great sadness. After leaving
him, I was struck by the appalling thought that this one
game of cricket might have left a scar on him for life.*

# The Biggest Defeat in First-class Cricket

It happened thirteen years ago this week, and that is the
appropriate time after which to commemorate it. Dera Ismail
Khan – or D.I.K. to old colonial hands – is on the west bank of the
Indus, itself the westernmost of the Punjab's rivers. The muddy
Indus flows softly in winter, little bigger than the Thames. But in
summer, when the snows of the Karakoram melt, the Indus
trebles its volume, filling the canals and irrigating the fields of
cotton and sugar-cane.

The town of Dera Ismail Khan – or D.I.Khan to its inhabitants –
consists of a long, dusty main street and a bazaar. It is mud-
bricked, one-storeyed and poor, its pride a Plaza cinema; and
baking hot, so that its people are swarthier than most other
Pakistanis.

But for want of anywhere else in those parts, the British made
the town an administrative centre, and so it remains. The Raj
lingers on in the bungalows and clubs (now Army property) of
the suburb; in the two mud-brick churches, each with but a
weekly service; and in the one-room municipal library stocked
with biographies of Palmerston and the Earl of Derby, unread
since 1947, and the complete works of Scott.

Little different, therefore, from any other Pakistani town in
which the Raj set up shop. But D.I.Khan once played a first-class

cricket match, exactly thirteen years ago: and they had the misfortune to lose it by the margin of an innings and 851 runs.

In the subcontinent, weirder sides have slipped through the net of first-class status: the Hindustan Breweries XI and the Maharashtra Small Savings Minister's XI (the savings were small, presumably, not the Savings Minister himself). In 1964, it was reasonable by such standards for the new Ayub Zonal Tournament to be accorded first-class status. In the first round D.I.Khan, instead of playing another small fish like Baluchistan, were drawn against the mighty Railways, the match to be played at the Railways Stadium in Lahore.

A D.I.Khan team was assembled, but they had no wicket-keeper until someone visiting his brother in the town volunteered. Eight of them travelled to Lahore by train, two by bus, and Inayet, their best bowler, set off on the 250-mile journey by motorbike.

Railways won the toss, batted, overcame the loss of an early wicket, and finished the first day at 415 for 2. Ijaz Husain made 124 and Javed Baber, out early next day, chipped in with 200. But when Javed was out, the rot set in as Railways collapsed to 662 for 6. Pervez Akhtar and Mohammed Sharif, however, revived Railways and took the score to 825 for 6 at the close. They slaughtered the enemy with a mighty slaughtering, and the morning and the evening were the second day.

It had occurred to the D.I.Khan team that a declaration was about due. They were exhausted, and it was only on the assumption that they would be batting that they went to the ground on the third day. But risking nothing, Railways batted on to 910 for 6 before declaring, with Pervez Akhtar, who had never made a century before, 337 not out. The declaration did not please Pervez because he had Hanif's world record of 499 in sight.

The bowling figures testify to a carnage. Whereas Anwar Husain represented penetration (46 overs, 3–295), Inayet was accuracy (59 overs, 1–279). They both bowled fast-medium. At one point, while walking back to his mark, Anwar, now an Army major, was moved to continue past it and to hide behind the sight-screen.

D.I.Khan's reply was brief. They were all out for 32. Railways then gambled on a lead of 878 and enforced the follow-on. This time D.I.Khan were less successful, being all out for 27. Ahad Khan took 9 wickets for 7 runs with mixed spin. Whereas Railways had batted for two and a quarter days, D.I.Khan were dismissed twice in two hours.

The cricketers of D.I.Khan were too tired and dejected to go home. They stayed in Lahore for several days recuperating, and then, on their return, by the waters of Indus they lay down and wept.

Two of the side gave up playing cricket after that match (or even during it, you might say, but that is unfair for they used no substitute fielders – they had none). And most of them left D.I.Khan in the course of time to find work, so that only three members still remain there.

Inayet lives in a back street of D.I.Khan. His full name is Inayet Ullah, but everyone knows him as Inayet Bowler. He is about 6 feet tall, with long strong fingers. His wife was ill. Whether it was that, or hashish, or his job in a bank, an intense sadness shrouded him.

He spoke in the local tongue, save for the odd word in English and the one sentence: 'The fielding was very poor.' He estimated that 11 or 12 catches were dropped, one of them Pervez Akhtar (337*) before he made ten, off his own bowling. When he said that, he seemed near the unspeakable heart of his sadness.

No one who has experienced a hard day in the field would mock these men of Dera Ismail Khan. Their endurance was more admirable than the easy records set up against them. It would not have been unusual in such cricket if they had conceded the match, or resorted to the common expedient of walking out in protest at an umpire's decision.

With their performance indelible in cricket's history and records, they and their successors live under an eternal stigma. They talk of the match, and smile about it, but with an obvious sense of shame. Ever since they have been ostracised by the Pakistani authorities, for suffering the most humiliating defeat in first-class cricket in the only first-class match they ever played.

27 November 1977                                                     *Scyld Berry*

*In 1979–80 Australia, England and West Indies played
the first triangular series of one-day matches, known as the
Benson and Hedges World Series Cup. It was the price to be
paid for the reconciliation between established cricket and
Kerry Packer. Television began to dictate the shape of the
game: six-ball overs instead of eight-ball, to allow for more
commercial breaks per hour. This piece was written from the
viewpoint of someone watching Packer's Channel Nine,
advertisements and all.*

# Cricket on Television

'Welcome to the Sydney Cricket Ground for today's match
between Australia and England in the Benson and Hedges World
Series Cup. It's the first game to be played on Boxing Day at the
SCG for 48 years, a splendid crowd is building up, and we'll be
right back in just a moment.'

'Hi, I'm Tony Packard Holden, and have I got news for you! I
have 5,000 used cars just waiting for you at unbeatable low, low
prices. So if you're looking for a car as good as new, you come
along to me, and I'll do it right for you-u-u-u-u!'

'Welcome back to the SCG, and over now to Tony Greig who's
been taking a look at today's wickets.' 'Thank you, Richie, and
hello everybody. Well, basically to me it looks a pitch of in-
consistent bounce and slightly uneven.' Far more eye-catching
is Tony himself in his bright yellow blazer, as he squats by the
pitch with a mike. The captains then toss, Mike Brearley calls tails
and Greg Chappell tells Channel Nine viewers that he has won
the toss and decided to . . .

'Hi! How would *you* like to collect this brand new set of cricket
cards? Neat, eh?' Introducing the cockiest kid in the whole
Antipodes, streaky of hair and squeaky of voice. He struts in front
of Max Walker, Greg Chappell and Rodney Marsh to extol the
qualities of Ardmona, 'the canned fruit that comes with the cream
of the world's cricketers'. He throws a can at Marsh, who tosses it
from glove to glove and drops it. 'Arr, nice one, Rodney,' says our

171

lad. Apparently the players' opinion of him after filming the ad was unprintable.

'Now it's over to Bill Lawry for the first ball of the day, to be bowled by Graham Dilley.' 'Good morning', says Bill as 2.30 strikes. The first over is a maiden to Julien Wiener, followed by 30 seconds on the roofing tile that two-thirds of Australians prefer.

Ian Botham bowls the second over, and an arrow points out his leg-side field. This one is a commendable idea for the uninitiated, which the BBC thinks of borrowing. Later we get a diagram of an inswinger so that housewives in Wagga Wagga will feel informed and stay tuned (that's not difficult with the other channels offering repeats of 'My Favourite Martian' and 'The Cisco Kid'). Or there is a diagram of the delivery of a left-armer like Derek Underwood who is about to . . .

'Hi, I'm Tony Packard Holden, and have I got news for you!' Tony is fast making a name for himself as the world's most inadequate man. He clenches his fist in embarrassment and has to keep pointing his arms at you for emphasis. After Tony, we get the hard-sell on New Improved Fab, a burst of roof tiles again (still preferred by two-thirds of Australians), and back to the action where . . .

Botham is bowling the second ball of his over, the first having been overrun by ads. No reference, of course, is made to having missed it. In a major step this season the Australian Cricket Board introduced the six-ball over, but Channel Nine often go one better with a five-ball over. This has provoked an uproar in letters to the editor throughout the land.

'Hi! How would *you* like to collect this brand new set of cricket cards? Neat, eh?' Rodney drops his can again. Now McDonald's is offering a poster of all three international teams, free with every burger purchase. Allan Border and Deryck Murray do the sales talk in verse to impress the masses. In a final poetic flash Border tells Murray that his couplets aren't rhyming. Cracks Murray, with all the wit that dazzled Cambridge University for two years in the mid-'sixties: 'I can't make rhymes/All of the times.'

When Wiener is out in mid-over we break for Paul Sheahan, former Australian batsman, to emerge in his MCC tie from a sign proclaiming 10¾ per cent, the interest rate his building society offers.

In Australia's innings there are 194 runs, 54 commercial breaks and 6 wickets, plus one ad flashed across the screen commanding: 'Enjoy your summer outing with baby in Snugglers.' It's a brainwash, like nodding off to sleep and being woken every three minutes, or reading *War and Peace* with cartoons after every page. As soon as you pick up the thread of the cricket action, it's taken from you.

Geoff Boycott's match-winning 86 passes before the eyes like roof tiles, burgers and the cocky kid's fruit, the mind having been saturated. His innings and Peter Willey's take England all but home, until wickets tumble and we flash to Evonne Cawley for a spiel on fly spray. There are plenty of fly sprays on the Aussie market, but Evonne with her favourite can is the hottest shot by far. A quick squirt and there's our fly in close-up, wriggling until its last. Arr, nice one, Evonne. By ESP or somehow, they always show this ad during England's middle-order collapses.

Not even the pleasure at England's eventual win could overcome the revulsion that seven hours of burgers, tinned fruit and baby Snugglers had induced. According to a Sydney professor, the average Australian spends two solid years of his life watching ads. Given that amount, the danger is that he would hardly mind if the cricket itself became tinned, instant and specifically designed for the mass market.

He may, however, be saved by the judiciary. The Australian Broadcasting Commission has applied for a court order restraining Channel Nine from exclusive Test and international match coverage. Neat, eh?

30 December 1979                                        *Scyld Berry*

---

*In an age of increasing specialisation, Tony Pawson was captain of Oxford and played for Kent from 1946 to 1953, scoring 3807 first-class runs at an average of 37; a football blue who played for Charlton Athletic; and subsequently a national fishing champion. Equally versatile at writing, as cricket and football correspondent of* The Observer, *he once reported a Test match and a First Division League match on the same day*.

# The Australians of My Experience

The famous Bodyline series of 1932–33 in Australia was the focal point of my schoolboy interest. England temporarily subdued the incredible Don Bradman and won a series of high quality fast bowling to packed leg-side fields.

Infamous it may be called now because of the bitterness it caused, and because the legacy of exploiting the intimidatory aspects of fast bowling is still with us. But then it seemed simply a great 4–1 victory. It was all the sweeter for us since Douglas Jardine, the stern unbending captain who relentlessly applied fast leg-theory (as Harold Larwood termed it) no matter whose head or heart it bruised, was an old boy of our Horris Hill preparatory school, and we had an extra holiday in his honour.

We ignored the injuries and the injured feelings and exulted for a change in a crushing English win. What impressed me as an 11-year-old was the pictured agony on Australian faces as the immaculate, unruffled Herbert Sutcliffe played the ball on to his stumps without removing a bail, before going on to make 194 and win the First Test. Equally satisfying was the delight on Bill Bowes's face as he removed Bradman first ball in the next Test. Then there was the emotional response to Eddie Paynter, taken ill to hospital, yet coming from ward to wicket and a battling 83 in the sweltering Brisbane heat to transform a losing situation into the decisive win.

In adult retrospect our admiration might more properly have gone to Gubby Allen, the amateur fast bowler who refused to be party to Bodyline tactics, than to the England captain. And indeed when we checked our hero's batting record at Horris Hill we found an unfortunate entry in a key match against Summerfields School: Jardine b Allen 0.

It was another and much older Australian campaigner who

coached me at Winchester, as he had coached my father. Rockley Wilson was a gritty Yorkshireman whose accurate bowling nagged the Australians, and whose witty tongue occasionally upset them. Rockley's exit line at a farewell party in Australia might more appropriately be attributed to Jardine: 'You must be upset I'm leaving, Governor.' 'Why in particular?' 'Because now *you* will be the most unpopular man in Australia again.'

My own experience was to be on the receiving end of the 1948 Australians' fast bowling and quick wit, as Bradman's side carried all before it. At Oxford I went in at 19 for 2, facing Bill Johnston and determined to play a captain's innings. Johnston was a left-hander with a bucking run and flailing arms, deceptive pace and late swing, who equalled Ray Lindwall's 27 wickets that Test series without ever matching his killer reputation. My first ball was wide to leg, but as I tried to glance it swung suddenly back to remove the off bail. As I passed the bowler he added insult to injury by saying, 'Sorry about that, skipper. It was meant to be an easy one to get you off the mark.'

I did get off the mark against those Australians when Kent played them at Canterbury. England had just been bowled out for 52 at The Oval, with Len Hutton batting throughout the innings for a mammoth 30, so it amused us to think we were certain to make more than England. On a plum pitch we were bowled out for 51 and I was fourth highest scorer with one.

The start had done little to settle my nerves. Our elderly opener, Leslie Todd, was a considerable character but of unpredictable mood. And his mood that day was not attuned to playing fast bowling. Lindwall's loosener of an opening ball pitched on his toe and all the Australians from long leg to cover were instantly airborne in a concerted appeal which left the umpire unmoved. 'Toddy', however, hobbled down the wicket and appeared to argue – with equal lack of success – that he had indeed been out.

He then shouldered his bat to the next ball which knocked out his middle stump, limped off to the dressing room, and announced he was too injured to take further part in the match. When a physiotherapist's examination failed to reveal even a bruise or to change his mind, he was suspended for the rest of the season by Bryan Valentine, the entertaining Kent captain

175

whose Test average of 64.85 remains the highest of any English-man batting five times or more.

For me the interesting contrast in that team was between captain and vice-captain. Bradman was totally dedicated to run-making and to winning, seeming always intent and unsmiling. Some 22,000 came to that Canterbury game as a farewell tribute. Yet 'The Don' could not just accept the compliment but had to make formal complaint that, by packing them in, the overspill had reduced the boundaries. It wasn't as if we were likely to find the boundary very often! When I talked later with 'The Don' he commented that he had been caught by Godfrey Evans early on but 'fortunately' no one appealed. To have walked in that situation would have seemed to him the act of a simpleton.

His deputy, Lindsay Hassett, had captained at Oxford and at first appeared just as dour. We had him out for a duck and he sat next to me at the tea interval, sullen and silent. When later I inquired which roller he wanted, he demanded the spiked one and made angry-sounding comment when I confessed the absence of any such implement.

A moment later he added, 'I wouldn't worry about it, son. We only use it for breaking up the roads, and I don't think we'll have to resort to that to get you lot out.' How right he was.

Hassett's humour survived the tensest situations. When his usually safe hands failed to hold successive catches at long leg in one of the Tests, he borrowed a policeman's helmet and parked it beside him in case a third came his way. His sportsmanship matched his humour. Early in that disastrous Oval innings, Compton slipped on the wet turf when going for a run. Hassett had the ball in his hands, but declined to take advantage and run out England's best bat as he was perfectly entitled to do.

31 August 1980                                                    *Tony Pawson*

---

*The Centenary Test at Lord's in 1980 paid the penalty for trying to imitate the Melbourne match of 1977. It was memorable only for the strokeplay of Kim Hughes and for the retirement of John Arlott. Shortly after lunch on the final day Arlott ascended the steps to the commentary box for the last time and described Dennis Lillee bowling to Geoff Boycott. He then went to live in Alderney, leaving us to wonder whether cricket commentary on the radio could continue without the most evocative of voices.*

# Cricket on Radio

When Saturday's play in the Lord's Test match was washed out in 1976, the BBC hit upon an apparent paradox. They found out that the harder it rained, the more keenly did listeners cling to their programme 'Test Match Special'.

Instead of being handed back to the studio that wet Saturday, listeners were regaled with a feast of Arlott, Bailey, Johnston and Trueman anecdote and memory. Rather than dampening the commentary team's enthusiasm, rain was fuel for it. They managed to assuage the disappointment felt by millions, and amongst those who professed themselves delighted was the Duke of Edinburgh.

It could only happen in cricket that, with the game abandoned, people should chat for hours with sense and humour, and that millions should tune in to hear them. Cricket's assets are its profundity and diversity, and its bringing to mind of happier bygone days, while John Arlott's voice evokes the lawn mower of hot afternoons.

Radio broadcasting of Test cricket is prodigiously successful, and the figure given last year [1979] of an average of half a million listeners quite misleading – if people watch the television with the radio on, as many do, the figures are given to television. Men who would only get out of bed if their wives went into labour willingly set the alarm for early a.m. to hear how England are faring in Australia. The radios hidden in desks, at school, or in the office, evince the same phenomenon: an incredible vicarious pleasure in hearing about what is happening on a cricket ground.

According to the BBC's cricket correspondent, Christopher Martin-Jenkins, the basic formula of cricket broadcasting has not changed since the pre-war doyen Howard Marshall: 'X runs in, bowls, the batsman does this and the score is that.' What has changed, and what distinguishes English commentary, is providing 'colour' – the wit and whimsy, where Australian commentators keep faithfully to description. 'Now there's a crisp bag at mid-wicket, blown over from the pavilion end – plain or smokey bacon would you say, Fred?' . . . 'And many thanks to Miss Jones of Whitehaven for her bottle of home-made cowslip wine . . .'

Perhaps, if loneliness is the social disease of our time, the programme's merit lies in providing access to civilised conversation. The chat-show has boomed: 'Start the Week', 'Stop the Week', anything with Robert Robinson and a handful of guests. But 'Test Match Special' holds the advantage, because the chat-show participants have no *raison d'être*, except to make a programme.

King of the conversationalists is, of course, John Arlott, now on the verge of taking his lawn mower into retirement. The voice, he says, became enriched 'with age and bronchitis'; when he started broadcasting in 1946 it was more metallic and the phrases came more quickly, though even then with poetic turns. It is hard to realise how uncommon his regional accent was on early radio, when Alvar Liddell was the model; now the soft regional accent à la Melvyn Bragg can be considered quite charming.

Arlott ascends to the top of the Lord's pavilion for the first of his last broadcasts, stops and mops his brow, heaves back his shoulders and wades straight in. 'I once tried not looking at the play before I went on the air and went up the stairs backwards – to give myself a fright, so my voice wasn't so deep.' But fortunately it stayed deep.

The broadcasters' popularity is apparent from the bundles of mail with which the MCC officials stagger into the box. 'Lucky we've got a bucket of water outside,' says the apprehensive producer fingering a package. Just as unsavoury in 1970 was excrement received through the post as a comment on some anti-apartheid views.

If Arlott is the Beethoven of the box, Brian Johnston is the Mozart; and just as a few cannot stand the sweetness of Mozart, there are many attracted by his bubbling vitality, who would not otherwise be attracted to the subject at all.

The Johnstonian style is said not to appeal much to West Indian listeners: the talk of cakes and delphiniums and maiden aunts in Whitehaven clearly has less relevance. But there again the prattle, perhaps the very inconsequentiality of it, has appealed to sections of the community not normally associated with cricket, who would confuse a run out with a not out, and might conclude that rioting had broken out amongst the commentary team if they heard that so-and-so had been hit in the box.

Johnston is the key factor, whose affability is the oil that keeps the wheels revolving. As a freelance he can keep working with the team for many more years; and then says the producer, Peter Baxter, 'if he does retire, it would help if he just sat at the back of the box'. He plays the foil to each of his colleagues, setting up comic situations, and bringing the best from others.

His continued presence will help tide over the initial post-Arlott era. The longer term future for cricket broadcasting is also bright in Arlott's view. The harsher reality becomes, the more unemployed there are, the higher the rate of inflation, the deeper the Soviet Union penetrates into the free world – the more people will want to escape into another world where 'tragedy' and 'disaster' are nothing more than hackneyed synonyms for a run out. 'It's an escape,' says Arlott. 'It's no coincidence that there is a high brick wall surrounding Lord's.'

Yes, broadcasting and the listening and the enjoyment, both of broadcasters and listeners, will surely continue so long as every cricket ball that is bowled is different from every other in pace and place of pitching. The secret is that cricket has infinite varieties: each ball, each cricketer and each game is unique. So there can never be one absolute opinion, and opinions if aired with sense and humour will always be worth listening to.

'And many thanks to Mrs Poole of Godalming for taking the trouble to write in to us about her delphiniums . . . Thanks also to Major Smith for sending us a very fine bottle from his collection of British wines.' By late afternoon half-eaten cheesecakes are piled high on ledges. Bits of wedding cake drip their icing. No wonder a doctor has just sent in a load of toothpicks. If 'Test Match Special' does pass away, it won't be from starvation.

Arlott, however, considers it more likely that cricket on radio will continue to be nourished by its partnership with television. 'The television may be on, but people will still listen to the radio – drip-feed listeners, housewives at the sink.' Unfortunately he himself will start increasing the listening audience next year, by one.

6 September 1980                                    *Scyld Berry*

---

*In a three-way conversation during the Lord's Test of 1981 between England and Australia, three Test cricketers assessed how the game had changed in their experience. Between them, that experience covered 50 years of Test history. Jack Fingleton played for Australia 1931–38; Len Hutton for England 1937–55; Bobby Simpson for Australia 1957–68 and again, in perhaps the most remarkable comeback known to Test cricket, in a home series against India and an away series against West Indies in 1977–78.*

# The Changing Game

Q. Have standards risen in the various departments of the game?

FINGLETON   Greg Chappell, Viv and Barry Richards would have been great, truly great, batsmen in any era, but maybe the net was wider in the past – lovely batsmen like Charlie Barnett, Compton, Nourse, Kippax, Jackson and McCabe who played three wizard Test innings. Bowling was more varied, slow bowlers had a seat at the table and were not just to pick up the crumbs. Men like Freeman, Grimmett, O'Reilly, Tayfield, Laker, Lock – too many to mention all – were indispensable in the attacks of their sides. It led, too, to footwork and a larger variety of strokes. That is one bad feature of modern cricket: spinners need not apply. In other days spinners would 'buy' their wickets whereas now there is too much emphasis on keeping down runs. In fielding the standard has risen sky-scraper high. Wonderful, delightful. In my time, various fieldsmen were hidden because they could bat or bowl. None of that now, everybody must be able to field. We had individuals who were outstanding, but now some six or seven are in every team.

HUTTON   We have some very fine cricketers today, and would have more if South Africa were still a Test-playing country. The only deterioration I can see is in the class of spin-bowlers. The leg-break bowler has disappeared from big cricket, and the slow left-arm spinners bear little resemblance to the exponents of the past. During the past 20 years or so, the fielding has improved considerably. The Australians and West Indians were always good, indeed brilliant in the field. England fielded much better *after* my time, and in the days of Brian Statham and Fred Trueman we had two fast bowlers who were fine fieldsmen, which was rare.

SIMPSON   In some areas, yes. The technique of defensive bowling certainly has improved. Batting, on the other hand, has not, with a general decline in the techniques of most batsmen. They move back and across the crease, which limits their range of stroke – Bob Woolmer is a good example. Batsmen should stand still, judge the length and play accordingly. The fielding of today is generally better though I doubt whether the throwing by Australians is much better. We used to throw stones a lot when we were young, and played more baseball.

Q.   How frequent were bouncers?

FINGLETON   Bouncers were very frequent from Larwood and Voce, but that was a part of their Bodyline plan. Every fast bowler reserves the right to bowl an occasional one but World Series Cricket unleashed too many. Dennis Amiss said 23 helmets were hit in that cricket. It is high time the umpires said, especially to the West Indians who are the greatest offenders, 'That's it, boys. Keep the ball pitched up or else.'

HUTTON  After the Bodyline tour of Australia in 1932–33, bouncers took a back seat in English cricket. A certain amount of rough stuff was always seen in the Yorkshire v. Notts match, particularly at Trent Bridge. Larwood and Voce could be nasty on occasions – no one could surpass the Nottinghamshire pair when they were in a bouncing mood. I first encountered sustained short-pitched deliveries in Australia during the 1946–47 tour. In England we had no fast bowlers for several years after the war but Australia had several who could bowl bouncers, including Lindwall who bowled the best bouncers I faced. They did not go 2 or 3 yards over the batsman's head; you had to play them or be hit. He also concealed his bouncer and would bowl no more than two per over. Many of the bouncers I have seen in recent years have been of poor quality, and some of these bowlers would have been better employed bowling length and direction.

SIMPSON  In my view more bouncers were bowled in the 'fifties and 'sixties due to the fact that there was virtually no restriction on their use. And from 19 yards or less, rather than 20, as now, because bowlers 'dragged' over the front crease. In 1965 in the West Indies, Hall and Griffith in their opening spells were averaging nearly three an over. Whereas in 1978, when I revisited the West Indies, the bowlers were limited to three every two overs.

Q.  Has the level of sportsmanship changed?

FINGLETON  Certainly there were not these modern slanging matches – players had too much respect for themselves, the game, the opposition and the umpires. That is not to say the air wasn't somewhat 'blue' at times when luck went one way or the other. Bill O'Reilly had a few choice things to say to the ether in Sydney in 1932 when Herbert Sutcliffe played a ball hard on to his stumps and the bails didn't fall. Herbert was then in the 40s and made 194. I don't think relations are as friendly as they were before the war, although they seem splendid so far this series. Fortunately, too, there has been a cutting down on exhibitionism in the field, which is a credit to the players and the Australian management.

HUTTON   During my career I was never insulted by a bowler, though there were occasions when I could see the bowler was very annoyed at a decision given in my favour. And there were occasions when the relationship between bowler and umpire was definitely near breaking point. I did not hear words exchanged in anger, but expressions can speak louder than words. Relations between players are probably better today than they have ever been. In Australia, in 1946–47, it came as a severe shock that close fielders were appealing for lbw and caught-behind decisions. This was a foreign language to me. My father had said, when I was a teenager, only the bowler and wicket-keeper should appeal for lbw decisions. In my early days with Yorkshire I found myself, I don't know why, at second slip. When in my youthful enthusiasm I appealed for lbw, first slip turned to me and asked if I had something stuck in my throat, and followed this remark by saying, 'It's a good job Lord Hawke's not here. Tha would NIVER play for Yorkshire again.'

SIMPSON   Verbal intimidation has always been a part of cricket in my experience. It was less obvious during my early days than now and also probably more subtle. Generally it consisted of by-play between bowlers, fieldsmen and wicket-keeper in sound of the batsman. Often the 'freeze' was used when nothing was allowed to be said to talkative batsmen who sought the comfort of conversation with the opposition to boost his confidence. Geoff Boycott once declared publicly that he liked to seek the solace of the dressing room corner before any innings to psyche himself up. Our answer was to have our twelfth man seek him out at this time to sign autographs. Verbal clashes between fast bowlers and batsmen have always been a healthy aggressive sign of total commitment. Many times Freddie Trueman questioned the status of my parents' union. Providing it is limited and not allowed to build up too much I feel this edge is good for the game.

Q.   Was it the custom for batsmen to 'walk' before the umpires gave them out?

FINGLETON   Never the custom, and I agree. Some who walk today stay put in a crisis and hope their reputation will influence the umpires. The umpire is there to say in or out and all should rely on him. True, this can be overdone. I know one batsman (not an Englishman) who never thought straddling his stumps was reason enough to leave the middle.

HUTTON  Walking was certainly not the custom during my period in first-class cricket. I have the utmost difficulty in naming a player who did not wait for the umpire's decision. Some batsmen lingered at the wicket longer than was considered in good taste but they were few and far between.

SIMPSON  Walking has always been a personal and controversial choice. I tried walking for some time but eventually decided to give it up because so many of the publicised 'walkers' didn't walk in crucial times and thus put more pressure on the umpires and the spirit of the game.

Q.  What kind of protection did batsmen have?

FINGLETON  Just the usual box and a strip of (mostly useless) crêpe rubber around the upper part of the body under the shirt. Helmets were unknown. Had they been available, I and my fellows would have rushed to use them against Bodyline.

HUTTON  The type of protection used by myself and most other batsmen was an abdominal protector and a thigh pad. I wore the best batting gloves available. The one big fear which all batsmen have against the Bouncing Billies is the same as the heavyweight boxer's: it is not the punch he can see that worries him, but the punch he doesn't see. So it is with the batsman. In 1938, in Johannesburg, I was struck on the head with the first ball I received from the Transvaal fast bowler; this put me into hospital for four days. In Sydney during the Second Test against Australia, in 1954–55, Frank Tyson was struck on the head by a delivery from Lindwall which Frank did not see.

SIMPSON  Protection has always varied according to circum-stances and individual style. During the Hall–Griffith onslaught in the 'sixties many players and particularly Colin McDonald and Colin Cowdrey chose to use chest and side protectors as well as the normal equipment. The danger of excessive protection is that it can be used as a 'crutch' by the batsman and he becomes preoccupied with being hurt. It is far better to develop your evasive techniques or attacking flair, for to be uncomfortable or to be hit can only boost the confidence of the bowler. During the hectic 1960–61 series against West Indies in Australia I was often criticised because of my unorthodox weaving technique against Hall. Yet I was one of Australia's most successful batsmen and was hit only twice above the hip, on the left side when I didn't move inside the ball quickly enough. It is almost impossible to be hit on the head if you watch the ball. Most batsmen are hit on the head when either hooking or taking the eye off the ball.

Q. Do close fielders field much closer now?

FINGLETON   Yes, some do but only because they are allowed to wear a helmet which, in my view, should never be allowed a fieldsman. We went up close, very close, as nature turned us out. I can still memorise the outline of Len Hutton's posterior as seen from a few yards away for hour after hour, day after day, at The Oval in 1938. No box, no helmet, just confidence in Bill O'Reilly and myself. If one keeps close to the ground at short leg one won't be hit. Big hits are up in the air – and one can always duck, though I didn't to Percy Santall at Edgbaston in 1938 and I still recall the crunch on my forehead. But helmets for fieldsmen, faugh! I can imagine what the good Doctor would have said of that. And, if helmets for fieldsmen, why not a sling for the bowler?

HUTTON   Fieldsmen have always fielded close to the wicket for *good* bowlers. I remember batting on a turning wicket against Tom Goddard at Bristol; I could almost touch the three short legs. Syd Barnes fielded almost in the batsman's pocket to the bowling of Ray Lindwall. Jack Fingleton couldn't have been much closer at forward short leg to the bowling of Bill O'Reilly. In recent years, however, I have seen many fielders close to the wicket for indifferent slow bowlers.

SIMPSON   More use is made of close fieldsmen today due to uncertain wickets. But they don't necessarily field closer. I have little doubt that the skills are much greater in this area than in previous years due to the extra emphasis placed on fielding close. Helmets should be outlawed for they give an unfair advantage to the fieldsman.

Q.   How does the over-rate compare?

FINGLETON   It was never a worry in my time and infinitely faster than today. It would have to have been, otherwise the game would be at a standstill by now, especially against West Indies.

HUTTON   The over-rate in my time was much quicker owing, I think, to the much greater use of spin-bowlers. I think games-manship and the changes in the lbw law have resulted in a slower tempo of Test and first-class cricket.

SIMPSON   The over-rate used to be generally in excess of 100 balls per hour. The slow over-rate is the greatest danger to cricket's popularity.

Q.   Are bowlers' run-ups too long?

FINGLETON   Yes, much too long by many. There should be a limit. How long does it take for a sprinter to work up maximum pace? Let it be the same for a bowler. He can hit his top speed in a short space. And it would be good, too, for his old age when many now soak their feet in hot water and salt.

HUTTON   Bowlers' run-ups are much longer than they used to be in pre-war days. Harold Larwood, in the early 'thirties, had the longest run in England. When I first saw him I thought his run-up enormous but delightful to watch, as was his action, the best I have seen. The West Indians always loved to run a long way – Constantine, Martindale – and their present fast bowlers like to run almost from the boundary. Much too long, I think, and very boring to watch.

SIMPSON   Most certainly they are. Excessive run-ups are a blight on the game and rob the public. Most bowlers, I believe, would benefit by shortening their run-up. Frank Tyson in 1954–55 was a case in point. At the start of the tour and including the First Test he ran from the sightboard with limited success. When he cut his run in half he was explosive and successful, and fully earned his nickname of 'The Typhoon'.

Q. Were congratulations for a bowler taking a wicket, or a fielder taking a catch, so pronounced?

FINGLETON   Overexuberance, from the soccer field, has come to stay. I suppose it suggests camaraderie, but it is overdone. Just a mere 'well done' or a slap on the back is good enough. I would love to have seen fieldsmen trying to slobber over Bill O'Reilly and some others when they got wickets, which they were expected to do. A cricket field is entitled to circumspect, more controlled behaviour. Some ebullience is permissible if a fieldsman takes a 'blinder' but he is there to take catches. Yes, the cackle, whoops, leaps and hugs should be cut. A man is a man, or is he?

HUTTON   Only on very rare occasions did I see any displays of jubilation when a bowler captured an important wicket – just quiet congratulations. Other countries were more demonstrative, particularly Australia from 1946 to 1953, when they carried all before them. They could behave as they wished, but not England: that sort of behaviour, back-slapping and so on, ended when prep school days were over.

SIMPSON   This new trend probably began with Richie Benaud. While it can be overdone I don't see anything particularly wrong with it. In many cases it has added a greater warmth to the game and extra player-involvement. These days players are expected to project personality much more than in the past and I see this as an extension of this player–crowd involvement.

Q.   What has been the biggest single influence on the game?

FINGLETON   It has to be Kerry Packer. He has taken over the game, he owns the game. He has bred a new type of Australian spectator who isn't interested in cricket's traditional skills. He wants limited-over cricket with close finishes, and as a result there is far too much of it.

HUTTON   I think it has been commercial television, of which Kerry Packer was just an extension. Commercial television increased the money in the game, where before the BBC and their Australian counterpart paid pretty low fees. It is such a powerful medium that women have become snooker fans who didn't know the right end of a cue. The influence of Packer in England has gone but that of television remains, encouraging limited-over cricket and an artificial number of tight finishes.

SIMPSON   Important as the effects of Packer and television have been, wickets have been as influential as anything on the game. They virtually dictate the style and quality of cricket and, unfortunately, over the past 20 years we have seen a decline in their standard, playing havoc with the game, and affecting its crowd appeal. This decline in wickets has caused a fall in the standard of batting and encouraged dull, military-medium pace bowlers. They prosper not so much through skill alone, but through helpful conditions.

5 August 1981

---

*The sweatshops of India that produce carpets and clothes for the British market in inhuman conditions have been exposed. Here is a description of a sweatshop that was producing cricket equipment in Jullundur when England played a one-day international there just before Christmas on their 1981–82 tour of India.*

# Cricket Factory

If the stocking to be opened on Christmas morning reveals an item of cricket equipment, the probability is that it was made in Punjab, in the city of Jullundur, where England's one-day international is scheduled for today. At least 99 per cent of pads and gloves now sold in England and three-quarters of all cricket balls are made in that part of India.

They say that Alexander the Great paved the streets of Jullundur, according to Kipling at any rate. So much for romance. Now the pavements have crumbled into dusty rubble, the buildings are utterly unlovely and the streets overflow with packing cases addressed to Slazenger's, Stuart Surridge, Gray Nichols, Duncan Fearnley and St Peter's (Yorks, not Rome).

One of the Raj's proudest achievements, the Grand Trunk Road, runs through Jullundur on its journey of 1500 miles from Calcutta to Peshawar; and beside it stands the biggest of Jullundur's sports equipment factories. The company which owns it is called Mahajan's, and has a curious history attached to it.

In 1925 Hans Raj Mahajan, father of the present managing director, began a sports factory in Sialkot, which has since become part of Pakistan. When Partition came, Mahajan, as a Hindu, had to flee Sialkot before he was able to sell his factory, so that he arrived in Jullundur with 25 rupees. The family business has since expanded to an annual turnover of 40 million rupees, with 80 per cent of its sales to Australia and the UK.

The Mahajans chose Jullundur as the site of their new factory because of the cheap labour available. Jullundur's refugee camp contained more than 50,000 Hindus who had fled from Pakistan, and the subsequent supply has been kept topped up by the drift from the countryside to the cities. With such resources at hand, no employer need tolerate for a moment the existence of a trade union.

None of the raw materials for cricket equipment is available locally, but the cheapness of labour outweighs any transport costs involved. Cane for bat handles comes from the Andaman Islands, cork from Portugal, leather from cows in Uttar Pradesh, and willow for bats from Kashmir, Assam and Bhutan. Mahajan's have also provided the official hockey balls for the last six Olympiads.

The English equipment companies, those well-known names, have only to specify their own designs and arrange for transportation. They can afford to air-freight from New Delhi rather than ship the products from Bombay. Then they mark up a profit margin of 100 per cent, or more.

Inside, this factory recalls those history books with pictures of early Victorian working conditions before the Factory Acts. The labour is cheap and is treated as such. Five hundred people work in one far from large building, sometimes 30 and 40 to a room.

An old unshaven Punjabi squats by a pair of scales weighing the half-made cricket balls, then adjusting their weight by adding or subtracting thread wrapped around the cork. Professional cricketers know that balls vary considerably in weight in spite of the rigidly prescribed standards, and after looking at the strength of the old man's spectacles one is not altogether surprised.

He folds his arms to speak, as he lost two fingers in an earlier accident; and he has to take time off at his own expense to speak, or go to the lavatory, or to eat, because all the workers are employed at piece-work rates. He is on one of the highest rates, for he is skilled and in a responsible position. He earns 72 paise for every dozen balls that he weighs and adjusts – which constitutes roughly an hour's work. And 72 paise, just under three-quarters of a rupee, is equal to 4p.

Further on in the maze, a dark-haired Punjabi girl with a ring through one nostril squats on the concrete floor with three other women, earning half as much as that man. She takes a cricket ball, squeezes lemon juice on it and polishes until it shines. But no ball is half so bright as her wistful smile.

Next door, a room no longer than a cricket pitch, by about 8 yards wide, contains 50 workers. They sit in four rows, stuffing synthetic wool into cricket pads, stitching, and sewing on buckles and the labels of those well-known English companies. Some of the younger ones could not be more than 9 or 10 years old; yet they all work a six-and-a-half day week.

The workers' only distraction comes from a radio in one corner of the room. It will usually pour forth the songs that the film stars sing, but now it is broadcasting commentary on England's current match. The irony is poignant: they make the equipment for a few paise, then it is sold and advertised for sums many times the cost price.

Of course, even the children want the work, since Jullundur can provide no better alternative for employment. And this is not a scandal like the Sri Lankan tea-pickers paid a pittance by a British tea company, or black workers in South Africa receiving a fraction of white workers' pay for the same job. The law of a free and open market does apply.

Nevertheless it would cost little to get the wage rates at least doubled for these workers. That would make one of the best Christmas presents of all.

20 December 1981                                          *Scyld Berry*

---

*Shiva Naipaul visited Sri Lanka en route to Australia, and was writing a book about his travels when he died suddenly of a heart attack. This piece was written for the colour magazine about the newest country in Test cricket. In the less than enchanted course of it, the author offers the reminder that sport is a social luxury.*

# Sri Lanka

Sri Lanka was suffering from its worst drought in 30 years. In the countryside around Colombo, the waterless paddy-fields baked in the sun. Village wells were drying up. Outbreaks of cholera and typhoid were being reported. In the heart of the capital a permanent haze of red dust overhung Galle Face Green. The talk everywhere was of the rain that would not come. But up in Kandy they were expending 10,000 gallons of water daily on the field where Sri Lanka would soon be playing its first Test match with an Australian touring cricket team.

'You will observe our priorities,' an acquaintance (who happened to be an enemy of the present capitalist-minded government) remarked. 'Who cares if the country goes to rack and ruin? So long as the cricket fields are green, what else matters?' Cricket, enjoyed by perhaps 20 per cent of the population, was part of the oppressive class structure that was slowly but surely going to strangle Sri Lanka. As such, it ought to be abolished.

At that juncture I was sympathetic not so much to the Marxist logic of the argument as to its conclusion.

191

Next afternoon at the Singhalese Sports Club, the headquarters of the Cricket Board of Control, my Press card was scanned with an odd mixture of suspicion and inertia and returned to me with a shrug.

'Everybody here,' said a non-reactive individual, 'is damned busy. We're all damned busy.' On the walls were fading photographs of vanished teams, vanished heroes. Turning my back on all those damned busy people, I walked out to the airy balcony. Down on the playing field, a wicket was being watered. A rosy dusk was beginning to illumine the sky.

These private Colombo clubs, of which there are about 25, have traditionally controlled cricket in Sri Lanka. Those who take their cricket seriously tend to be urban and overwhelmingly middle class, though some attempt is now being made to change this, to broaden both its social and geographical appeal.

In a society where 1300 rupees a month (about £40) is considered a good wage, and where half of the population earns 300 rupees or less a month, the financial attractions of modern cricket (and I leave aside the kind of bait dangled by the South Africans) are obvious. If you have the talent, it offers an alluring vista of escape from the debilitating and endless struggle for existence. It is so much better to be a successful cricketer than to be earning a pittance in the Survey Department after 25 years of service; it is so much better to be a cricketer than an unemployed, not-too-literate university graduate. Cricket holds out a possibility of international recognition denied Sri Lankans in most spheres: the island offers little glamour to the vast majority of those condemned to live there.

How wonderful to be a 'teen star' like Arjuna Ranatunga – who scored a half-century against the Australians in a one-day match – and have this sort of prose appear about you in one of the local newspapers: 'Ranatunga, the whizz-kid of local cricket, smashed an exhilarating 55 in 39 deliveries to send Sri Lanka soaring to a magnificent four-wicket victory.' The Australians had met their match in this 'Wizard of Ours . . . the teen star who bopped them.'

If Ranatunga had not been a teen star, his thoughts, like those of so many other Sri Lankans, might have turned towards the Middle East: in Dubai it is possible to earn eight or nine times the average Sri Lankan wage. (The whore-houses of Colombo, I had

been assured, had been emptied by the Middle Eastern exodus.)
The 30,000 migrants living in the Gulf states are a valuable source
of foreign exchange and a buffer against social unrest – always
just round the corner in Sri Lanka.

For those who are able to play it, cricket offers a fantasy of
possibilities – a fantasy that has begun to acquire a new solidity
with the granting of Test status. Cricket is not played in Sri Lanka
because of any post-imperial nostalgia. The clubs are only
nominally oases of exclusivity. Many are shabby, fly-blown places,
battling to make ends meet. The young men who play cricket
may, by the standard of the island, constitute an élite. But they are
a peculiar and modest élite; an élite on the make.

Again and again I was told with a mournful air of pride that Sri
Lankan school cricket was considered among the best in the
world; that the best schools gained prestige less from their
academic performance than from their performance on the field.
So what happened to all that talent after school? It ran off and
disappeared because precious jobs had to be found; families had
to be maintained. The struggle for existence took precedence.
But now, with Test status, with the odd tour by teams of
international class, it was hoped that this would gradually change.
Young men could now join the Army, the Navy, the Air Force, the
police – and continue to play cricket for the teams fielded by
their employers. I stared out into the deepening, rose-red dusk,
watching precious water soak into the turf.

The Australians dominated the sports pages of the newspapers.
They had sent a good team. Nearly all the big names had been
included – Greg Chappell, Dennis Lillee, David Hookes, Rodney
Hogg, Kepler Wessels. Chappell was saying all the right things: he
had heard so much about Sri Lanka and had always wanted to
visit the island; he and his team had no intention of underrating
the opposition. It was all terribly pleasing. In turn, the Sri
Lankans could point to Sir Garfield Sobers. He had come to
advise them, to exhort, to boost morale. 'Togetherness' was one
of his major themes. He spoke of the damaging effect inter-island
rivalry had had on West Indian cricket. He appealed to his
charges to consider Test cricket a 'national duty'.

The local commentators, falling into the spirit of the occasion,
described his remarks as opportune. What Sir Gary had said

about the West Indies was, apparently, all too sadly the case in Sri Lanka. Players and selectors had suffered from 'unfair and vulgar criticism'. An unnamed Sri Lankan cricketer commented, 'I, for one, just feel like chucking in the game ... if hoots and bad remarks are all we get from our own people for playing for the country.' The atmosphere was charged with a pre-connubial tension. I was reminded of the irritability, the excitability, that precedes an Indian wedding.

And yet, in the end, it all turned out to be slightly deceptive.

On the day of the first one-day international, the police issued extensive traffic regulations. I feared the worst. My imagination conjured up images of chaos. I saw multitudes thronging the approaches to the Sara Stadium, I saw bad-tempered policemen on bad-tempered horses. I saw stampede and mayhem. It was not at all like that.

The Sara Stadium turned out to be located in the midst of one of Colombo's most squalid squatter colonies. In the doorways of dark-interioned hovels lurked young men and women with painfully meagre bodies. Children splashed in fetid pools, squatted in the roadside dust. The morning air was tainted with the smells of ordure.

'Bad people, sir,' my driver murmured obsequiously.

'Why are they bad people?'

'They should not be here, sir. It is not their place.'

'Where is their place?'

He did not know and he did not care. We were watched with lethargic hostility from the doorways. Nearby rose blocks of mossy apartments bordered by broad, stagnant gutters, ornamented with mounds of refuse. A few days previously there had been stampede and mayhem in this locality. The blocks of flats ringing the stadium are occupied by Air Force personnel and their families. Assorted disagreements – I was not able to discover the exact points of contention – had arisen between the Air Force families and the squatters. The former, losing patience, had opened fire on the latter and gone on a rampage. Some of the hovels were burnt down, squatters were killed. The Army and the police had moved in, establishing a kind of martial law in the vicinity. Reflections on Test cricket and national duty receded as we crawled past groups of soldiers armed with rifles. I stared at a colourful portrait displayed on the roadside. It commemorated a squatter child murdered during the disturbance.

Within the stadium, the crowd was disappointingly small and subdued. There were reasons for this. Tickets were expensive, some costing 200 rupees; the match was being broadcast on the radio and televised. Also, it happened to be the Singhalese and Tamil New Year and so large numbers of people were 'out of station', enjoying, in this season of drought, the high-altitude delights of the hill country. A line of low stands fringed part of the ground, conveniently overlooked by the Air Force tenements – they probably had the best view of the game. I hoped they would not suddenly take into their heads to open fire. A licensed jester, with a Sri Lankan flag, paraded the perimeter of the field, shouting encouragement. Occasionally, a fire cracker exploded.

At lunch, the Sri Lankans were pleased. The Australian total was modest and half the side was out. The afternoon drawled on ('Good shot, sir, damned good shot'), pursuing its luminous path to dusk.

It seemed that Sri Lanka could win. When the possible became probable, the crowd livened up, detonating their fire crackers with selfless prodigality. When the probability became a certainty, the police converged on the boundary.

I quite forget who won the Man-of-the-Match award.

19 June 1983                                        *Shiva Naipaul*

PART 5

# *Obituaries*

*WG died in 1915, when the nation's mind was on things other than cricket, to wit the King's appeal for more troops in a message that was printed alongside this obituary. But space was found to eulogise the life of the most remarkable of all cricketers. Grace was 67 at his death, and had played his final first-class match only seven years before. Three years before that, in 1905, he had known his greatest tragedy when his son, William Gilbert (junior), died after an appendicitis operation.*

# W. G. Grace

The greatest of all cricketers has passed away. No doubt when peace returns to the world great batsmen and great bowlers now unknown will win laurels at Lord's and The Oval, but there can never come another W. G. Grace. He was unique and unapproachable. Not again may one look for the combination of qualities that produced his superlative excellence. Apart from his genius for cricket he had every physical advantage, including a strength of constitution that defied fatigue. It is on record that once, after passing the whole night by the bedside of a patient, he stepped on to the Clifton College ground and scored 200 runs without turning a hair. Nature was abundant in her gifts to him, but he worked very hard to make and keep his position.

Even in his comparatively young days he required a lot of practice. Once or twice, from unavoidable causes, he had to start the season with less preparation than usual, and his batting fell off 50 per cent. Fame came to W. G. Grace very early in life. He was not quite 17 when in 1865 he was picked for Gentlemen v. Players at The Oval and Lord's – rather more for his medium-pace bowling than for his batting. He did very well, helping the Gentlemen to gain their first victory at Lord's since 1853.

In the next year he jumped to the top of the tree as a batsman, scoring in two matches at The Oval 224 not out and 173 not out. Illness gave him a temporary check in 1867, but from 1868 right on to 1877 he enjoyed a measure of success till then undreamt of.

That was the most brilliant part of his career. His name was in everyone's mouth, and hundreds of people who had never before given a serious thought to cricket learnt to love the game from watching him bat. When in 1871 he played for the first time at Nottingham, the crowd at Trent Bridge beat all records.

After 1877 there came a change. WG was thinking of giving up cricket and settling down in life as a surgeon. The appearance in England of the first Australian XI and the astounding success that attended them had the effect – so it has always been understood – of keeping the great cricketer in full activity. At any rate, there was no more talk of retirement. WG started, as it were, on a second career, and from the first meeting of England and Australia at The Oval in September 1880, down to his last game in Nottingham in 1899 he only missed one Test match. During all these years he was great – the Australian bowlers found few batsmen so formidable – but he was not quite the same as in his youth. Increased weight told against him – a good deal in batting and to a sad extent, as time went on, in fielding.

Even when Test matches were no longer for him, WG went on playing, managing the London County team at the Crystal Palace for some years, and at The Oval in 1906 he scored 74 in his last Gentlemen v. Players match – a happy and fitting celebration of his fifty-eighth birthday. After that he quitted the scene, content-ing himself with a little club cricket and golf.

The miracle of his life happened in 1895. He was nearly 47, but in some strange way he renewed the strength of his prime. He scored a thousand runs in the month of May, and if the weather had kept dry all the summer he would beyond a doubt have approached his biggest records. Despite the handicap of wet wickets he had an average for the season of 51.

A detailed account of WG's doings in the cricket field would demand far more space than can be spared in these troubled times. All the statistics of his career have been published and are readily accessible. By universal consent WG as a batsman stood far ahead of all his early contemporaries and of all who had flourished before his day. In comparing him with the greatest batsmen of recent years – Ranjitsinhji and Victor Trumper, for examples – it must always be borne in mind that when WG first won his fame wickets were not as they are now. Modern methods

200

of preparation were unknown, and the heavy roller had scarcely been seen. A first-rate pitch could always be found at The Oval, but some of the wickets at Lord's were rough and dangerous to a degree. WG on the subject of his own powers was modesty itself. Never did a boastful word escape his lips, but he was once heard to say that few modern batsmen would have stood up to Freeman and Emmett as he and C. E. Green did on one eventful day at Lord's in 1870.

Of all the fine innings that WG played against the Australians, perhaps the best was his 165 for the Gentlemen in 1888. The Derby being treated with great respect at Lord's in those days, the match was left drawn on the second day. On the Monday evening WG was 150 not out, having actually scored his last 50 runs in about half an hour. He had not given such a display for a dozen years. He was only meeting Turner and Ferris for the second time, and he earned their heartfelt respect. Turner was reported to have said it was worth journeying from Australia to see such batting. WG went to Australia twice, with his own team in 1873–74, and as captain of Lord Sheffield's team in 1891–92. He was also the bright particular star of the amateur side that, with R. A. Fitzgerald as leader, had such a glorious trip to Canada in 1872. In a social sense that was, on the testimony of all concerned, the pleasantest cricket tour on record. WG was young then, and many were the jokes about his after-dinner speeches. Well, the great man is dead at 67. Not long ago one would have expected him to live another ten years at least. Still, he had a wonderful life, and his name can never be forgotten.

24 October 1915                                             *'The Don'*

---

*The author, a biographer of Hobbs, was well equipped to write this obituary when, four days before Christmas 1963, news came through of the death of 'The Master'. John Arlott had also helped to set up 'The Master's Club', which had as its object the rendering of honour and respect to Hobbs.*

# Jack Hobbs

Sir John Berry Hobbs, who has died a few days after his eighty-first birthday, was the greatest batsman and best-loved man of modern cricket. His knighthood, the first bestowed on a professional cricketer, honoured not only great technical skill but a gracious character.

Jack Hobbs was a simple man. The idea that he, the eldest of the 12 children of a net-bowler at Fenner's, was a great man always seemed to him an odd, and slightly amusing, idea which existed only in the minds of others. 'But it pleases them, you know...'

Hobbs scored more runs (61,237) and more centuries (197) than anyone else in first-class cricket; and more than any other Englishman on the high plateau of the game, which is Test play between England and Australia.

In 1920, when a Surrey opening bowler did not arrive for a match with Warwickshire, Hobbs went on with the new ball and took 5 wickets for 21 – and then scored 101.

He was top of the first-class bowling averages that year, which made him laugh. For nearly 30 years his speed in the pick-up, and the accuracy of his whippy, low throw, made it perilous to run a single to him at cover point.

The number of his runs is the more remarkable since he did not play first-class cricket until he was 22, lost four seasons to the 1914–18 War, and virtually missed two more owing to injury and illness.

When he was 51 and on the verge of retirement, he played in George Duckworth's benefit match, against Lancashire, the county champions, and scored the only century made against them at Old Trafford that season – and 51 not out in the second innings.

When A. W. Carr fell ill during the 1926 Old Trafford Test against Australia, Hobbs took over the captaincy: but, in all but name, he captained England many times and with much wisdom.

On figures as well as in memory, he and Herbert Sutcliffe were the finest pair of opening batsmen Test cricket has known; and, for Surrey, first with his fellow Cambridge man, Tom Hayward, then with Andrew Sandham, he shared the majority of his record number of century openings (166).

Sir Jack would never enter any discussion which compared him with W. G. Grace, though he liked to think he inherited 'The Old Man's' batting technique. By a happy coincidence, in his first match for Surrey – against the Gentlemen of England – he and WG were on opposing sides.

A. C. MacLaren analysed Hobbs's technique in a book aptly titled *The Perfect Batsman*. Neat, quizzical looking, wiry, quick in his assessment of the bowled ball, he came without hurry to the ideal position to play any stroke: and he had them all.

Against any bowling, and even on bad wickets – where his ability lifted him above Bradman – he wore an air of ease. Often one had to observe his partner's difficulties to appreciate the sensitive skill of Hobbs.

During the 1920s it seemed as though he could make a hundred at will. Yet he gave little thought to records. He played with enjoyment and humour; his mischief, which was completely without malice, brought laughter to many grave cricket fields.

After he sent his poignant letter of resignation to Surrey in 1935, his life changed. He devoted much time to his sports goods business in Fleet Street, which he controlled in detail, never too busy to choose a bat – and choose it with care – for a schoolboy.

He played little cricket, though the last time he picked up a bat, in 1941, he scored the last of the 47 centuries he could remember making outside the first-class game. Until last year he played golf regularly with his old companion, Herbert Strudwick; he cherished an unfailing feeling for old friends, and a genuine consideration for those his charity could not bring him to approve.

He settled in Hove, where for the last few years of her life he tended his sick wife with a moving gentleness. As a player, he had considered it professionally advisable not to drink or smoke. Freed from those responsibilities, he relished an occasional cigar and his own, unusual brand of fat cigarettes: he would take a hock with his dinner and given the excuse of a visit from a friend he would mildly shock himself by opening a half-bottle of champagne at mid-morning.

A shy man, he was embarrassed by public appearances, and

with a single annual exception avoided speech-making. Reluctantly but pleasantly, he made two sound broadcasts and one
television programme.

Eventually his knighthood and the volume of his correspondence convinced him that, whatever his feelings, he would
henceforth be regarded a public figure. Every letter he received –
and hundreds came from people he had never known – was
answered in his own rather painful hand; every autograph
demanded of him was given, every gesture acknowledged.

Hesitantly at first, but eventually with great gusto, he consented
to become the permanent guest of honour at the lunches of 'The
Master's Club', formed in his honour in the early 'fifties. It was
understood that there were no speeches at these luncheons, and
only the single toast of 'The Master'. But one year he stood up
and, after his thanks 'for the honour you have done me', addressed
himself separately to everyone present, recalling some bygone
incident to each person's credit. Thereafter, his speech was the
great event of the year for the club.

On the cricket of his contemporaries he was shrewd and
amusing. Of one famous bowler he said, 'Ah, now he spun it a lot:
a dangerous bowler but, you know, he never seemed to bowl so
well if you hit him over the top of extra cover two or three times
in his first over.'

The words used by Nyren, an earlier cricket immortal, about
another, David Harris, apply just as precisely to Jack Hobbs: 'I can
call to mind no worthier, or, in the active sense of the word, not a
more "*good* man".'

22 December 1963                                              *John Arlott*

---

*One cold March day in 1965, when feeling all the more
desolate for the length of winter and the absence of summer
joys like cricket, R. C. Robertson-Glasgow committed suicide.
He was not the first cricketer, nor the first writer of comedy,
to do so. Here his successor as cricket correspondent, Alan
Ross, pays tribute.*

# Raymond Robertson-Glasgow

The thing about R. C. Robertson-Glasgow that you noticed first was his reverberating laugh. He had, when speaking, a disconcerting habit of thrusting his face right up close to yours, never moving his eyes away, and then, swaying away out of reach like a boxer, of throwing his head back and laughing.

It was a laugh that penetrated all corners of a pavilion, a laugh that, pinning its recipients like butterflies to a setting board, had no gainsaying.

R. C. Robertson-Glasgow was, with C. B. Fry and Neville Cardus, in the great line of prolific cricket talkers. A mine of information and anecdote on all subjects, he used freedom of speech to the full. He died, suddenly, on Thursday in the Thames Valley that, with Scotland, Somerset and Oxford, was the place closest to his heart.

He was a man of great sweetness and charm, of abiding loyalties and infectious enthusiasms. His pleasures were convivial company, sport, country life and the classics, roughly in that order, and his supple and elegant prose, correspondingly rich, derived unostentatiously from the study of Latin elegiacs and Greek prose.

He was devoid of pomposity and, as a journalist, never succumbed to the temptation of Johnsonian exhortation or portentous moralising about the dubious relationships between cricket and empire-building.

If he had faults, they were in the direction of levity, a refusal to treat Test matches as warfare or as anything other than civilised fun. The higher strategies tended to leave him cold; of civilised fun he can have had precious little from English cricket in the last decade, when, perhaps wisely, he had preferred the complexities of rustic Pangbourne society to the devious machinations of the international Test circuit.

As a cricketer he reached in his prime the very edge of the England side and that at a time, in the mid-'twenties, when quickish bowlers of quality were far thicker on the ground than now. At Charterhouse he made plenty of runs, but he played four seasons for Oxford mainly as a bowler, though his appearances at

Lord's, ironically enough, brought him only 2 wickets for 250 but a batting average of 36.

He joined Somerset in 1920, playing regularly for five years and spasmodically for 15, and he must have been, at his best, a fine bowler indeed of fast-medium inswing.

He had a high rollicking action with plenty of life and movement off the pitch. I batted against him for Oxford when he was 40 and he was still lively enough to catch me a fearful crack on the knee and momentarily jeopardise my fitness for Lord's.

Later, in more relaxed contexts, we often fielded or rather covered at slip, and he seemed to get as much enjoyment out of these as when he was bowling to Hobbs and Sutcliffe, or sharing the glamour of those Oxford years when his companions were G. T. S. Stevens, R. H. Bettington, L. P. Hedges, C. H. Knott and B. H. Lyon and his Cambridge opponents included A. P. F. Chapman, J. L. Bryan, C. S. Marriott and the Ashtons.

But, good cricketer though he was, it was as a writer that he staked out his claim for cricketing immortality. With Cardus, he helped to raise cricket reporting from journalism to an art.

He wrote concisely and wittily, his sentences suitably con-structed, the observation and imagery and technical comment absorbed effortlessly into a flowing style that showed no joins. He, like Cardus, saw cricket in terms of human character, as an interplay of personalities that were themselves the expression of divers social attitudes and environments.

His writing for the *Morning Post* for the seven years before the war and for this newspaper for the seven years after it, until 1953 when I inadequately succeeded him, his autobiography *46 Not Out* and his various volumes of *Cricket Prints*, were all marked by a rare generosity of spirit, a remarkable blending of the lyrical and the comic.

In some ways a reactionary, disconcertingly contemptuous for one so tolerant and scholarly of all forms of modern art and progressive thought, he embodied in his prose classical virtues and humanist values. I have by me as I write his book of sketches, *The Brighter Side of Cricket*, presented to me in 1935 for captaining a successful preparatory school team.

If I am to be honest, I must put it, incongruous though it may seem, among Lamartine, Rimbaud, D. H. Lawrence, Scott Fitzgerald, Hazlitt and Auden (whom he hated), as one of the earliest books that influenced me, and which I have reread with the most pleasure.

7 March 1965                                                          *Alan Ross*

---

*This is a touching tribute from a Yorkshireman to a Lancastrian. George Duckworth kept wicket for Lancashire from 1923 to 1938, and in 24 Test matches for England.*

# George Duckworth

George Duckworth, who died last week, came from Lancashire. Anyone who did not realise this after being in his company for ten minutes was either an illiterate or a fool.

God Almighty decided some 64 years ago that Lancashire needed a wicket-keeper. I don't think He had England in mind; I think He was primarily concerned with Lancashire.

No one was better physically endowed for the task than Duckworth. He was short and stocky; the ground was near; and his appeal was the most frightening noise any batsman had to endure. He also had, for a small man, an extraordinarily large pair of gloves. When I first saw him behind the stumps I thought he could never drop a catch with those enormous gloves.

The first words he said to me were, 'You're out.' This was in my first Yorkshire and Lancashire match. No young batsman likes to be out, but it hurts very much more when a great man tells you so, and it was particularly painful to me as I had already received a broken nose.

My first sight of Duckworth was in 1930, when I watched for ten hours at Headingley while Don Bradman made 334. In 1954, when I took the team to Australia, I was very lucky to have

George as the assistant manager. His advice, I would say, was the vital factor in our success on that tour. In the ill-fated Brisbane Test match, when Australia won by an innings and Brisbane was to me the most depressing place on earth, my friend and comforter was George Duckworth. Two hours after the end of the game, he and I were cruising down the Brisbane River, a Yorkshireman and a Lancastrian in the depths of gloom on a showboat on the river in Brisbane.

At that time I realised what a great little man George was. He had innumerable friends in Australia. Wherever he went, they would come to see him. The greatest Australian rugby league players always made a point of seeing George at least once during our tours.

He learned his trade with Lancashire at a time when cricketers did not wear suede shoes or run motor-cars. To keep wicket for Lancashire during the early 'twenties required a man of substance. Mistakes behind the wicket were not allowed to happen and few wicket-keepers could have known how tough it really was to keep to that wonderful Lancashire attack. Duckworth kept wicket superbly to some of the greatest bowlers the game has ever known: Cecil Parkin, Dick Tyldesley, Ted McDonald – the most beautiful of bowlers – and Harold Larwood, Maurice Tate, Wilfred Rhodes and many others. I used to love to hear George talk about these men.

I said to him once, 'Why are you so tough, George?' He replied, 'Len, when I started with Lancashire there were some tough chaps about and I was just a little lad from Warrington. If I hadn't done something about it, I'd have been trampled under foot in a couple of weeks.' He added that he was nowhere near as tough as he looked or sounded. I found this to be true. When we managed to win the Test series in Australia, George's cheerful face – red from the Australian climate, like the setting sun in the tropics – was overwhelmed with joy.

9 January 1966                                                            *Len Hutton*

---

*Lord Learie Nicholas Constantine died at the age of 69. In first-class cricket he scored 4475 runs at 24, and took 439 wickets at 20. In Test cricket his record was not so good: 635 runs at 19, and 58 wickets at 30. But they only prove how inadequate records are when it comes to evaluating a cricketer as an entertainer.*

# Learie Constantine

Of all the cricketers I have seen and played against, none intrigued or fascinated me more than Learie Constantine, the most natural cricketer I ever saw.

If any man was born to play cricket it was Learie, not the long drawn out five- or six-day Test, but the Saturday afternoon league match where time and speed – and particularly speed – are of vital importance. This was a man of speed whether batting, bowling or fielding.

The first time I ever saw or played against Constantine was at Lord's in 1939. Having heard and read so much about him, I sought first-class advice about him from my guide and comforter, Maurice Leyland, who knew the man from Trinidad inside out. 'Watch his slow ball, it's a googly which he disguises very carefully. And be very wary about running sharp singles if the ball is within his reach.'

On that morning of beautiful sunshine at Lord's in 1939 Constantine opened the bowling to me from the Pavilion end. I knew he was fast and had a very good slow ball, but he had something else that nobody had told me about. The fact that he always bowled with his shirt sleeves down did not concern me much. It was his extraordinary way of looking up at his hand at the moment of delivery that bothered me.

This was something I had never seen before and something I have only seen done by Constantine. I managed to survive my first encounter with the great man, who tried a number of slow deliveries, all of which were genuine googlies and did turn down the slope a little.

I had read Learie Constantine's book which he wrote in the early 'thirties called *Cricket and I*. In this book he said that Hobbs never played at a good length ball pitched one inch outside his off stump. In one of my early matches for Yorkshire I thought I would do what my idol Hobbs did, but found to my consternation that my off stump was knocked out of the ground in both innings for my first pair in first-class cricket.

I was coached and listened carefully to all that was said to me. Constantine received coaching but gave one the impression that he could well have done without it. He was a law unto himself, enjoying every moment of his game and spreading joy amongst cricket followers wherever he played.

I had seen some very fine fielders before seeing Learie, but he was by far the best I had seen. He moved as only a West Indian can move. He ran as though his feet did not touch the ground. His limbs appeared boneless. He coiled them from time to time and then darted and sprang like a panther, gathering the ball for a throw at the wicket. At that he had no peer.

Whether batting, bowling or fielding he was quick. I do not think he could play a maiden over. His batting was undoubtedly something which Learie invented himself. He would hit a ball for six off his middle stump and then cut the next one past second slip off the leg stump with a flick of his rubber wrists.

If any cricketer played his own game it was Constantine. He learnt his cricket from nobody and taught it to nobody. He played his own game and in so doing brought light to West Indian and Lancashire League cricket.

4 April 1971                                                          *Len Hutton*

---

*Herbert Sutcliffe was the author's opening partner for Yorkshire for most of the period from 1934 until the Second World War. Here one great Yorkshireman, and England batsman, affectionately salutes the passing of another.*

# Herbert Sutcliffe

The Sutcliffes and the Huttons were cricketing families in Pudsey, a small textile town in West Yorkshire. My father played with Herbert for Pudsey St Lawrence when Herbert was a teenager. In those early days Herbert worked hard at his cricket. A great believer in practice, he moved to the Pudsey Britannia club because the practice wickets at Pudsey St Lawrence were of doubtful quality.

Herbert, together with Jack Hobbs, were my boyhood heroes. My first innings with Herbert was a most wonderful experience for me, an uncapped Yorkshire player. I was thrilled to be at the crease with him, but so frightened that I might do something foolish. Herbert was most kind to me, although my stay was far from outstanding. A young player could not have wished to receive more encouragement than I did on that occasion. This was the spirit that prevailed when I entered first-class cricket in 1934.

For several years I was closely associated with George Hirst, who taught me a great deal. The practical side was to come later: this I found from associating and playing with Herbert. He was ambitious, very correct in all he did on and off the field, but never so ambitious that he forgot that he was playing a team game. He was always willing to help those with ordinary ability. After making a century and deciding to give his wicket away, he would give it to the bowler whom he thought deserved it.

On my twenty-first birthday, Herbert and myself, against Leicestershire at Hull, were 315 undefeated at tea on the first day. After tea on our way to the wicket, Herbert said to me, 'We will go for 556.' At that time 555 was the world record partnership for the first wicket, of which he himself was the joint holder. His remark so shattered me that I was bowled third ball after tea. I was never forgiven. Two years later in 1939, against Hampshire at Sheffield, we were again 315 for 0 when again I did something foolish. This was the end. I came to the conclusion that I was not born a record-breaker.

Herbert Sutcliffe was the finest hooker of the short-pitched ball I have seen. Don Bradman was the finest puller in front of square

I have seen, but Hebert hit the ball behind square to perfection. His technique was not faultless: the bat was picked up in the direction of third slip, but – and this is important – he managed to bring it down straight more often than not. His stance at the wicket prepared him for the short-pitched ball, open with the weight on the left leg. This enabled him to move quickly into position for the hook stroke.

The change in the lbw law in 1935 brought some problems to this great player. After a period when Herbert was caught playing back to the inswinger, he changed his technique and remained the best opening batsman in England until the Second World War ended his remarkable career.

It is impossible not to learn something from close association with a man of outstanding talent. Herbert introduced me to the art of running between the wickets. His judgement of the short single was supreme. Each and every one was completed with the minimum of effort and not a single hair out of place.

He was at his best playing against Lancashire or Australia when every run had to be earned. Nothing was given away in these contests, which pulled out that magnificent fighting spirit. Herbert had the big match temperament in abundance. The fact that he might have given a chance or missed the outswinger by a wafer was forgotten seconds later; barracking was a waste of time. Deep down I am sure he enjoyed the bellowings from the Sydney Hill.

At 13 years of age I was taken to his home, a seven-iron shot from the house where I was born, to purchase my first cricket bat, which was duly autographed by the master himself. This bat was a magic bat. I made my first half-century with it, also my first century. No bat since had quite what that one had: I used to sleep with it under my pillow.

It is sad indeed to lose a friend, particularly a long-standing one. I had known Herbert Sutcliffe as long as I had known my parents and brothers. He led me through those early days of doubt and indecision to the promised land. I thank you, Herbert. May God bless you.

29 January 1978                                                   *Len Hutton*

*Jack Fingleton died at the age of 73, greatly lamented. This obituary of him was written by the Sports Editor as he then was, and still is at the time of publication, Peter Corrigan.*

# Jack Fingleton

One day last April there appeared among *The Observer*'s sports desk mail an article bearing the name of Jack Fingleton.

It was obviously a mistake. Fingleton, an Australian opening batsman of pre-war fame, had been writing for *The Sunday Times* for many years, establishing himself as a major cricket writer and dragging rare envy and admiration from that newspaper's rivals.

But, even as the article was being handed over for readdressing, another look at the covering letter revealed that Jack had really meant it to be delivered to the 'Sporting Editor, The Observer'. It read:

Dear Sir, In 1946–47, the first English cricket visit after the war, I covered the tour for your newspaper and greatly enjoyed it . . . then the sports editor of *The Sunday Times* contacted me when I came to England in 1948 and said he was so tired of being asked at his weekly conference why he didn't have somebody in Australia to offset this chap Fingleton that he decided to book me up himself and for years I have written for that newspaper.

He went on to give one or two reasons why he was no longer writing for them and added:

Anyway, here is an article which you might or might not want . . . I saw your newspaper often when I was in England last summer and I greatly admired the guts of your Sport, sound and sensible, not seeking stunts or display.

If the article doesn't suit you, there's no worry. Just send it back and no harm is done at all. If you use it, it is a matter for you whether you use my name over it or a 'Special Correspondent'.

To have a Fingleton piece thus labelled would be like Stradi-varius signing himself 'a violin-maker'. He proceeded to write for us throughout the summer and the autumn, happy to take part with Sir Len Hutton and his countryman Bobby Simpson in one or two special features, while completing his autobiography for Collins, *Batting from Memory*, which was published only a week or so ago.

'It is driving me up the wall,' he wrote to us. 'Still, I was an opening batsman and not used to giving up easily although one gets very bored with it, as I did with continuous opening and the spectators with me. No matter . . . it is life.'

The week before last we tried to contact him at his home near Canberra to ask for his thoughts on the Lillee kicking incident. There was no answer. Last Sunday we learned he had died the previous day.

Jack Fingleton was 73. He has the record of scoring centuries in four consecutive Test innings in 1935–36. Against England in 1936 he put on 346 with Don Bradman for the sixth wicket at Melbourne and his Test figures were 1189 runs, with five hundreds and an average of 42.46. In Australia he was respected for his political writing as well as his unique cricket prose.

He would have had a tribute in these columns even without his late defection into our company. But we like to think he enjoyed his brief time as part of this motley collection of dreamers and seekers of truth and wisdom, as much as we were proud to have him.

29 November 1981                                    *Peter Corrigan*

# Index

Brisbane xxx, 7, 111, 114–17, 208
BBC 177–80
Broadhalfpenny Down xxv
Brown, D. 61, 133
Brown, W. A. 12, 114
Bryan, J. L. 206
Buller, Syd 161
Burtt, T. 162
Butcher 52, 125

Cambridge University 14, 46, 104–7
Canada 201
Cape Coloured 47
Cardus, Sir Neville xxvi–xxviii, 144–5, 205–6
Carey, M. 65
Carr, A. W. 100–2, 104, 202
Carris 107
Catt, T. 68
Centenary Test 176
Ceylon 153–4
Chandra 71
Chapman, A. P. F. 98–9, 104, 142, 206
Chappell, G. 130, 171, 180, 193
Chappell, I. 130
Charlton Athletic 173
Chester, F. 162
Close, B. 66, 127–8
Cockney North 6
Cockney South 6
Compton, D. C. S. xxix, 10–13, 15, 66, 109, 114, 117, 176, 180
Constantine, Lord (L. N.) 26, 29, 186, 209–10
Cook 99
Cook, G. 133
Cornell, J. 166
Corrigan, P. 213
Cottam, R. 133
Cotter, T. 56, 147–8
County cricket 155–7
Cowdrey, Colin xxi, 24, 65, 118–21, 154, 159, 184
Cozier, T. 28
*Cricket and I* 210
Cricket Association 72
Cricket Board of Control 192
*Cricket Prints* 206
*Cricketer, The* 55
Crompton, N. 119–20.

Crystal Palace 79

*Daily Mail* 119
*Daily Telegraph, The* 24, 65, 104
Davidson, A. 54, 127
Davie, M. xix–xx, xxx, 37, 43, 118, 163
Davies, Dai 162
Davies, J. 69
de Saram, F. C. 154
Dera Ismail Khan 168–70
Dev, Kapil 135–6, 138
Dexter, T. xxi, 49, 120–1, 126–8, 160
Dilley, G. 172
Dipper, A. E. 94–5, 98
Dixon 105–6
d'Oliveira, B. 47–9, 69, 130
Douglas, J. 59, 97–8
Duckworth, G. 202, 207–8
Dujon, J. 26, 135
Duleepsinhji, K. S. 142, 149
Durham University 42
Dye, J. 133
Dyer, A. W. 23

Edgbaston 24, 77, 160, 185
Edrich, W. J. 13, 109–12, 114–15, 117
Edwards 130
Eggar 107
Emmett 121, 201
England xxvii, 7, 12–14, 16–17, 20–5, 34, 36, 38–9, 43–4, 47, 49, 51–2, 54, 58, 61, 64–5, 68, 70, 80, 93–7, 99–102, 107–17, 123–31, 141–7, 149–52, 154, 160–1, 164, 168, 171, 174–5, 180–2, 200, 202, 212
women's team 74–5
English Sunday League 56
Essex CCC 22
Evans, G. 12, 67–70, 162, 176
*Evening Standard, The* 120

Fagg, A. 111, 160
Farnes, K. 114
Fender, P. G. H. xxi, xxviii, 12, 141
Ferris 201
Fingleton, J. H. xxi, 114, 180–7, 213–14
Fitzgerald, R. A. 201
Fleetwood-Smith, L. O'B. 12, 109, 111–14
Flood 122

216